# MAPPING THE WORLD'S VEGETATION

SYRACUSE GEOGRAPHICAL SERIES, 4

# MAPPING THE
## *Regionalization of*

# WORLD'S VEGETATION
*Formations and Flora*

### David J. de Laubenfels

SYRACUSE UNIVERSITY PRESS       1975

Map by A. W. Küchler, "Natural Vegetation," from
Edward B. Espenshade, Jr., ed., *Goode's World Atlas*,
9th ed., copyright © 1949 by Rand McNally & Company,
Chicago, Illinois, pp. 16-17. Reprinted by permission
of Rand McNally College Publishing Company.

Map from Ronald Good, *The Geography of the Flowering
Plants*, copyright © 1947 by Longman Group Ltd.

Map from Preston E. James, *One World Divided*, 1st and
2nd eds., copyright © 1964, 1974 by John Wiley & Sons,
Inc.; reprinted by permission of John Wiley & Sons, Inc.

**Library of Congress Cataloging in Publication Data**

De Laubenfels, David John    1925-
    Mapping the world's vegetation.

    (Syracuse geographical series; no. 4)
    Bibliography: p.
    1. Vegetation mapping.    2. Phytogeography.
I. Title.  II. Series.
QK63.D44            581.9            75-25934
ISBN O-8156-2172-8

SYRACUSE GEOGRAPHICAL SERIES, 4

iv

# Contents

# List of Figures

# List of Maps

# Preface

As a geographer I have always enjoyed knowing about the patterns of the physical environment on the earth's surface. These patterns are displayed in textbooks, and I have spread them before many classes of students, explaining why they matter. One must always accept much knowledge from the experts because there is much more to know than anyone can confirm for one's self. Nevertheless, I have always wanted to see for myself as much as I could and especially of vegetation and plants — to see a tropical grassland and a tropical rainforest with my own eyes. Inevitably what I found was not always what I expected to find. Surely some of my disappointment resulted from my own misinterpretation of what had been written, but perhaps some of what had been written was wrong. Such perceptions provided the basis for much research and have been the stimulus for the book presented here.

Travel, as much as I have been able, has been a way of life for me. As a youngster my family took me on extensive trips over the United States in 1931, 1933, and 1942, particularly the West. The army did more of the same in 1944 and 1945. Then I went on my own in the summers of 1946 and 1947, first exploring all corners of the United States and then invading Canada and Mexico. Research for my doctoral dissertation took me all over South America in 1952, but especially to Chile. A major focus on vegetation began during a research trip to Australia and nearby areas in 1957. The major part of the field research for the work presented here was carried out in 1964 and 1965. First studies were made in the western parts of the United States and in Mexico, then operations were transferred to eastern Australia and such nearby areas as New Guinea, New Caledonia, and Fiji. In the summer of 1973 a plant-collecting expedition took me to new areas, including Java, Malaya, Sarawak, and Formosa. At this time I took the opportunity to test many of my conclusions derived from earlier research. Various trips to Europe have contributed little in the way of observations because I did not see much that could be called wild vegetation. Even though I have not seen every region in the world I have written about, I have seen and studied all the types of vegetation discussed.

At the beginning it was my senior colleague, Preston E. James, who encouraged me to investigate the patterns of vegetation. He knew that few geographers were studying such matters and he realized that a better understanding was both possible and needed. Later, the support and encouragement of Donald W. Meinig has been very valuable to me in carrying this work to completion. The major field research was supported by Syracuse University by way of a sabbatical leave, and costs of preparing the manuscript for publication were borne by the Department of Geography. In the field I have contacted numerous foresters and botanists, often going into the field with them. These include Dr. Hugh S. McKee, M. Schmid, M. Corbasson, Selwyn L. Everist, Lindsay Smith, S. T. Blake, J. S. Womersley, Dr. W. D. Jackson, Martin Bannister, Dr. Engke Soepadmo, Dr. A. J. G. H. Kostermans, Paul Chai, and many others. Nature itself has been my greatest teacher, and I only hope I have seen it clearly enough to advance our knowledge a bit further.

*Syracuse, New York*                                             David J. de Laubenfels
*Spring 1975*

# Introduction

Vegetation is the plant content of area, and as a fundamental and major component in the character of the earth's surface, it is of intrinsic scientific interest. Because vegetation varies, often greatly and in numerous ways, from place to place, the mapping of vegetation is a basic scientific task. Mapping requires the establishment of general categories and the delineation of regional boundaries between categories. Maps of world vegetation have long been a standard item in atlases and in textbooks and other studies dealing with the physical character of the earth. Yet these maps differ in the way they generalize about vegetation, and accompanying literature simply does not give satisfactory definitions and explanations for the regionalizations depicted. Thus a fresh examination of the regionalization of vegetation on a world scale is needed.

The result of such examination has been an elaboration of two distinct regional vegetation systems. These are consonant with two widely used schemes, and although they introduce some innovations, they substantially confirm the larger part of commonly used maps. The primary goal of this book is the systematization of the regional categories, their character, and relationships, and explanations for the origin of the distinctions are also suggested. Thus, the maps and rationale place world vegetation mapping on a more satisfactory scientific basis.

The most general motivations for mapping vegetation can be placed in two categories: an interest in learning about the plants themselves, and an interest in learning about the physical environment in general (Grigg 1965; Küchler 1956, 1973). The first relates to the study of *floristics*, dealing with assemblages of species; the second relates to the study of *form*, dealing with plant physiognomy as in some way responsive to other elements of a physical environment. To a considerable extent there has been a relationship between each of these motivations and the scale of mapping. Studies in floristics have made use of large-scale maps by which species associations can be best depicted, whereas the usual complexity of such associations over large areas has meant that most small-scale mapping of vegetation has only made use of form. Nevertheless, both of these basic approaches to the study of vegetation have led to the development of regional schemes for use on a global scale. The one involves major floral regions, usually called realms or kingdoms, as well as subdivisions of these; the other involves categories of vegetation formations.

There are of course other reasons for mapping vegetation (Küchler 1967). Economic considerations may bring about the mapping of some particular aspect of the plant cover. Foresters and lumbering interests must constantly differentiate between commercial and non-commercial stands, and the commercial stands must further be divided into specific types (Zon and Spearhawk 1923; Hadden-Guest et al. 1956). Actually, small-scale lumber maps have very little practical value because little particular information can be shown. Nevertheless, such concerns have influenced vegetation mapping in general, as for example in the use of terms like "hardwood" and "softwood" to designate categories. Another use of vegetation maps stems from interest in the relationships between culture and plants. Much can be learned about the past activities of man from his imprint on plant growth, especially from large-scale maps (Denevan 1961; Robbins 1962; Johannessen 1963). Disturbance by man is nearly universal to some degree on the natural vegetation, and the character and distribution of man's interference with plant growth can probably yield far more than we yet know about many early cultures. Other interests arise from such fields as military strategy, land-use planning, and recreation. But interesting as these avenues might be for explorations in vegetation mapping, this book is confined to the analysis and evaluation of the two main general systems, formations and flora.

A definite and rather standard approach will be used in the examination of world patterns of vegetation. The first step is to work through the literature to discover what has been said, partly to document the assertion which has been made that proper justification of available regionalizations is lacking. The next step is to analyze the factors that relate to regional differentiation to discover just how and in what ways vegetation is organized. Finally, the facts will be assembled into more rational regional systems of vegetation.

The history of vegetation geography began with a generally unified approach, diverging with time into several directions of study that are often treated rather independently today. The two parts of this study will be apparent both in the origins of each line of thought and in the patterns that each leads to.

The factors which differentiate vegetation formation from one place to another contrast with the factors supporting floristic regionalization. For formation, the physical form or physiognomy of individual plants must be considered. Many other factors have also been used, and it becomes necessary, therefore, to examine this range of characters to see how they relate to vegetation formation. For flora the basic factor is the taxon (species, genus, family, etc.) whose distribution is involved. A flora is a grouping of taxa, and it is necessary to discover how taxa group. For both the form characteristics and the grouping of taxa, the geographer must look at boundaries, if there are any, for without discontinuities there are no discrete categories of phenomena. Continua can be regionalized, of course, but vegetation categories and boundaries have consistently been presented, so this book might be thought of as a test of the proposition that vegetation categories do exist.

Vegetation can be separated into regional units with distinct boundaries in at least two ways. There is a system of vegetation formations — each formation sharply marked off from the others and each occupying distinct areas on the surface of the earth. Flora also segregate into contrasting regional assemblages whose boundaries, it turns out, are usually at the same time formation boundaries. This book, then, will define the formation types and the major floristic groups, as well as present maps which show their respective distributions.

# MAPPING THE WORLD'S VEGETATION

# PART ONE

## *Vegetation Formations*

# 1

# The Evolution of World
# Vegetation Formation Maps

I T IS A WIDELY HELD ASSUMPTION that vegetation or vegetation formations are integrators of all the factors of the natural environment, particularly climate, because plants, the elements of vegetation, are fixed on the surface of the earth where they must enjoy or endure their environment. A knowledge of vegetation can be very important in assessing or understanding man's habitat and his interaction with it (Poore 1963).

The significance of vegetation mapping has been appreciated in Europe, where there are whole institutes devoted to the preparation of vegetation maps. But a danger arises in assuming the relationship between vegetation and its total environmental system, the ecosystem, and then confusing the two (Herbertson 1905; Penck 1910). Few ecologists today would accept the dictum of Clements (Clements and Shelford 1936, p. 24; Weaver and Clements 1938, pp. 89-91; Blumenstock and Thornthwaite 1941; Beadle 1951; Whittaker 1957; Morgan and Moss 1965) that vegetation formations are definite organic entities produced and delimited by climate; that physiognomy, floristic composition, and habitat are all aspects, expressed in developmental stages, of an ultimate organism, the climax formation (Clements 1963, p. 124). (The wording "climax formation" is redundant, *climax* and *formation* as used by Clements being synonymous.) Yet many maps in current use called "vegetation maps" in fact portray ecosystems (Fosberg 1961, p. 32) and thus by implication or direct statement equate vegetation with the habitat, more particularly with climate (Egler 1957; Tosi 1964; Mather and Yoshioka 1968). When such

3

maps are used as vegetation maps, the correlation of their patterns with those of other environmental components will produce specious conclusions. Few attempts to handle world vegetation distribution free from habitat involvement have been made, and yet if vegetation's generally conceded significance to the natural environment is going to be tested and properly used, vegetation must first be mapped independently (Fosberg *et al.* 1961).

The mapping of vegetation, the sum total of the plants in an area, has evolved along with the growing body of information about plant distribution, the modern period beginning essentially with Humboldt (1805), who introduced the term "association" to describe a regional vegetation assemblage (Grisebach coined the term "formation" in 1883, p. 160). Obviously the quality of the maps could be no better than the data available, and it must be admitted that serious gaps still exist in our knowledge of the simplest details of the vegetation patterns in some parts of the world. Of greater interest, however, are the systems used to present the patterns of vegetation, because these systems determine what information is available on the resulting maps and therefore also what is omitted. Furthermore, by dictating what is required, these systems have some effect on the kinds of observations that are made and compiled.

## EARLY IDEAS

In the middle of the nineteenth century, proper vegetation formation maps of the world were not yet possible. The few maps then in use showed vague temperature zones or blocked out individual regions based on floral content, not vegetation formation, although there was a suggestion in some of relationships between flora and form (Grisebach 1866 — this map is reproduced here as Map 1 — 1872; Drude 1884, 1890). (Zones are still in general use in western United States based on C. H. Merriam 1898. For a discussion of floristic maps including some of the earliest maps of vegetation, see the second part of this study.) It was generally understood that plants differed with latitude in some sort of correspondence to the long-used climatic zones of *torrid, temperate,* and *frigid.*

Thus, the influential classification of de Candolle (1855) set forth five basic types of plants in terms of their physiologic response to climate. He proposed four temperature types: *megatherms*, or plants requiring continuously high temperature and abundant moisture; *mesotherms*, or plants needing only a moderate amount of heat and moisture; *microtherms*, or plants tolerant of shorter summers and colder winters; and *hekistotherms*, the plants of the polar zone (beyond the limit of trees). Between the first and second of the temperature types, in recognition of their common zonal position, de Candolle (1874) placed the *xerophytes*, or plants that tolerate dryness but need at least a short hot season, which were later divided into the three subtypes: *desert plants*, *steppe plants*, and *xerophytic trees and bushes* (actually the terms *hydromegatherm* and *xerophil* were used originally, but modified later). By incorporating a major category of moisture deficiency, de Candolle made a significant addition to the simple system in use since Greek times, the importance not being the recognition of the difference between moisture-requiring and drought-tolerating plants, which was not a new idea, but the status he accorded this distinction. The separation of the temperate zone into a subtropical zone and a subpolar zone was also an addition to the Greek system of three zones. De Candolle's classification did not result directly in a map but was used as a basic framework for later studies, such as the widely used climatic classification of Köppen.

A rather detailed but somewhat confusing treatment of vegetation was presented by Engler (1882) on the same map which delineated his floristic regions. The categories of vegetation are called physiologic plant groups with obvious reference to de Candolle, but the key includes additional factors. A category such as, "conifers and dicotyledonous broad-leaved trees rather evenly divided in forming forest, but the latter generally in greater richness of form," is a bit perplexing (it occurs in Japan and around the Great Lakes). Some categories are supplied with names after a description such as, "thick communities of moist and warmth requiring plants (hydromegatherms). — Tropical Urwälder," which in this case is equivalent to tropical rainforest. More than one term is sometimes used as, "brush and grass, forming steppe and prairie." In this latter case it should be noted that not all grasslands are included. In spite of the cartographic detail of this map, a logical system for vegetation classification does not emerge. The reader senses a groping for categories on the part of these authors.

An emphasis on moisture zones was presented in a map by Hinman in 1888 (p. 332) reproduced here as Map 2. Five forma-

Map 1. Vegetation regions of the world according to Grisebach (1866). Each of the 24 regions is independent but the possibility of a system was originally indicated by similar colors. Four regions with dry summers are in shades of blue, three treeless temperate areas are in shades of yellow, and three tropical

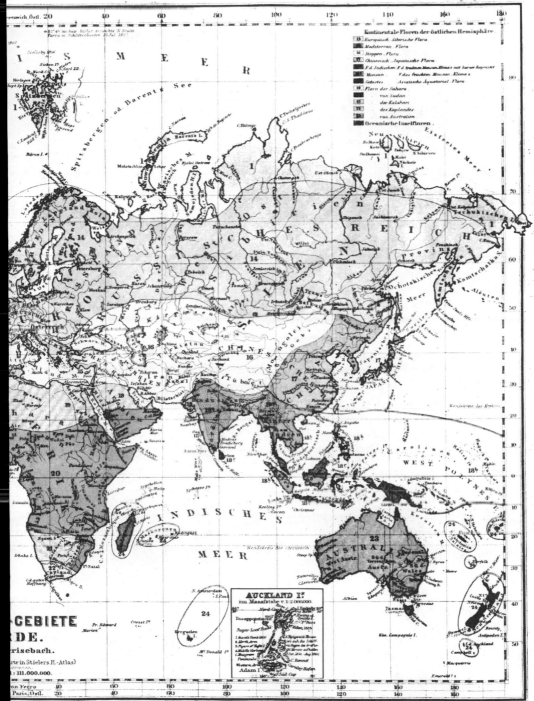

areas with trees are in shades of dark green. There are other tropical areas
with trees which have distinctive colors so that the suggestion of system is
incomplete.

tion zones (regions) related to moisture were presented: *very dense forest, dense forest, open forest, meadow lands,* and *deserts, tundra, ice fields* (these last three grouped into one category).

By the beginning of the twentieth century the study of vegetation was separating into three directions or emphases, two of which concentrated on mapping (Eckert 1925; Schroeter 1912; Raup 1942; Wace 1967), and the other focused primarily upon process (Whittaker 1962). This latter discipline was given the name plant ecology, and its numerous adherents busied themselves with the response in restricted areas of plant species and associations to local differences in site, to each other, and to the environment in general. The older name of plant geography has been retained by those botanists who are concerned with the distribution of species and of floras and what this can reveal about plant history and plant systematics. The third division involving vegetation formation distribution, the subject of this part of this work, has been something of a stepchild. Normally it is treated as a sideline by plant ecologists, plant geographers, climatologists, or geographers in general. Plant form is logically a concern of ecologists. They frequently incorporate large-scale distributional factors in their research, while distribution is a fundamental part of geography and geographers as much as anybody make and use small-scale maps of vegetation patterns.

## THE FIRST MAPS

The first of the modern vegetation maps was published by Wagner and Sydow (1888, plate 8) and reproduced here as Map 3.* This surprisingly precocious map has nine categories which correspond in every case to types in common use in the middle of the twentieth century; it deviates only by omitting the Mediterranean scrub. A semblance of system is applied in that there are three groups of three divisions each: the first (unnamed) could be called poor vegetation; the second is labelled "temperate"; and the third "tropical and subtropical." The first group is divided into *tundra,*

---

*A map drawn by the famous A. Engler in 1908 (Chisholm and Leete, plate 7) essentially follows this map but adds the "maqui" (Mediterranean type) and several unique categories such as "prairie" in North America only and "rather bare" tropical steppe in the Sudan only.

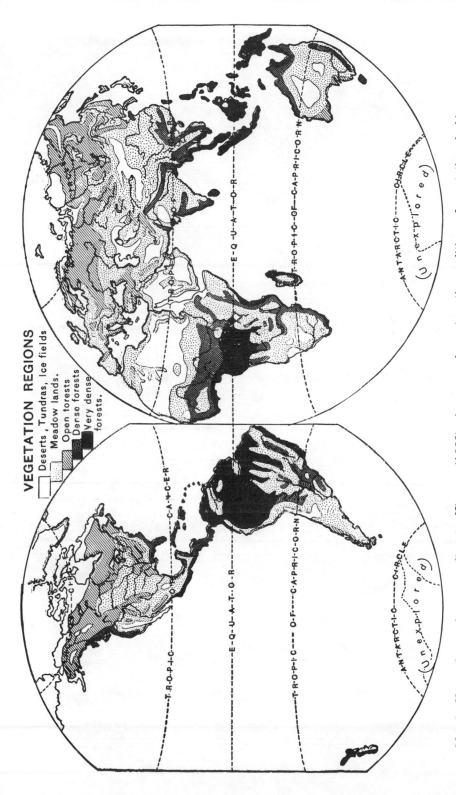

**VEGETATION REGIONS**

- Deserts, Tundras, Ice fields
- Meadow lands.
- Open forests
- Dense forests
- Very dense forests.

*Map* 2. Vegetation regions according to Hinman (1838). A very early systematic rendition of vegetation, lacking a temperature category. The specific categories and their boundaries could well be improved by revision.

ERLÄUTERUNGEN
ZUR
HAUPTKARTE

Tundren
Hochgebirgsflora
Vegetationsarme
Gebiete (Wüsten)
Grasland
Vorherrschend   der ge-
Nadelwald   mäss.
Wald (Laub und   igten
Nadelwald) und   Zone
Kulturland
Grasland   in trop.
Wald und   u. subtro-
Kulturland   pischen
Urwald   Gebieten

(Grenzen nach Engler)

Jährl. Regenmenge
unter 20 Centimeter
20 _ 60
60 _ 130
130 _ 200
über 200

REGENMENGE
nach Loomis

Eiswüs

Nord Pacific Str.

Nord Passat Trift

Aequatorial Gegenstrom

Süd Passat Trift

Sargasso

Nord Passat

West-Wind Trift

Antarktische Strom

Kap Hoorn Str.

Relativ warme Strömungen
Relativ kühle Strömungen
Kalte Polar-Strömungen
Packeis und Eiswände

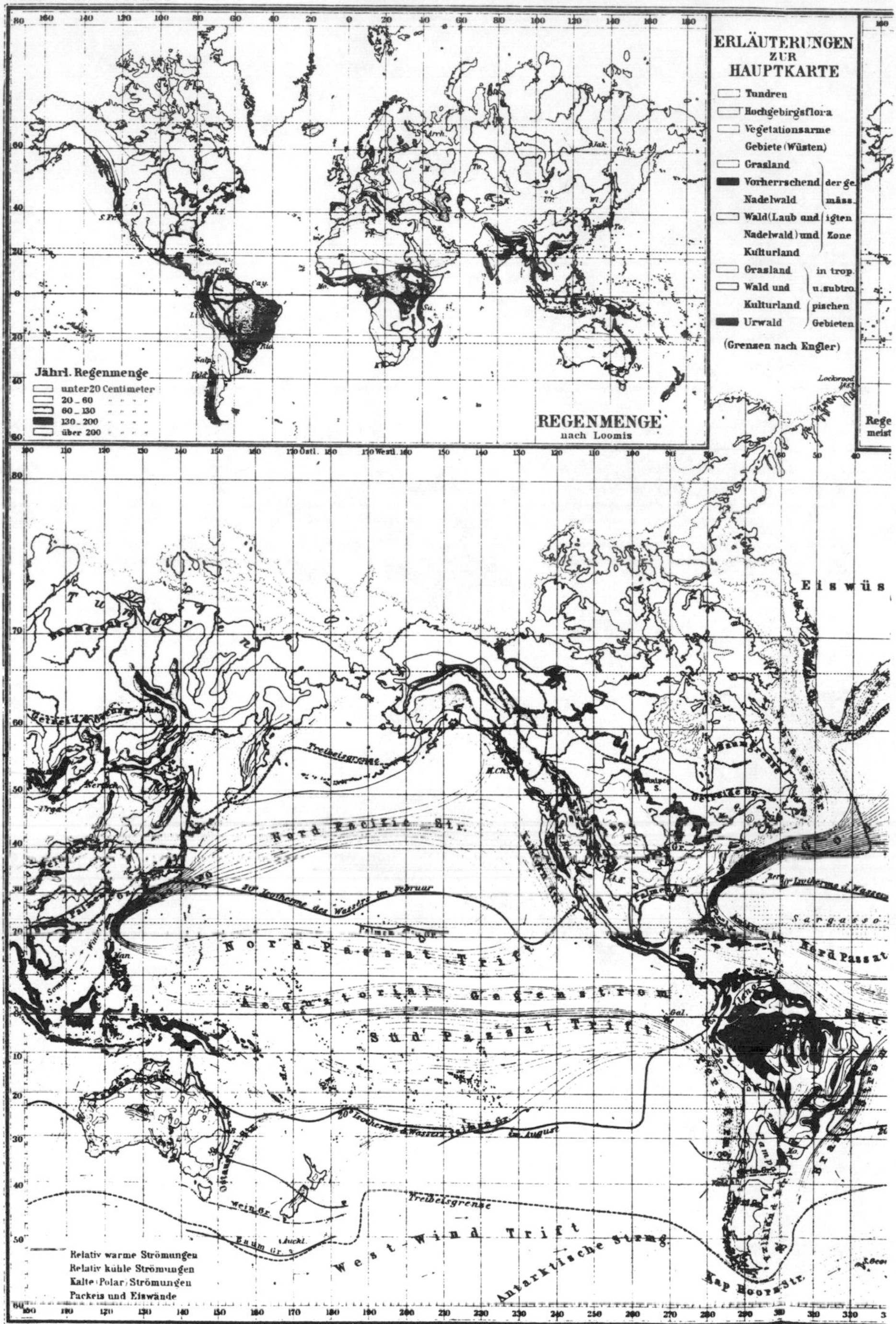

Gezeichn. v. V. Geyer      Mafsstab im Aequator für die Hauptkar

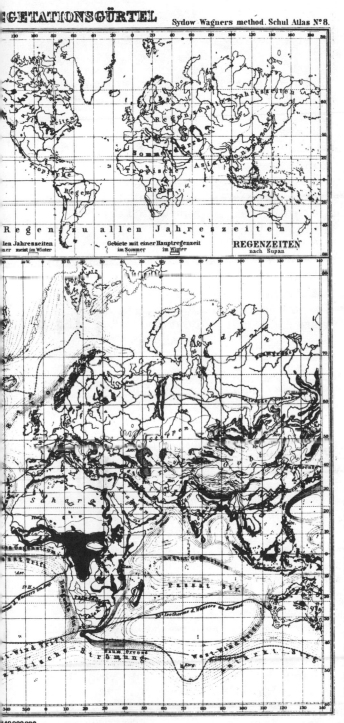

*Map 3.* The Sydow-Wagner map of vegetation (1883?). The signature, "Lockwood 1883," could mean that the plate was produced that year. The atlas in which the map was included first appeared in 1888. This map is certainly the earliest to use a full range of the vegetation categories that were widely accepted in later years. Earlier maps were incomplete and generally lacking in system. The boundaries on this map are attributed to Engler.

*high mountain flora* (alpine), and *desert;* the second into *grassland, dominantly needle forest,* and *mixed leaf and needle forest;* the third into *grassland, forest,* and *rainforest.*

More systematic and much better known is the world map of vegetation formations produced by Schimper (1898), who considered this original map to be a preliminary outline, and in terms of distributional data it is somewhat vague (Map 4). The familiar division between the tropic, temperate, and polar zones constitutes his primary separation, with the last represented by the one formation, *tundra.* For the first time on a world map the vegetation of the tropical and temperature zones is then apportioned to the distinct formation categories *rainforest* (or luxuriant rainforest), *forest* (or less luxuriant rainforest), *woodland, grassland,* and *desert.* For each of these except desert there is a tropical and a temperate variety. Two transitional categories appear — *park-like landscape* and *semi-desert* — generally without distinct boundaries. High mountains are represented by the category *alpine desert* and thus there is a total of thirteen formation types. Schimper regarded these broadly distributed subdivisions of vegetation as climatic formations and differentiated them from the edaphic or local formations, the distinction that still tends to separate the vegetation geographer from the plant ecologist.

Two years after Schimper's map was published, Köppen (1900) put forth the first of his climatic classifications (Map 5). He had seen elements of symmetry in Grisebach's map of 1866 in that certain of the twenty-four provinces in similar positions had similar vegetation. For example, *the Mediterranean, Cape, California,* and *Chile* provinces formed one such group, the *Steppe, Prairie, Pampa* and *Kalahari* formed another, and still further combinations were suggested (sometimes by similar color tints) with respect to tropical forests or middle-latitude forest. Köppen's classification was an attempt to combine some of the detail of Grisebach within the framework of de Candolle. Thus Köppen accepted the temperature divisions of *tropical* (megathermal), *warm temperate* (mesothermal), *subarctic* (microthermal), and *polar* (hekistothermal) together with the moisture divisions of *forest* (not xerophytes), *tree savanna* (xerophytic trees and shrubs), *steppe,* and *desert.* By combining each of the four moisture divisions with each of the temperature divisions except for the *polar* area which had only the two which were without trees, he produced fourteen types. He placed the first category of moisture from de Candolle's dry climates *(xerophytic trees and shrubs)* into his various humid climate groups. He, in effect, rotated the moisture gradient in the higher latitudes so that in response to cold one proceeded pole-ward from *oak forest* to *birch* (also called *needle forest)* in the microtherms, followed by *tundra* and then *eternal snow* (or *cold desert)* for the hekistotherms. Several other categories or sub-divisions were added to the basic groups so far described. There were two *high mountain tundra* types (tropical and temperate), as well as *upland savanna,* and *coastal deserts with frequent fog. Low-land tundra* and *subarctic forest* were each divided between northern and southern hemisphere because of (continental) differ-ences in the seasonal temperature range, the *warm temperate forest* and *warm temperate woodland* were each divided into warm summer and mild summer phases, and two additional types with cool instead of mild winters were distinguished from the warm temperate forest, one with a dry late summer. With these latter types, which have no obvious relation to vegetation or the basic scheme expanded by Köppen, he achieved a total of twenty-four climatic types.

The maps of world vegetation by Andree (1906) closely resemble a simple interpretation of de Candolle's classification (Map 6). There is *tropical forest, subtropical forest, temperate forest,* and *tundra* along with *lighter tropical forest and savanna, tree poor and grassland,* and *desert steppe.* To this is added *sand and stone desert, high mountain flora,* and (curiously) *temperate mountain forest.* This is the first world vegetation scheme with a barren desert type of category. Except for the barren desert and the temperate mountain forest the categories paralleled those of Schimper in distribution but with several combinations. The *sub-tropical forest* (as per de Candolle) corresponds to Schimper's *temperate rainforest* plus his *sclerophyllous woodland;* the *lighter tropical forest* and *savanna* to Schimper's *(tropical) grassland* plus his *xerophyllous woodland.* The transitional categories are ab-sorbed. The result, although still rather generalized, is more detailed and precise than that of Schimper.

Certain principles clearly manifest themselves in the organiza-tion of the works so far described. There may be some variation, but the different categories of vegetation unequivocally are set into a temperature series and a moisture series. Specific names for most of these categories were becoming emphasized, names like *rainforest, savanna, steppe, desert,* and *tundra.* In each case the

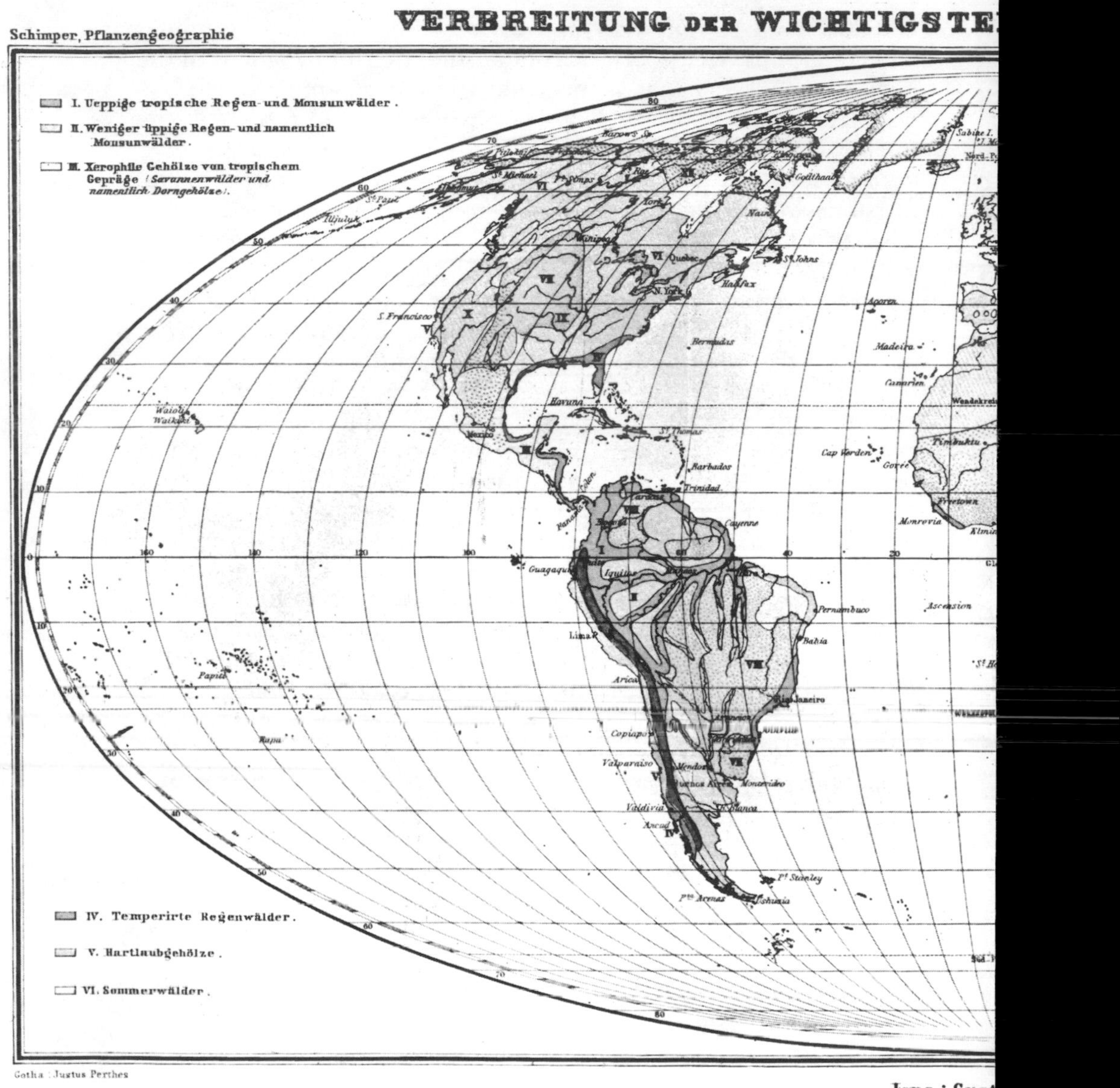
Schimper, Pflanzengeographie
VERBREITUNG DER WICHTIGSTE
I. Ueppige tropische Regen- und Monsunwälder.
II. Weniger üppige Regen- und namentlich Monsunwälder.
III. Xerophile Gehölze von tropischem Gepräge (Savannenwälder und namentlich Dorngehölze).
IV. Temperirte Regenwälder.
V. Hartlaubgehölze.
VI. Sommerwälder.
S. Francisco
Quebec
St Johns
Halifax
N. York
Bermudas
Azoren
Madeira
Canarien
Havana
Mexico
St Thomas
Barbados
Trinidad
Cap Verden
Goree
Freetown
Monrovia
Cayenne
Iquitos
Pernambuco
Ascension
Bahia
Lima
Arica
Copiapo
Valparaiso
Mendoza
Montevideo
Valdivia
Ancud
Pt Stanley
Pta Arenas
Ushuaia
Papiti
Rapa
Timbuktu
Gotha: Justus Perthes
Jena: Gust

*Map 4.* Vegetation formations according to Schimper (1898). Although this map is basically systematic, there are two intrusive transitional categories.

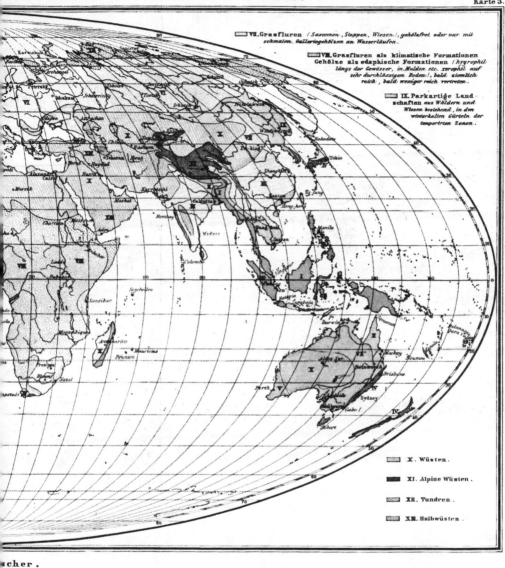

VII. Grasfluren (Savannen, Steppen, Wiesen), gehölzfrei oder nur mit schmalen Galleriegehölzen an Wasserläufen.

VIII. Grasfluren als klimatische Formationen Gehölze als edaphische Formationen (hygrophil längs der Gewässer, in Mulden etc. xerophil auf sehr durchlässigem Boden), bald ziemlich reich, bald weniger reich vertreten.

IX. Parkartige Landschaften aus Wäldern und Wiesen bestehend, in den winterkalten Gürteln der temperirten Zonen.

X. Wüsten.

XI. Alpine Wüsten.

XII. Tundren.

XIII. Halbwüsten.

scher.

Boundaries in many areas are vague, which is an honest reflection of the limited available knowledge at that time.

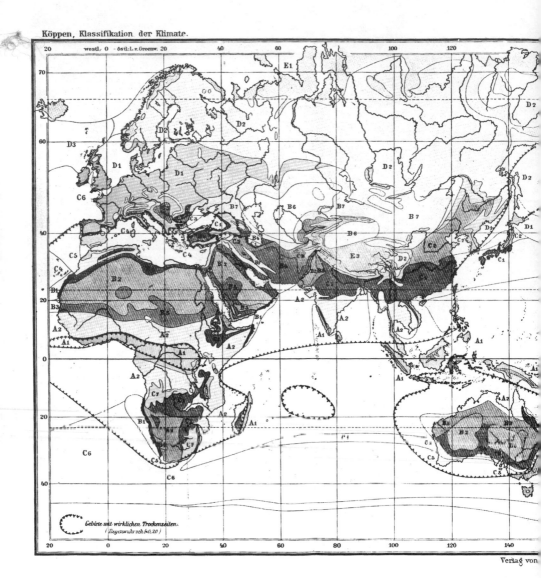

*Map 5.* The climatic regions of Köppen (1900). Because Köppen's climatic
regions are essentially based on vegetation, his map is as much a vegetation

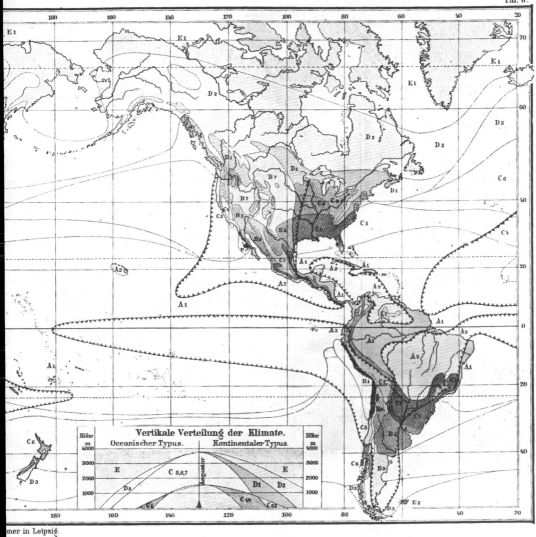

oner in Leipzig.

map as a climatic map. There is a plethora of minor categories that makes the
result much too complicated.

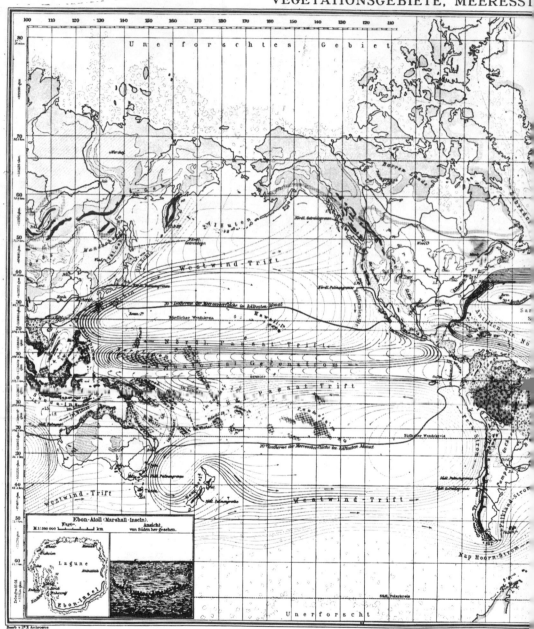

*Map 6*. World vegetation according to Andree (1906). The primary importance of this atlas map is that it refines the earlier attempts to map vegeta-

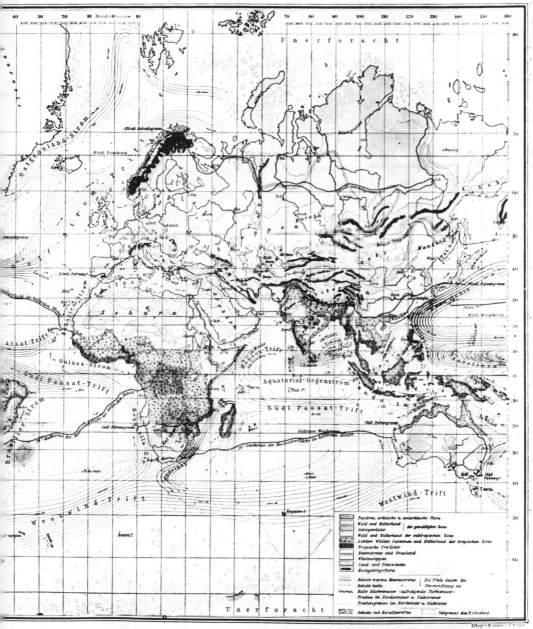

tion. There are fewer categories than used by Schimper (10 instead of 13)
and the boundaries are more carefully delimited.

classification is not perfect because certain disharmonious categories intrude. Perhaps the mountain distinctions can be accepted, in that altitude is being recognized as similar to latitude in the effect on temperature.


## LATER DEVELOPMENT

Greater precision concerning actual patterns of vegetation was achieved during the early part of this century through regional studies of continents or major parts thereof. Some important examples of these are Harshberger (1911) on North America, Shantz and Zon (1924) on the United States, Bartholomew (1917) on Europe, Shantz and Marbut (1923) on Africa, and a series of maps by Vidal de la Blache and Gallois in the *Geographie Universelle* (1927-46). These maps tend to differ from the world representation by freedom from the necessity to conform to a universal system and therefore they characteristically contain unique sorts of vegetation such as *prairie, southern pines, taiga, tall grass-low tree savanna, caatinga,* and *mallee.* Several series of continental maps were published during this period (Hardy 1920; Unstead and Taylor), but because each map had a separate title, unique categories could still be retained in spite of the tendency toward uniformity imposed by their group association. A carry-over even can be seen on world maps compiled from such sources, where the legend is encumbered with endemic elements (Jones 1923; Herzog 1933; Linton 1951; Eyre 1963, pp. 277-99).

During this period maps were also published that retained a world system of vegetation classification, but these showed remarkably little difference from their predecessors. Undercurrents of vegetation category stereotypes and parochial influences were developing in such maps. One source of variation arose from the fact that Schimper had two moisture sequences of forest in but two temperature zones while de Candolle called for only one level of forest to be divided among three zones. In order to provide for three zones, the equivalent of Schimper's *temperate rainforest* was placed between *temperate forest* and *tropical rainforest* (equatorial and tropical forest) and called *subtropical forest* or *rainforest* or even *temperate rainforest.* This procedure leaves the *lighter tropical forest* in an anomalous position as the only second-level forest, or conversely one may consider rainforest as a strictly tropical phenomenon, as do Finch and Trewartha (1936). Later their vegetation map was simplified by elimination of the tropical steppe area, calling the savanna tropical grassland, and grouping the lighter tropical forest with the thorn forest. Another alternative is to accept both levels of forest and three temperature zones, as does Schimper and von Faber (1935). There is no subtropical forest on this map but savanna woodland is extended into the corresponding position.

The more usual practice is to drop either the lighter tropical forest or the low-latitude steppe, so that the four moisture levels are retained. This gives either the sequence in the tropics of *rainforest, savanna, steppe,* and *desert* or *rainforest, forest, savanna,* and *desert.* There seems to be no consensus as to the equation of savanna with either tropical steppe or with tropical woodland. Quite a few maps have thorn forest (caatinga) located in one or more areas within the savanna zone. Occasionally the subtropical forest is omitted completely and, because steppe and desert are not normally subdivided, the result is to eliminate the subtropical temperature zone completely.

Some sort of temperate or middle-latitude forest, mostly in the northern hemisphere, is a regular component of all vegetation maps, although it may occasionally be combined with other kinds of forest. In 1900 Köppen instituted a south to north sequence from this forest to cold desert with levels corresponding to those of the wet-dry sequence. This produced a *needle forest* region which was in harmony with the taiga or northern coniferous forest that is identified on continental maps, as well as on Wagner's world map. The idea of a polar woodland corresponding to other subhumid forest or woodland zones is consonant with the general thinking of de Candolle and Schimper. However, as this subdivision of forest became general on world vegetation maps it was expanded to include all areas of conifer dominance. A few authors, such as James (1929, 1935), divided the conifers according to zone, but, with the conifers, a phylogenetic concept came almost universally to supersede the zonal concepts previously involved. Along with the distinction of *coniferous forest* or its equivalent, there was the category of *mixed coniferous and broadleaved forest,* sometimes combined with *broadleaved forest* on the maps.

The subtropical woodland was early identified with the dry summer areas, an obvious and distinct climatic area. As the world

# KLIMATE DER ERDE

von

## W. Köppen

Maßstab 1 : 60 000 000
(Mittelpunktmaßstab)

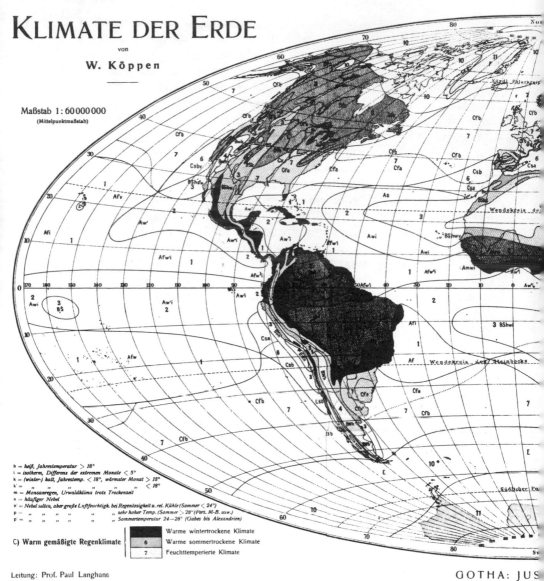

h = heiß, Jahrestemperatur > 18°
i = isotherm, Differenz der extremen Monate < 5°
k = (winter-) kalt, Jahrestemp. < 18°, wärmster Monat > 18°
k' = „ „ „ „ „ „ < 18°
m = Monsunregen, Urwaldklima trotz Trockenzeit
n = häufiger Nebel
n' = Nebel selten, aber große Luftfeuchtigk. bei Regenlosigkt u. rel. Kühle (Sommer < 24°)
n" = „ „ „ „ „ „ sehr hoher Temp. (Sommer > 28° (Pers. M.-B. usw.)
p = „ „ „ „ „ „ Sommertemperatur 24—28° (Gabes bis Alexandrien)

C) Warm gemäßigte Regenklimate
| 6 | Warme wintertrockene Klimate |
| | Warme sommertrockene Klimate |
| 7 | Feuchttemperierte Klimate |

Leitung: Prof. Paul Langhans

GOTHA: JUS

*Map 7.* The climatic regions of Köppen (1918). The elimination of many
categories allowed Köppen to make a more systematic classification in this

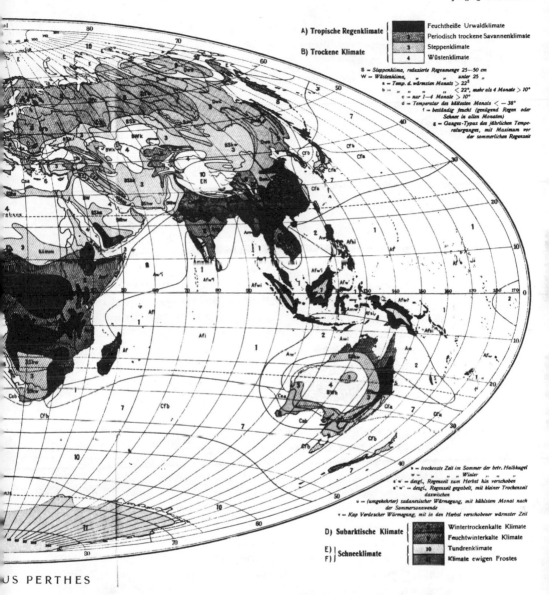

A) Tropische Regenklimate

B) Trockene Klimate

Feuchtheiße Urwaldklimate
Periodisch trockene Savannenklimate
Steppenklimate
Wüstenklimate

S = Steppenklima, reduzierte Regenmenge 25—50 cm
W = Wüstenklima, " unter 25 "
a = Temp. d. wärmsten Monats > 22°
b = " " " " < 22°, mehr als 4 Monate > 10°
c = nur 1—4 Monate > 10°
d = Temperatur des kältesten Monats < —38°
f = beständig feucht (genügend Regen oder Schnee in allen Monaten)
g = Ganges-Typus des jährlichen Temperaturganges, mit Maximum vor der sommerlichen Regenzeit

s = trockenste Zeit im Sommer der betr. Halbkugel
w = " " " " Winter
s'w = desgl. Regenzeit zum Herbst hin verschoben
s"w = desgl. Regenzeit gegabelt, mit kleiner Trockenzeit dazwischen
u = (umgekehrter) sudanesischer Wärmegang, mit kühlstem Monat nach der Sommersonnwende
v = Kap Verdescher Wärmegang, mit in den Herbst verschobener wärmster Zeit

D) Subarktische Klimate

E) / Schneeklimate
F) /

Wintertrockenkalte Klimate
Feuchtwinterkalte Klimate
Tundrenklimate
Klimate ewigen Frostes

second attempt. Most of the categories are meant to correspond with vegetation types, and revisions of this system are generally designed to perfect this correspondence.

maps became more detailed, the woodlands of the dry summer areas were given prominence and other subtropical woodland areas were glossed over or ignored. Virtually the only exception is the map by De Martonne (1927) which, although sketchy, clearly does not limit this vegetation type to the one climatic category. Quite a repertoire of titles is applied to the subtropical woodland as narrowly conceived, including *sclerophyll forest* or *woodland, evergreen hardwood forest,* and *Mediterranean scrub forest.* Although originally created as a subhumid zone on the humid side of the steppe, as currently delineated it normally abuts the desert.

## THE ROLE OF THE CLIMATIC MAP

By the mid-twentieth century the vegetation map of the world, through small changes, had evolved into an assemblage of specific kinds of vegetation with certain zonal qualities but no longer with the obvious and direct symmetry of a half-century before. However, a strong relationship to the climatic map of Köppen had become apparent, and this was not accidental.

In 1918 Köppen published a new classification of climate which closely paralleled his earlier attempt but which differed in emphasis and definitions (Map 7). The four-part temperature and one-part arid framework based on de Candolle was retained. Each major climatic zone was then divided so that a total of eleven primary climates were recognized. Several secondary climates were suggested and a number of subdivisions of the primary climates were added. Among the eleven, the *tropical rainforest, savanna, steppe, desert,* and *warm temperature rainy without a dry summer* were equated with the corresponding vegetation types of Schimper (the last being his temperate rainforest), even though Köppen's maps show greater correspondence of pattern to later vegetation maps than to the vague map of Schimper. Köppen's *tundra, eternal frost* (plantless), and *subarctic* (forest) also correspond to popular vegetation types. Because Köppen looked upon this classification as not to be dominated by vegetation, he expressly states that the differentiation of his *subarctic dry winter* and his *warm temperate dry winter* (wet summer) climates are not reflected in vegetation. It is significant that these nonvegetation-related climatic distinctions among his major divisions are precisely the ones most commonly ignored by users of his system. On the other hand, the summer temperature distinctions, which he relegated to a subsidiary role, are often raised to primary importance. Thus, (with their vegetation correlations) we have *Cfa* (subtropical forest), *Cfb* (temperate rainforest), *Dfb* (temperate forest), *Dfc* (taiga). The secondary climatic type *monsoon rainforest* was created to accommodate those areas with a rainforest type of vegetation in spite of a distinct dry season, because of a high total annual precipitation.

The use of Köppen's climatic classification in connection with vegetation distribution maps is a standard practice. It is common for textbooks when discussing natural patterns to suggest that a close similarity exists and perhaps to construct a hypothetical continent with idealized climatic patterns, as Köppen himself did, and then to compare it with a similar diagram of vegetation. There is more than a suggestion here that categories are selected which produce a happy correlation, an exercise in circular reasoning. Further, there have been numerous discussions of the Köppen classification where modifications are suggested in order to create more harmony with details of the vegetation distribution (Leighly 1949; Hare 1951; Ackerman 1941; Rubner 1938; Trewartha 1954, pp. 223 38).

## THE ADDITION OF NON-CLIMATIC FACTORS

With the introduction of *coniferous forest* as a category of vegetation, there is the possibility of independence from climatic consideration in ordering the plant cover of the earth. Conifer or *needle-leaved evergreen* trees can be distinguished without reference to climatic statistics, suggesting the contrasting category of *broadleaved deciduous* trees. This leads to all sorts of leaf-type distinctions as, for example, those used by Rübel (1930, pp. 52-53), ranging from *needle leaf forest* through *summer green deciduous forest* (temperate forest) and *raingreen deciduous forest* (tropical forest) to *laurel forest (broadleaf evergreen sclerophyll forest* or subtropical forest). The tropical rainforest is, of course, a *broadleaf evergreen hygrophytic forest.* James observed that the tropical seasonal forest was not entirely deciduous, and so on his 1935 map

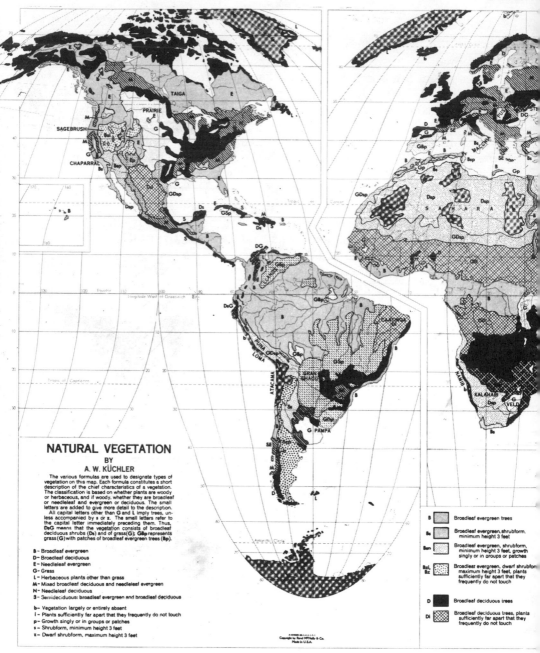

## NATURAL VEGETATION

### BY
### A. W. KÜCHLER

The various formulas are used to designate types of vegetation on this map. Each formula constitutes a short description of the chief characteristics of a vegetation. The classification is based on whether plants are woody or herbaceous, and if woody, whether they are broadleaf or needleleaf and evergreen or deciduous. The small letters are added to give more detail to the description.

All capital letters other than G and L imply trees, unless accompanied by s or z. The small letters refer to the capital letter immediately preceding them. Thus, DsG means that the vegetation consists of broadleaf deciduous shrubs (Ds) and of grass (G); GBp represents grass (G) with patches of broadleaf evergreen trees (Bp).

B – Broadleaf evergreen
D – Broadleaf deciduous
E – Needleleaf evergreen
G – Grass
L – Herbaceous plants other than grass
M – Mixed broadleaf deciduous and needleleaf evergreen
N – Needleleaf deciduous
3 – Semideciduous: broadleaf evergreen and broadleaf deciduous

b – Vegetation largely or entirely absent
i – Plants sufficiently far apart that they frequently do not touch
p – Growth singly or in groups or patches
s – Shrubform, minimum height 3 feet
z – Dwarf shrubform, maximum height 3 feet

Copyright by Rand McNally & Co.
Made in U.S.A.

| | |
|---|---|
| B | Broadleaf evergreen trees |
| Bs | Broadleaf evergreen, shrubform, minimum height 3 feet |
| Bsn | Broadleaf evergreen, shrubform, minimum height 3 feet, growth singly or in groups or patches |
| Bzi, Bz | Broadleaf evergreen, dwarf shrubform, maximum height 3 feet, plants sufficiently far apart that they frequently do not touch |
| D | Broadleaf deciduous trees |
| Di | Broadleaf deciduous trees, plants sufficiently far apart that they frequently do not touch |

Map 8. World vegetation according to Küchler (1949). Here is a major break with tradition, the categories selected without reference to climate. For most

Legend:

| | |
|---|---|
| Broadleaf deciduous, shrubform, minimum height 3 feet | |
| Broadleaf deciduous, shrubform, minimum height 3 feet, plants sufficiently far apart that they frequently do not touch | |
| Broadleaf deciduous, shrubform, minimum height 3 feet, growth singly or in groups or patches | |
| Broadleaf deciduous, dwarf shrubform, maximum height 3 feet, growth singly or in groups or patches | |
| Broadleaf deciduous, shrubform, minimum height 3 feet. Grass and other herbaceous plants | |
| Broadleaf deciduous trees. Grass and other herbaceous plants | |
| Broadleaf deciduous trees. Broadleaf evergreen, shrubform, minimum height 3 feet | |

E — Needleleaf evergreen trees

Ep — Needleleaf evergreen trees, growth singly or in groups or patches

G — Grass and other herbaceous plants

Gp — Grass and other herbaceous plants, growth singly or in groups or patches

GBp — Grass and other herbaceous plants. Broadleaf evergreen trees, growth singly or in groups or patches

GD — Grass and other herbaceous plants. Broadleaf deciduous trees

GDp — Grass and other herbaceous plants. Broadleaf deciduous trees, growth singly or in groups or patches

GDsp — Grass and other herbaceous plants. Broadleaf deciduous, shrubform, minimum height 3 feet, growth singly or in groups or patches

GSp — Grass and other herbaceous plants. Semideciduous: broadleaf evergreen and broadleaf deciduous trees, growth singly or in groups or patches

L — Herbaceous plants other than grass

M — Mixed: broadleaf deciduous and needleleaf evergreen trees

N — Needleleaf deciduous trees

ND — Needleleaf deciduous trees. Broadleaf deciduous trees

S — Semideciduous: broadleaf evergreen and broadleaf deciduous trees

Ss — Semideciduous: broadleaf evergreen and broadleaf deciduous, shrubform, minimum height 3 feet

SsG — Semideciduous: broadleaf evergreen and broadleaf deciduous, shrubform, minimum height 3 feet. Grass and other herbaceous plants

Szp — Semideciduous: broadleaf evergreen and broadleaf deciduous, dwarf shrubform, maximum height 3 feet, growth singly or in groups or patches

SE — Semideciduous: broadleaf evergreen and broadleaf deciduous trees. Needleleaf evergreen trees

b — Vegetation largely or entirely absent

purposes there are too many categories. It could be called an analytical rendition of vegetation.

MODIFIED VAN DER GRINTEN PROJECTION

TROPICAL RAINFOREST

LIGHTER TROPICAL FOREST
(SEMIDECIDUOUS)

TROPICAL SCRUB FOREST

SAVANNA (TROPICAL GRASSLAND)

PRAIRIE

STEPPE

DESERT

*Map 9.* Generalized vegetation map representing those widely used in the mid-twentieth century. The variation of any one map from any other or

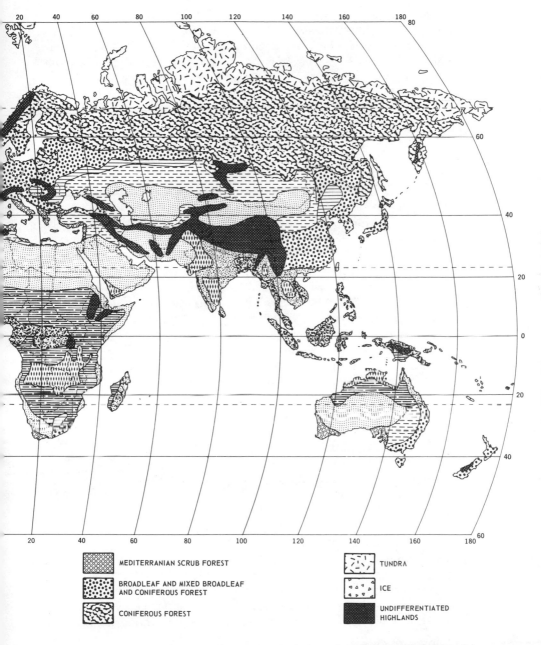

| | | | |
|---|---|---|---|
| MEDITERRANIAN SCRUB FOREST | | TUNDRA | |
| BROADLEAF AND MIXED BROADLEAF AND CONIFEROUS FOREST | | ICE | |
| CONIFEROUS FOREST | | UNDIFFERENTIATED HIGHLANDS | |

from this generalization is remarkably slight although definite differences do occur. A comparison with Köppen's map of climatic types also shows substantial agreement.

he employed the term *semideciduous*, which has been widely used since. Other possible leaf distinctions are *broadleaf evergreen sclerophyll woodland* (Mediterranean scrub forest) and *deciduous xerophytic woodland* (tropical thorn forest). A further bold step was taken by Küchler (1947a, 1949a, 1949b) in an attempt to create a vegetation map entirely free of climatic considerations (Map 8). Küchler created a map without temperature zones but with all trees and shrubs categorized with respect to leaf type, broadleaf or needleleaf and deciduous or evergreen, with provisions for combinations.

In recent times several vegetation classifications with numerous (more than thirty as compared with the usual fewer than twenty) categories having been constructed (Linton 1951; Eyre 1963; Schmithüsen 1959. See also regional classifications in Montoya Maquin 1966). In part these may make use of most or all of the distinctions which have already been discussed. Not only do they have temperature zones with moisture subdivisions, but they have leaf types segregated as well, not to mention elevation effects. Also included are various or even many special or endemic formations designated by the name of a location or a particular plant, and formations based on more than just vegetation. These profuse collations are in part not classifications, but more of a "round-up" of everything the author felt should be mentioned.

## RECENT TREATMENT

By the mid-twentieth century there had developed a very standardized notion of the world vegetation map (Finch *et al.* 1957; Kendall *et al.* 1962; Williams 1963; Philbrick 1963; Fullard and Darby 1969; Whittaker 1970; *etc.*). Each version is, naturally, different in some way from the others, but the similarities are overwhelming (Map 9). The *tropical rainforest* is always one category. *Lighter tropical forest* or *semideciduous forest* is often present. *Tropical scrub forest* is sometimes differentiated. *Savanna*, sometimes called *tropical grassland*, is a regular category. *Prairie* and *steppe* are sometimes separate or else combined into a type called *grassland*. *Desert* is a constant inclusion. *Mediterranean scrub* under some name is always mapped along with some kind of *middle-latitude forest*. *Coniferous forest* is sometimes limited to boreal regions, but *tundra* is accepted by all. *Ice cap* usually rounds out the map which, therefore, has about a dozen categories. Quite a range of factors is suggested by these names which do not fall into any readily apparent system. Of course, it can always be argued that system is present and only obscured by labels, but no clear system is revealed by the text in those cases where such maps are accompanied by a text.

A somewhat different approach was used in my own map of world vegetation (de Laubenfels 1964). Only seven categories of plant cover appear, based on the dominant layer of growth (Map 10). Like the map of Küchler, climatic factors are avoided, but the total character of the plant cover is suggested as the criterion rather than certain physiognomic features. The vegetation is ordered from *rainforest*, with the absence of mechanisms for dormancy, *seasonal forest*, with still a continuous tree canopy, *woodland*, with discontinuous tree canopy, to *desert*, with a discontinuous cover of plants. *Tundra* is accepted (with some lack of consistency) for the cold treeless areas. Abundant trees with a grass cover are placed in the *woodland-savanna* (parkland) category, while, where herbaceous plants dominate, the term *grassland* is applied. *Brush* is not mapped separately, being included in the woodland and the tundra areas because it is too scattered to be distinguished at the world scale. The more open savannas are grouped with grassland. With the nearly self-evident division of the world into tropical and middle-latitude zones, the usual complement of vegetation types can easily be accounted for. Elements of cover characteristics, of course, are involved in many earlier maps, but this is the first world map to attempt a classification based on cover-types alone, unless certain highly generalized maps with but three or four categories be considered (Polunin 1960, p. 213). Implied here is dissatisfaction with other factors used to subdivide world vegetation, and it will be the purpose of succeeding parts of this book to weigh these various factors and assess their significance.

## FACTORS IN MAPPING VEGETATION FORMATIONS

In practice a great many factors have been used in the construction of vegetation maps of plant formations. As groundwork for

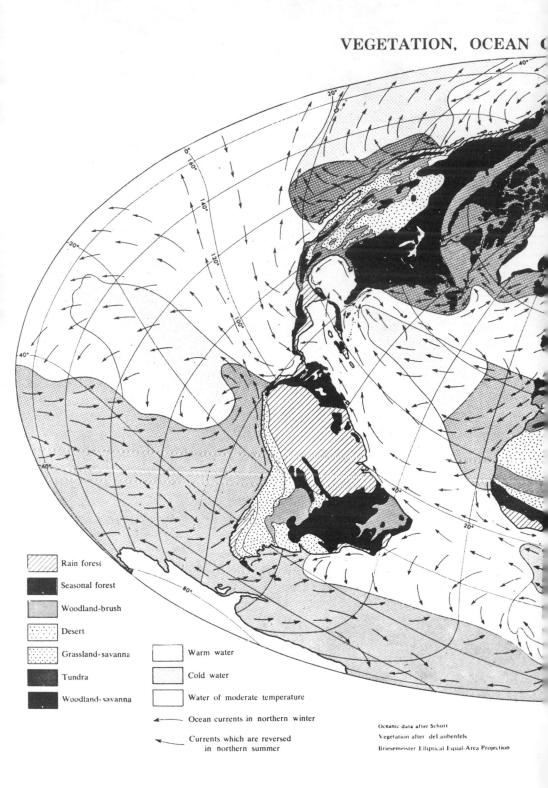

**Rain forest**

**Seasonal forest**

**Woodland-brush**

**Desert**

**Grassland-savanna**

**Tundra**

**Woodland-savanna**

Warm water

Cold water

Water of moderate temperature

Ocean currents in northern winter

Currents which are reversed in northern summer

Oceanic data after Schott

Vegetation after deLaubenfels

Briesemeister Elliptical Equal-Area Projection

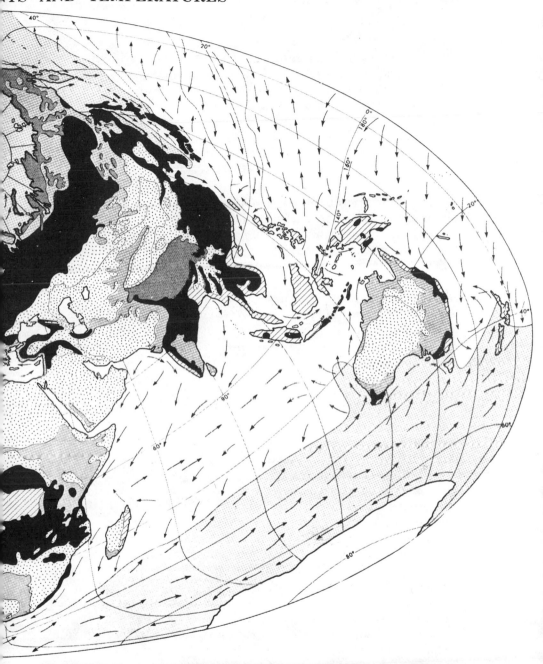

*Map 10.* World vegetation according to de Laubenfels (1964). A first attempt at an integrated vegetational system. The inclusion of *Tundra* as a category is inconsistent.

analysis, these can be categorized into their major types. From the early days a relationship between plants and environment has been suggested; so vegetation is commonly segregated, in part, in terms of *external factors*, that is, relevant environmental characteristics. Constantly stressed is the fact that any vegetation is a composite of individual plant species; so attention is given to *phylogeny* in categorizing vegetation. More directly related to the physical makeup of plants is their *form*, while in combination there is produced different kinds of vegetation *cover* over the ground.

The interaction between plants and their environment is a very important reason for studying vegetation because there is no question but that strong relationships exist. The external factor most frequently associated with vegetation is climate. The earliest vegetation maps had zonal temperature and moisture distinctions. More complicated climatic combinations are made concerning the relationship and severity of moisture and temperature seasons; thus specific climatic types emerge which are said to have characteristic vegetational responses. The environment of plants also includes soil and, especially on large-scale maps, all sorts of edaphic vegetation types are identified. Soil, of course, is not independent of plants. Landform is yet another factor, with slope, exposure, and elevation all having their effect on plant growth in some way.

Plants with a common ancestry share various characteristics, the more closely related, the more similar they are. For whatever purpose a vegetation map is produced, plants that are related will tend to fall together to some degree within the elements of the classification. Some broad generalizations have been made about such major groups as conifers, grasses, palms, and others. Inasmuch as these generalizations are correct they might properly take their place alongside other factors in differentiating vegetation.

As elements of the landscape, the most obvious character of individual plants is their form (Cain and Castro 1959, pp. 255-85). There are many aspects of form, the most important of which are leaf shape, branching structure, and size. Leaves have been generally divided into broad as against small (needle or scale shaped) and into deciduous or evergreen. Descriptively underlying the separation of some kinds of vegetation is the branching structure, including the relation of secondary branches to the trunk in size and position and the degree of branching. The branching structure of some plants is quite distinctive, at least with respect to the associated plants. Size is very important, especially as it relates to the difference between trees, bushes, and shrubs. Other form factors include special organs, such as thorns, or special functions, such as water storage.

Cover involves plant form but considers the assemblage of plants together over an area. Cover can be distinguished by layers, the three most important of which are the canopy, the understory, and the ground cover. In a given area any one of these can be continuous, discontinuous, or absent. The several resulting combinations can be further separated by other factors such as the extent of permanence of the elements. Other layers have been recognized and various degrees of discontinuity can be established (Richards 1952, pp. 19-39).

It must not be overlooked that any of the factors of vegetation might be pertinent to any of the objects for which a vegetation map is to be produced. We shall evaluate each for its contribution, if any, to an understanding of the response of vegetation to environment. Factors which may not seem to represent a vegetation response may, nevertheless, involve such a response masked by a poor or misleading label. On the other hand, apparent responses can turn out to be illusory. Each of the various factors identified above will be examined in turn in the following chapters.

# 2

# External Factors Used in Vegetation Mapping

I N MAPPING VEGETATION, factors which are not in themselves elements of vegetation are commonly identified. It is at
least implied in such cases that the external factor stands for or
sums up other factors which are in fact vegetational. That this is
not necessarily true is indicated by the fact that environmental
references have been explicitly avoided in some vegetational
classification schemes, as was seen in the introductory discussion.
There is no doubt that correlations exist between the environment
and the vegetation, but unless external environmental terms represent definitely understood vegetational characteristics, their use is
at least confusing and probably misleading. The external factors
which have been used to differentiate vegetation are dominated by
various aspects of climate, with other important factors being soil
and landform. The particular aspects of climate generally employed
in classifying vegetation include zonal divisions of temperature
(tropical and temperate) and two special vegetation-climate complexes, the Mediterranean type and tundra. Moisture inferences,
such as rainforest and desert, are understood as much in the form
of the plant cover as they are in climatic terms and therefore need
not be considered here among the important environmental
references in vegetation classification.

## DIVISION OF VEGETATION BETWEEN TROPICAL
## AND TEMPERATE ZONES

Many plants, especially cultigens, are essentially limited to or excluded from the tropics, because many tropical plants are frost

sensitive while extra-tropical plants may need certain day-length variations or temperature cycles in order to complete their own growth cycle. The idea follows that if plants are largely differentiated by temperature zones, then vegetation formations should also be so ordered. Nearly all vegetation maps segregate tropical from temperate forests, the most notable exceptions being Bartholomew, Küchler, and de Laubenfels. Bartholomew, however, approaches the treatment of Unstead and Taylor, who show only one category of tropical forest by having very little forest other than rainforest in the low latitudes. It is common to treat savanna as tropical grassland and contrast it with steppe (middle-latitude grassland). Even when grassland is differentiated from savanna, the tropical grassland is usually distinguished from middle-latitude grassland. Woodlands and thorn forest are not always mapped or they are identified with particular regions, but nevertheless, they are not likely to be found grouped into any unit that extends from the tropics through the middle latitudes. Even desert on detailed maps may be separated into two latitudinal types. It is a question, then as to what exactly the purported vegetational differences are and how valid they appear to be. Let us consider each of these in turn, that is: forest, rainforest, grassland, woodland, and desert.

*Forest*

Considering forest in the narrow sense, with rainforest kept aside as possibly a different sort of problem, it is notable that most of the major forest regions are not only isolated from one another, but are also definitely in or out of the tropics (Map 13). Therefore, the division of forest by latitude is no great problem, it is for the most part obvious on a vegetation map, whether or not an identification of low- and middle-latitude types is made. There are places, however, where forests bridge the temperature zones and the question still remains, should a distinction be made as to the kind of forest by latitude.

A search of the literature yields almost no statements that would explain why forests nearer the equator should be marked off from those outside of the tropics. The two zones are nevertheless treated separately and sometimes described in detail. The field of distinctions narrows virtually down to the fact that deciduous forests of the continuously warm areas tend to have tree flowering during the leaf-absent period (Polunin 1960, p. 440). Of course, many trees with a winter leaf fall have a conspicuous crop of flowers before the new leaves unfold (but not during the dead of the winter) and the dry season of the low latitudes is certainly not in every place nor continuously marked by floral displays. Comments concerning leaf form variations or references to tendencies toward layering with respect to tropical forests are neither directly contrasted with extra-tropical forests nor do they suggest any characteristics that are not familiar outside of the tropics. Therefore, it is notable that Schimper said, after discussing the effects of moisture on vegetation and of heat on flora, "only in the polar areas is the temperature important as a climatic cause of a type of vegetation — in the cold desert or tundra" (1903, p. 160). It is apparent that the division of forest is essentially floristic, not based on form.

There are three places where the forests of the higher latitudes come in contact with forests of the lower latitudes — Central America, Southeast Asia, and Australia. Southern Brazil and South Africa might be considered additional cases where bits of forest extend beyond thirty degrees latitude and considerable areas do experience some frost. The situations in Central America and Southeast Asia are similar in that the zone of contact is narrow compared to the much more extensive distribution of the respective floras northward and southward and in both cases also highly mountainous, so that moisture and other factors are intertwined with temperature considerations. Both cases seem to involve an impingement of separate floras developed well isolated from one another in distinctive sets of environmental complexes. Nevertheless, there is overlap as, for example, the mesquite which forms important woodland in central Texas and the pine which extends well south in savannas in the lowland of eastern Nicaragua, not to mention oak, which is found at higher elevation, not only in northern South America but also beyond the equator in New Guinea and as low as four thousand feet.

The situation in Australia, however, is instructive in that a broad forest zone extends along the eastern part of that country from northern Queensland without interruption south to Victoria with outliers beyond in Tasmania to the south and in New Guinea to the north, the northern part being undoubtedly tropical and the southern part most definitely not. The zone is about evenly divided between tropical and temperate reaches by whatever

*Figure 1*. Australian forest east of Melbourne at 38° latitude. The area experiences regular winter freezes. This is a "fire climax" forest but the grass has not been burned in several years.

criterion might be applied. From north to south the flora and the physiognomy are virtually unchanged. The forest is strongly dominated by eucalypts but there are important associated trees including *Acacia* (wattle), *Casuarina*, and *Callitris* (cypress-pine). These latter three, although involving tree species, are more often shrubby and are joined by such widespread shrub types as *Banksia*, cycads, and grass-trees. Species vary from north to south and with respect to habitat, but important species extend through most of the latitudinal spread of the forest, as the forest red gum *(Eucalyptus tereticornis)*, ironbark *(E. crebra)*, spotted gum *(E. maculata* and varieties), she-oak *(Casuarina cunninghamiana, C. torulosa)*, and cypress pine *(Callitris columellaris = C. hugelii* and *C. intertropica)* (Forestry and Timber Bureau 1957). There is no sorting out of species based on frost-prone or frost-free areas or any other discernible division. It would be very difficult to distinguish in terms of form a series of pictures taken from north to south, assigning to each one its correct approximate position over

*Figure 2.* Australian forest north of Ingham at 18° latitude. No freezing reaches this area. The forest stand is typical of eastern Queensland. The foreground is part of a railroad right of way.

a mere random guess (Figures 1 and 2). The same diagnosis could apply to any latitude of this forest: (a) a generally open stand of evergreen trees, but not so dispersed as to allow continuous bands of sunshine to reach the ground beneath the trees; (b) shade not very dense with continuous ground cover of mostly grass; (c) crown well above the ground, trees sixty and more feet high; (d) scattered juvenile trees of shrubby tree species; (e) occasionally more dense apparently where fire has not been recent and with a greater variety of small understory trees but with only a thin cover of grass and other herbs (Williams 1955, pp. 8-11).* Certainly the

*The various types of dry sclerophyll forest and (mixed) woodland used by Williams cover most of the area under discussion. His descriptions attempt to avoid the effects of disturbance, and the dry sclerophyll forest is not reported for Queensland but is mapped in Queensland in the issue "Forest Resources" of the *Atlas of Australian Resources* (1954), and I have seen it in many places and as far north as the Atherton area. The woodland is "subdivided arbitrarily" into temperate and tropical groups on the former map but it is not so divided on the forest resources map. In most of Queensland frost is rare or unknown ("Temperatures," *Atlas of Australian Resources,* 1953).

same kinds of trees with the same forms can cope with the variations associated with latitude, temperature, and whatever else might be effective.

Each plant association is unique, but it is questionable whether any physiognomic generalizations can be found to separate tropical forests from forests in the middle latitudes. Anyone familiar with both regions is likely to be struck by the similarities. Polunin (1960), for example, compares the monsoon forests with temperate deciduous forests in their general aspect. My impression has frequently been the same. Because of this, and because in the standard literature, where tropical forests have been separated from middle-latitude forests, there is no specified definitive difference given, while the description of one or the other can be shorn of environmental references and applied virtually whole to the other, one must conclude that the separation of tropical forests from middle-latitude forests does not communicate any useful information about the vegetation form and does not belong on a vegetation formation map. The identification of specific floras is quite another matter, but does not correlate with the temperature zones either.

*Rainforest*

Classical rainforest probably occurs only in the wet tropics where the vegetation need not adapt to the potential of either killing drought or killing cold. Yet rainforests, variously called subtropical or temperate, are often mapped and described. As a matter of fact, it has not been entirely clear what factor or factors mark off the rainforest from other kinds of forest. This problem will be examined more fully later, but assuming for the moment that there is such a thing, the possibility of latitudinal distinctions needs to be examined.

Rainforest other than lowland tropical is differentiated in the literature from the tropical variety only by degree (Polunin 1960, pp. 350-54, 438; Dansereau 1957, pp. 86-87; Richards 1952, p. 369). There are fewer tree species in such rainforests and these trees are more likely to have coriaceous leaves which, further, tend to be small. Tree buttresses are generally absent and there are fewer lianas. A distinct seasonal rhythm of growth is admitted. Most of these differences are to be found in the tropical highlands and all these differences are no more than a matter of degree compared to the norm of the tropical lowlands. Leaves in the lowland tropical rainforest canopy have to endure withering sunshine at midday and are characteristically coriaceous in this formation. Rarely more than a minority of the trees have buttresses in this formation, nor are buttresses unknown elsewhere. The number of lianas is quite variable both in and out of the tropics. Seasonal rhythms accompany a large part of the tropical rainforest (Richards 1952, pp. 319-20). Individual rhythms unlinked to the performance of other species are the rule where the forest is free from an integrated seasonal wax and wane. There does not appear to be any absolute character to separate the various kinds of rainforest.

The typical tropical rainforest cannot be said to be dominated by any particular one or a group of species, the most obvious distinction presented by the temperate rainforest. A closer look at the tropical rainforest, however, reveals many areas where the tree canopy is in fact dominated by one or a few kinds of trees (sometimes a group of closely related species). Many and possibly all such areas have mild edaphic or climatic limitations for plant growth, while recent disturbance may also be a factor. In northern South America such communities as the Mora forest and others have been recognized as being absolutely dominated by a single species, some in seasonally flooded areas, others in sands (Richards 1952, pp. 236-43, 254). A similar situation exists in the Congo related to edaphic conditions (Richards 1952, pp. 257-58). In parts of Burma and the Philippines those forests largely dominated by a broad range of trees of the dipterocarp family are reduced to dominance by several species of *Dipterocarpus*. Such areas generally form the margins of the rainforest. I have seen forests in New Guinea at intermediate elevations, where classical mixed rainforest is usually found, to be dominated by an association of oak, tan oak, and *Nothofagus*, three closely related genera. Under the canopy was an apparently normal rainforest structure, a solid growth of numerous species of understory trees, and little or no ground cover of herbs. The same situation develops where the rainforest is disturbed and some opportunistic species first occupies the area or where some commercial tree is planted. It probably makes little difference to the riot of understory plants whether the protecting canopy is monospecific or gregarious.

Temperate rainforests and their equivalents in the tropical highlands are very similar to one another and sometimes are represented by closely related species — as between New Guinea and New Zealand (Van Steenis 1953, p. 314. Mountain forests may be stunted by exposure but this is not necessarily their condition). A common factor is uniform coolness, and along with this goes less chance of dryness, so that moss and other epiphytic growth may be well developed. Under the protection of the canopy a wealth of understory trees or large bushes can grow. In such places herbs are insignificant. The hemlock forests of western Washington are an example of this where numerous species of small shade-requiring trees form a continuous cover along with large ferns and juveniles (Franklin and Dyrness 1969, p. 48). The same can be said of the rainforests of New Zealand (Cockayne and Turner 1958, pp. 11-12).

Those forms of vegetation called rainforest that grow outside of the tropics are related structually and often floristically to highland rainforests which themselves pass gradually into lowland rainforest and indeed closely resemble an important segment of the lowland rainforest. The temperate rainforest is a formation that is not unique to middle-latitude areas whether or not it can be included into a broad category called rainforest. Mixed rainforest without any clear-cut dominants, on the other hand, is strictly a tropical phenomenon.

*Grassland*

The almost universal current practice is to separate grasslands into tropical and temperate types. The temperate grasslands may be called steppe and on some maps are divided into tall grass and short grass or prairie and steppe. Tropical grassland is usually called savanna and on some maps a steppe zone or short grass savanna may be differentiated along the dry margins (primarily in Africa). Grasslands and savanna are not the same thing, and so the question here becomes, are the savannas limited to the tropics and are the grasslands excluded therefrom? Quite a few mountain grasslands are found in the tropics, but because they can be considered as extensions of higher-latitude conditions, they cannot be used to settle the question.

The original use of the term *savanna* was probably for a grassy opening, but the usual meaning has come to be a mixture of trees and grass (Fuson 1963). The trees may be numerous or sparse, tall

*Figure 3.* Oak savanna northwest of Santa Barbara, California. Without occasional fires many more trees would become established. The trees here reflect the prevailing wind direction from the left.

or shrubby, evenly distributed or clumped, or a mixture of these. Characteristically there are galeria forest strips along river courses, especially where there is a low floodplain with a high water table. By contrast, grassland is clean, a pure stand of grass and other herbaceous plants without trees of any kind.

Several kinds of vegetation prominent in the middle latitudes fit the definition of *savanna*. In the dry summer subtropics are open stands of trees ranging from grassland as one limit to forest as the other limit (Figure 3) (Dansereau 1957, pp. 91-92; Finch *et al.* 1957, p. 421). These have been called woodland or parkland, or more frequently are lumped together under Mediterranean vegetation. In the dry continental interiors are similar stands of scattered trees whose density has varied historically. The yellow pine is an important example, of which vast areas were or are covered by stands called woodland but which certainly fall within any definition of savanna (Figure 4) (Cowlin *et al.* 1942; Phillips

*Figure 4.* Yellow pine savanna in Montana. These "parklands" characteristically survive on bluffs. The stand will rapidly become forest with the suppression of fire.

1963) The third example of middle-latitude vegetation that might be called savanna is formed by the belts of considerable extent, between forest and grassland in such areas as the Prairie Provinces of Canada, western Missouri, and the northern Ukraine. These belts called parkland are considered to be transitional, but then so might be many tropical savanna belts. Other middle-latitude savannas can be found, as for example the pinyon-juniper woodlands of North America, which are sometimes quite open with grass, or similar woodlands of *Pinus gerardiana* in India (Dogra 1964), and eucalypt savannas in Victoria and Tasmania (Figure 5). Floristic considerations are exactly the same as for forests discussed above.

Treeless grassland occurs in the lowland tropics. The most notable area is in the Llanos of Venezuela where vast unbroken grasslands occur, especially toward the Colombian border (Hueck 1960; grassland with wood elements are mapped separately from "steppe" grassland). Comparable areas probably also exist in

*Figure 5.* Eucalyptus savanna in central Tasmania. Because eucalyptus is so fire resistant such open stands are not widespread. Note the similarity to Figure 3.

Colombia. On a more restricted scale, I have seen beautiful clear grasslands in the Markham Valley in New Guinea (Figure 6) (See Van Steenis 1958*a*). Among the vast savanna stands of Africa there also appear to be treeless areas of somewhat limited extent (Rattray 1960; grassland is treated separately from grasses associated with savanna or woodland. See also Shantz and Marbut 1923, pp. 10-11). All variations between undoubted savanna through very scattered trees to totally treeless conditions occur in grassland areas anywhere, as in the African case and also in Australia where vast areas of Mitchell grass form a mosaic of very open savanna and treeless grassland. There is nothing about continuously high temperatures that insures that trees will always be present in grassland regions.

Grasslands can be said to be more common as a naturally growing vegetation outside of the tropics whereas savanna is certainly the more prevalent of the two in areas closer to the equator. One is reminded of the great interior grasslands of North

America, the steppes of inner Eurasia, the grass pampas of Argentina, Uruguay, and nearby Brazil, and the veld of South Africa. The tropical savannas of the interior of Brazil and the vast savannas of the Sudan and East Africa stand in contrast. The list of trees, large or small, which can withstand both drought and cold and fire must be limited, and it is understandable that treeless grassland might be more prevalent in the higher latitudes where to the equivalent of everything that must be endured in the arid lower latitudes is added sharp cold. But the difference is a matter of degree and it is quite clear that grassland and savanna are not segregated each to their own latitudinal zone.

## Woodland and Desert

Neither woodland nor desert is regularly differentiated in the literature by latitude, but this distinction is sometimes made (Linton 1951; Eyre 1963). In the case of woodland, certain specific formations are indicated on the maps when a subdivision is made; in the case of desert the division seems to follow a blanket separation of all tropical vegetation regions from their middle-latitude counterparts. For both cases the intended nature of any distinction must be gained by inference, because explanations are not forthcoming.

According to labels, tropical woodlands are thorny and deciduous, those outside of the tropics are evergreen and sclerophyllous. These distinctions may apply to certain specific places but not to the whole zones in question. Many evergreen woodland plants exist in the tropics, with or without thorns. The pepper tree *(Schinus)* of Peru and other parts of Latin America is a good example of an evergreen thornless tropical woodland tree of some importance. In the drier valleys of the eastern sides of the Andes all combinations of evergreen and deciduous woodlands occur (Weberbauer 1936). On the other hand, some rather persuasive sharp points make themselves felt on deciduous mesquite plants in Texas or Central Chile or on single-leaved pinyons in Nevada and elsewhere. Deciduous oaks form woodland from the Great Plains (Wells 1965) through Arizona to California, where they mix with evergreen oaks and other deciduous plants like the California walnut.

It is hard to imagine what difference other than floristics in a general sense can justify the separation of low-latitude from

*Figure 6.* Grassland of the Markham Valley in New Guinea. Nearby areas with no difference in climate support rainforest. The grasses here are regularly burned in order to induce fresh growth that will be palatable for cattle.

middle-latitude desert vegetation. One thinks of cactus and euphorbia as prominent on warmer desert margins, but these plants extend in reduced numbers into higher latitudes. Surely a stand of scattered shrubs and ephemerals must belong to the same formation, no matter what sort of temperature variations might be endured. There is every reason to believe that a latitudinal division of desert vegetation is arbitrary.

## Summary

In the Introduction it was seen that temperature zones were accepted as applying to vegetation before any clear notion had developed as to what the distinct vegetation formations might be. It was recognized that there was a floristic relationship with latitude, and it is important to realize that Schimper, who did as much as anyone to lay the groundwork for an understanding of the geography of plants, clearly indicated that the latitudinal divisions applied to floristics and not to vegetation in the sense of form. Yet, the idea of the control of temperature on vegetation has been so persuasive that corresponding formations are time and again seen differently. Scattered trees in grassland in the United States is called *grassland* if it is possible to ignore the trees and woodland or *parkland* if not. But *grasslands* in Venezuela are *savannas* even if there is no tree in sight. Woodlands in Brazil are *xerophytic scrub* or *thorn forest;* woodlands in Chile are *sclerophyll forest* or *Mediterranean scrub.* Partly evergreen forest in the low latitudes can be called *semi-deciduous forest*, but the same thing at higher latitudes would be *temperate forest* or even *subtropical rainforest.*

Not every author of a vegetation classification has made latitudinal distinctions and precious few definitions or even suggestions as to the basis for such separations can be distilled from the literature. Even by inference the yield is small. After weighing the evidence, it cannot be fairly said that there is any kind of vegetation formation in the middle latitudes that can be successfully segregated from corresponding tropical types in terms of any available information. It is only possible to identify floristic divisions and the unique features that separate any given plant or set of plants from any others. It is clear that the latitudinal divisions made can be adequately explained as a carry-over from earlier thinking. Aside from the fact that a more extreme type of rainforest is restricted to the tropics (*not* divided into any zonal types), the low and middle latitudes share the same kinds of vegetation formations.

## SPECIAL VEGETATION-CLIMATE COMPLEXES

Two special vegetation types have come in the literature to be virtually synonymous with their corresponding climatic types: under the name *Mediterranean vegetation* is understood the evergreen woodland and brush of dry summer sub-tropical areas, while the vegetation type *tundra* is associated with the cold areas beyond the tree line, the name originating in northern Europe. There can be no doubt that regions with the combined properties indicated do exist, in contrast to neighboring areas. What is to be investigated concerns the possible uniqueness of the vegetation in each kind of region.

## Mediterranean Vegetation

The vegetation of the dry summer subtropical climate is remarkably similar in physiognomy for each of the widely separated regions where it is found. In detail it is made up of a mosaic of several different forms, partly because most such regions occur in broken country. Two of the forms are primarily identified with Mediterranean-type climate areas, the sclerophyllous woodland and the dense brush. By *sclerophyllous* is meant small, broad, evergreen leaves that are thick and leathery. The brush, presumably because of its uniqueness, is known locally by special names such as *garigue* and *maqui (macchia)* in the western Mediterranean, *chaparral* in California, and *matorral* in Chile. The term *Cape macchia* is applied in South Africa, while the *mallee* of Australia is in reality a woodland, there being no corresponding brush development in that occurrence of the climatic type. Associated clearly with the two distinctive vegetation forms are two others: grassland, especially in broad flat areas, and savannas, usually called *parkland*.

The Mediterranean-type climate, with mild moist winters and hot dry summers, is considered unique in the opportunities and limitations it presents to plant growth. Moisture, available in considerable quantities, is nevertheless not to be had when the more favorable temperatures occur, yet the winter is not so severe but that much of the time plant activity is possible. Evergreen plants, their leaves properly protected against the relentless summer sun, are available for photosynthesis at least in the spring and fall if not over the whole winter. Many authors, starting with Schimper, have emphasized the role of climate in plant development in these areas, giving prominence to the characteristic leaf type. At best this is an exaggeration.

The vegetation of the dry summer subtropics is by no means exclusively evergreen. Particularly in California deciduous trees are important under this climate. Probably the three most important kinds of tree in the California woodlands are live oak *(Quercus agrifolia-*coastal, *Q. wislizenii-*inland), blue oak *(Q. douglasii)*, and digger pine *(Pinus sabiniana)*. Of these the blue oak is deciduous.

There are other related but less important species corresponding to each, as well as other shrubby trees among which are included the California walnut *(Juglans californica)*, California buckeye *(Aesculus californica)*, and California redbud *(Cercis occidentalis)*, all neither evergreen nor rare. In the Mediterranean, although over-shadowed in importance by evergreens, deciduous plants do occur, such as *Pistacia terebinthus* (Schimper 1903, p. 523). The most common plant in central Chile, probably increased through disturbance, is the espino *(Acacia caven)*, and it is not the only deciduous shrub known there (Hueck 1966, pp. 329-30).

Nor are evergreen trees and shrubs in the summer dry areas always broad leaved. Needle leaves and scale leaves, more extreme-ly xerophytic, are usually prominent where the corresponding climate occurs. Needle-leaved pines are especially noticeable in the northern hemisphere, followed by scale-leaved cypresses and junipers as well as various flowering shrubs whose leaves approach these forms, such as rosemary *(Rosmarinus officinalis)*. Quite a variety of needle-leaved shrubs or trees occur in the comparable parts of Australia, including species of *Hakea* and *Banksia* as well as *Grevillia* and *Acacia* (these genera also have species with broad leaves). Scale leaves are represented in Australia by the genera *Casuarina*, *Callitris*, and others. Illustrations by Schimper (1903, p. 525) suggest that Cape Province in South Africa has similar forms to those of Australia. In Chile a scale-leaved cypress *(Libocedrus chilensis)* is important along the margins of the forest zone, while some more or less needle-leaved shrubs occur among the brush species, and cactus is quite common.

A *chaparral* or *maqui-like* vegetation is hardly unique to the dry summer sub-tropics. A considerable proportion of the California chaparral has developed over difficult serpentine soils, and its dwarf form may be stabilized or nearly so in such areas. An exactly analogous situation obtains in New Caledonia over serpentine soils but under a vastly different climate, one which supports tropical rainforests in adjacent better soils (Figure 7) (Sarlin 1954). In fact, dense brush vegetation is to be found in many areas, not the least of which is Arizona (Figure 8) (Nichol 1952). It often comes as a surprise to those indoctrinated in the concept of a distinct Mediterranean vegetation to find extensive chaparral across the middle of Arizona where it is accompanied by oak woodlands, not to mention expanses of grass and savanna, just like California, but with precipitation concentrated in the summer.

*Figure 7.* Maqui on serpentine soils in southern New Caledonia. The dwarf conifer *Decussocarpus minor* is growing in water in the center of the picture and is about three meters high. The maqui appears to the left and in the background. Where better soils occur there is rainforest.

Oak chaparrals can also be seen in western Colorado (Eyre 1963, p. 130).

A different view of the vegetation of the dry summer areas emerges when adjacent semi-arid areas are inspected. Leaving aside the large area of the Mediterranean borderlands and southwestern Asia, where the vegetation is so highly disturbed that its reconstruction is quite problematical, one finds strong relationships between neighboring dry climate vegetation areas. The case of Arizona has already been mentioned. The most common tree of the Arizona oak woodlands is a (sclerophyllous) live oak *(Quercus emoryi)*. Other oaks, deciduous and evergreen, are found, including the canyon live oak *(Q. chrysolepis)* which is also widespread and common in California. Additional trees related to California types are present, including juniper, cypress, and pine. In South America the common Chilean *espino* extends across large areas of

*Figure 8.* Chaparral near Globe, Arizona. Rainfall here is concentrated in the summer. Old burned twigs are in evidence.

*monte* in nearby Argentina (Hueck 1966), and other evergreen and deciduous species of Chile have related species in the Argentina summer rainfall woodlands. The same relationship occurs in South Africa, where closely related and morphologically identical species range from the Cape east and northward into the tropics. An example is the cedar *(Widdringtonia).* All the important tree types of the Australian forests — eucalypts, banksia, wattle, she-oak, and cypress-pine — are represented by analogous morphological types in both the dry summer areas and the other semi-arid reaches growing as woodland rather than forest. Not infrequently, the same species will extend into different climatic regimes (Forestry and Timber Bureau 1957). The thing to be learned here is that leaf type and structure of dry summer subtropical vegetation have in each region as much in common with nearby semi-arid regions of a different seasonal rainfall pattern as they have with other regions of similar climate, possibly even more.

Woodlands and dense brush, with a variety of leaf possibilities, grow in more than one sort of region with impoverished climatic moisture or impoverished soil, not being restricted to dry summer type areas at all. Perhaps one could make a case for a sclerophyllous type of leaf tending to be more common in that type of climate area, although the case has previously been so overstated that the implication is questionable. Certainly there is no such *kind* of vegetation as a Mediterranean-type woodland.

## Tundra Vegetation

The tundra is the cold polar area beyond the tree line; the term was used originally in northern Russia and then applied all around the Arctic Ocean because there is no regional difference east and west (Küchler 1947*b*, pp. 205-206; Kimble and Good 1955, p. 89). The same vegetation continues southward along mountain alignments in western North America and in Siberia, where it is usually treated as the same category on vegetation maps over the vigorous objections of some experts (Polunin 1960, p. 409; Küchler 1947*b*; Troll 1941, pp. 60-64. The appropriateness of combining tundra and alpine vegetation is well argued by Eyre 1963, pp. 95-96, 104-105). When the mountain areas are treated differently, their vegetation beyond the tree line is usually called *alpine*, but is sometimes divided between other categories such as *grassland* and *desert*, which may be further identified as a mountain variety (Linton 1951; Küchler 1949*a*). The reasons given, if any, for separating high-latitude tundra from high-elevation vegetation of a similar nature involve the habitat of the vegetation and are thus not appropriate for categorizing vegetation.

The plant cover beyond the tree line has considerable diversity which can be generalized into three main categories (Polunin 1960, pp. 380-99). In the first place, specialists in the far north are generally limiting the word *tundra* to grassland-covered areas (in spite of the original meaning of barren, that is treeless, ground). A wide array of mostly grass-like herbs are included here, among which are true grasses and sedges. More common toward the woodland boundary but also intermixed in complicated mosaics with the grasslands are the brush formations. There being so few plant varieties, one can speak of birch scrub, willow and alder thickets, and heathland. In the southern hemisphere different plants are involved. The third general category of vegetation is the cold desert, made up of fell-fields and barrens, the former being more complex. These cold deserts are concentrated at the highest latitudes. In the mountains, corresponding to these three categories of polar vegetation, are the alpine meadow, mountain brush cover, and barren mountains.

There are two important areas in the world well equatorward from the polar tundra zone where high mountains rise above treeless lowlands without an encompassing cloak of trees. The northern flanks of the Tibetan Highlands are for the most part treeless; grasslands verging on desert clothe both the uplands and the lower slopes. The Andean highlands of Peru, Bolivia, Argentina, and northern Chile support extensive grasslands which give way westward to high-elevation deserts, beyond which are low-elevation deserts. Of course, there are different species of plants at different elevations, but one is very perplexed to know, in terms of formation, just where low-elevation grassland becomes alpine meadow, or where low-elevation desert becomes alpine desert. It only happens that at this point in the history of the world there are no lowland grasslands or deserts extending poleward and adjoining tundra grassland and polar deserts. If they did so join, as they apparently did during the last glacial period, how then would they be separated as vegetation formations?

Tundra is the vegetation beyond the tree line. Without a tree line the question arises as to what sort of vegetation the tundra represents. Is it distinguished by the presence of sedges, lichens, and cushion plants? Obviously these items are not everywhere found within the tundra nor are sedges and lichens unique to grasslands, brush, or deserts in the tundra zone. It seems reasonable to suggest that beyond the tree line are to be found at least three major kinds of vegetation formation and that these three are not by any means confined to the tundra (and alpine) zone but are well known in many other parts of the world.

*Summary*

Geographers have long felt very comfortable about the two categories of vegetation, "Mediterranean woodland" and "tundra." To be sure, they are both often mosaics, but they contrast strongly, for the most part, with neighboring regions and each has very definite climatic characteristics. But climate is not vegetation and when vegetation alone is considered the terms are really not unique at all. To inflate presumed distinctions does not gainsay the fact, and the implication is fairly clear that knowledge of the climatic distinctions has strongly influenced the decision to distinguish these two kinds of vegetation.

## EDAPHIC AND LANDFORM VEGETATION TYPES

References to edaphic or landform factors in vegetation classifications are much less pervasive than the use of climate to indicate the nature of the plant cover, but they do occur (see, for examples, Eyre 1963, Linton 1951, Hardy 1920, and Beard 1944). Some aspects of the relationship of vegetation to landform have already been mentioned, and the examples of lack of correlation between certain climatic factors and vegetation have established that the use of external factors is quite likely to be inappropriate. There is no reason to suppose otherwise for the role of soil or of surface configuration.

It is well known that soil can have a powerful influence on the associated plant cover. Vegetation formations of greater or lesser luxuriance than that of surrounding areas may be induced by advantages or disadvantages impressed by the soil. Such variations are not ordinarily thought of as entirely new formations but merely azonal occurrences (Boyko 1947). A different set of species may accompany special soil chemical concentrations, especially salt. In form these are not necessarily different from other plants, even those nearby.

Special edaphic vegetation types are implied by the use of terms like *marsh, swamp, mangrove,* and *heath* (Heinselman 1963, definitions on pp. 373-74). Description of each of these examples makes clear that local moisture conditions or certain plant species or both are involved. Marsh is a wet grassland. In some parts of the world marshes are cut for hay, and rice is essentially a marsh grass. A swamp is a forested wetland. The trees in a swamp, growing in standing water, in most cases also form forests in drier conditions, that is, free of standing water. Mangrove is a stand of a very special group of trees that can endure tidal fluctuations of water level and various amounts of salt. Mangroves are not always a tangle of growth but when allowed to develop can form a definite forest cover. Heath is a brush cover of ericacious plants which in warmer climates reverts to forest when undisturbed. To be sure, there are some special vegetation types which do merit distinction, and *bog* may be one of them.

Landforms can influence vegetation through elevation effects on temperature and by the consequences of aspect and exposure. Most of these factors merely introduce local contrasts involving common vegetation types (Boyko 1947). Mountain forest may differ in species composition in the same way that species vary by latitude, but there is no reason why lowland formations should not occur at higher elevations. It is often noted that mountain trees are dwarfed, but this is strictly a matter of soil and exposure and not elevation (Van Steenis 1953, p. 314; Richards 1952, p. 373; Grubb and Whitmore 1966). One may ask, as will be done later, just what attention should be given to variations in stature, but other factors are generally involved in the *elfin woodlands,* as these ridge formations are often called. Mountain ridges have a way of being immersed in clouds much of the time and the heavy humidity thus provided supports marvelous festoons of epiphytic plants: mosses, herbs and even woody plants so thick that it may not be easy to tell which leaves belong to the host plant. The distribution of elfin woodlands or cloud forest must necessarily be very localized, even though it has the qualities of a distinctive type.

The effects of soil and of surface configuration are mostly local. The widespread types, when they occur, are not of any unique character among vegetation types not so affected. The more extreme example of this is alpine vegetation which, as discussed above, is made up of formations comparable to those found in polar areas. Distinct vegetation types of uniquely local occurrence, although they may merit recognition, cannot be treated on a world scale and will therefore not further occupy our attention.


## CONCLUSION

The examination of a series of external factors used to designate categories of vegetation has yielded a harvest of non-relationships. Most latitudinal divisions do not relate to vegetation formations. Special vegetation categories — that is, "tundra" and "Mediterranean scrub" — are not distinct categories at all. Except for perhaps special local types, landform and soil do not express vegetational distinctions. Taking the list of traditional vegetation units of world systems, and pruning the external factors therefrom, one is left with a tighter group. The remnants include *rainforest, evergreen seasonal forest, broadleaf deciduous forest, semi-deciduous forest, coniferous forest, mixed broadleaf and coniferous forest, woodland* (evergreen and deciduous), *savanna, grassland,* and *desert.* To these must be added *brush,* which previously was usually subsumed under other categories. Some authors combine among these units and perhaps add others.

The exercise of invalidating various external factors as indicators of vegetation is not meant to imply that correlations do not exist. The role of special local formations has already been admitted. Attention should also be directed to such a series as *rainforest, seasonal forest, woodland,* and *desert.* Clearly these form a sequence related to moisture (Schimper 1903, p. 160), but significantly they call to mind specific formation characteristics and distinctions and are not, ordinarily, defined by moisture characteristics, in spite of the reference to moisture in some of these terms. The conclusion here is that when vegetation has been classified using external factors as criteria, the categories produced have been mostly inadmissible and such a practice should be avoided. Certainly if clear-cut vegetation characteristics exist which correlate with external factors, it would be more logical to use the vegetation characteristics for criteria rather than the non-vegetational factors. This is especially true if one of the main uses of the vegetational classification is going to be an analysis of the relationships between vegetation and other factors.

# 3

# Taxonomic Factors Used in Vegetation Mapping

T HE PHYLOGENETIC RELATIONSHIP OF PLANTS is one of their fundamental attributes and thus may in some way be related to vegetation formation. But, phylogeny itself is determined, ideally, by the facts of evolutionary relationships which include many features, such as microscopic wood structure and developmental stages of the gametophyte and embryo, which cannot be considered as aspects of vegetation form. To be sure, any group of related plants, being less than all plants, will lack some of the qualities which can be ascribed to the totality of the plant world. Reference to a given taxonomic group thus restricts the attributes of the vegetation formed by that group to those characteristics possessed by that group. The possibility exists that a taxonomic group may possess characteristics or combinations of characteristics not shared with other plants or at least rare and sporadic among other plants. This latter can be the only justification for designating a taxonomic group as the criterion for a distinct vegetation-formation type and, therefore, will be used as the measure of the validity of any taxonomic categories which may be included in vegetation-formation classifications.

A great many taxonomic categories have appeared on vegetation maps. Those referring to a specific stand of plants may be dismissed with the realization that any unmixed stand of plants considered must have a unique phylogenetic expression. Rather, of concern are classes of vegetation formation characterized by some taxonomic reference (see, for example, Wagner 1957 — monocot, dicot, herbs, and ferns; Küchler 1949a — herbaceous

61

plants other than grass; Linton 1951 and many others — coniferous forest; Beard 1944 — palms, bamboos, cactus, and pine; Schimper and von Faber 1935 — heath; see also Humboldt 1817). By far the most prominent of these is the type called *coniferous forest. Coniferous woodland* is sometimes separated and an analogous category of *mixed* (coniferous and non-coniferous) *forest* is widely used. The term *grassland* might be considered a taxonomic reference, though the addition of *land* is often understood to remove such a restriction (Dansereau 1957, pp. 95-98; Polunin 1960, p. 443). Other kinds of herbs, such as sedges and ferns, are given prominence. Additional groups singled out include palms, bamboos, cactus and heaths, while a thorough search would undoubtedly unearth more examples.

## CONIFEROUS FOREST

Coniferous trees dominate wide tracts of forest in various parts of the world. By restricting consideration to forest, a brush dominated by conifers, which does occur, is omitted. The implication is that coniferous trees as a class display some essentially unique characteristic or characteristics compared to other forest trees (de Laubenfels 1957). Conifers are cast, usually by inference, as needle-leaved evergreen plants of the cooler areas of the world. The fact that conifers reproduce by means of cone-like structures or that most conifers have rather soft wood (but trees with soft wood are not by any means necessarily conifers) need not be of concern here because these are not characteristics of vegetative form. None of the imputed distinctions are constant characteristics of conifers nor are they substantially unique, even though each is admittedly well developed among the conifers.

In the first place, conifers are not always evergreen. The majority are, to be sure, but important exceptions occur, one of which, the larch, is differentiated in a few vegetation classifications (Küchler 1949a as *needle-leaf deciduous;* Eyre 1963). Among *all* trees, evergreenness is much more common than deciduousness.

No matter what criteria are used, conifers are neither exclusively nor overwhelmingly needle leaved (de Laubenfels 1953). A liberal definition of needle leaves, including scale leaves and narrow leaves, would embrace a substantial part of the conifers (Küchler

*Figure 9.* Redwood forest, northern California. Despite the great height of these trees, the stand cannot be considered a rainforest. Rich alluvial terrace soils make possible the remarkable growth.

1949*a*, p. 203) and of course a generous array of non-conifers (Davies 1964). But many conifers have undeniably broad leaves. An important example is the kauri *(Agathis sp.)* which dominates extensive rainforest areas from Borneo to New Zealand (Van Steenis 1958*a*). Two commonly associated conifers are *Podocarpus neriifolius* ("oleander leaved," it extends to Nepal and South China) and *P. amarus.* This last tree is of interest because, although it is a conifer, in the juvenile form it has especially well-developed drip tips on the leaves like so many flowering rainforest trees (Richards 1952, pp. 84-85). In the subtropical parts of the United States horticulturalists are very familiar with *P. macrophyllous* and *Decussocarpus nageia* from the warmer parts of China and Japan.

The early use of conifers on vegetation maps was related to the identification of a boreal forest, sometimes called the northern coniferous forest. Conifers are usually important (represented by just a few species) in northern forest areas. Later this restriction

*Figure 10.* A rainforest emergent in New Caledonia. A clearing in the foreground has opened the canopy so that the crown of the emergent tree can be seen. The tree is the broadleaved conifer, *Agathis lanceolata.*

of the use of the term "coniferous" was relaxed, because conifers are important in other parts of the world as well. The implication tends to persist, however, that conifers are essentially plants of cold areas (Li 1953). There are two major floristic divisions of the conifers, a northern and a southern hemisphere group. The first group is part of a circumpolar flora, well developed in cooler areas. There are numerous subtropical conifer elements in this flora, however, including most of the redwood family and the cypress family, as well as the true cedars and some pines. Certain pine species, in fact, are pioneers after fire or in sandy soils within the lowland tropics of Central America and Southeast Asia to Sumatra. The southern hemisphere conifers are anchored in the tropics, although there is a small high mountain group in Tasmania and New Zealand. The largest part of the austral species grow in rainforests and, although many extend to some elevation along with the rainforest in general, where moisture conditions are adequate

*Figure 11.* Juniper woodland in central Oregon. Trees block the distant view but the open ground cover is evident.

at low levels they can be prominent right down to sea level, I have verified this in study of the forests in Fiji, New Caledonia, Borneo, and Northern Queensland (de Laubenfels 1969). Lowland species of conifers also occur in New Guinea, Malaya, and the Philippines.* It turns out, when individual species distributions are studied carefully, that these conifers are generally lacking in disturbed areas, which means particularly the drier sites and the lowlands. There are tropical highland conifers, admittedly, but tropical conifers are by no means confined to the highlands.

The form and habit of coniferous trees, apart from the leaves, include a complete range of variation of basic possibilities. There are stunted trees at the tree line *(Picea* sp., *Larix* sp., *Pinus* sp.), semi-arid woodland, or even desert trees *(Juniperus* sp., *Pinus* sp., and *Callitris* sp.), trees of well-developed forest canopy (many

*Information for this statement is derived from extensive study of herbarium specimens with the information noted thereon and from numerous technical taxonomic publications.

*Figure 12.* Okefenokee swamp, Georgia, in the springtime.    The spring growth of the swamp cypress has only begun to appear making the trees seem rather dismal.

kinds), rainforest emergents (Araucariaceae), rainforest canopy trees and understory trees (Podocarpaceae, Taxaceae), and trees of the elfin woodland *(Phyllocladus* sp., *Libocedrus* sp., and *Dacrydium* sp.), to mention some of the more important forms with the leading representative groups (Figures 9-12). Conifer trees occur in a wide variety of swamp conditions and are famous for including opportunistic types which follow disturbance of the forest or thrive in difficult soils. It is not reasonable to include in a classification of vegetation formations a distinction based on conifers. It does not suggest any identifiable form factor at all.

## OTHER TAXONOMIC DESIGNATIONS

The use of taxonomic designations other than coniferous has been sporadic in vegetation classifications of generalized formation types. A number of these can be considered to show the difficulties involved in their use.

GRASS: except for bamboo, the many kinds of grass are herbaceous plants with generally strap-shaped leaves. They are so common and aggressive among herbaceous assemblages that the name *grassland* has come into general use for most such cover types. It has already been mentioned that other herbaceous plants usually accompany the grasses and that the term *grassland* is not meant to exclude that fact. Where there is enough light and moisture to support a continuous cover of herbs, grasses will usually be present, and the term *grassland* as it is understood is perfectly acceptable. There are, however, numerous other herbaceous plants related and not related that share essentially the same form as grass. For example, the common lawn weed, "knot grass" *(Polygonum aviculare)* is not at all related to true grass. The high arctic grasslands may have few or no true grasses, although the grass-like plants in this case are close relatives.

FERNS: there have been ferns around far longer than most other kinds of plants and they exhibit some considerable diversity. There are tree ferns and epiphytic ferns. There are tough ferns that can stand prolonged drought and there are delicate maidenhair ferns with little leaflets. Herbaceous ferns take many forms and flowering herbs frequently parallel these.

PALMS: the invocation of the term *palm* immediately brings to mind a particular plant form. The well-known image of palm trees is that of a single bole with a crown of huge compound leaves. It is not that simple, however, because palms are not always like that and plants like that are not always palms. There are bushy palms like the common palmetto of Florida and nearby states. There are vine palms like the insidious rattans or lawyer vines. In east Africa there are palm trees that have numerous branches. On the other hand palm-like trees include many cycads, tree ferns, and plants of the banana group. The basic form of a palm tree without branches is actually rather common among dicotyledonous plants of the rainforest understory (Richards 1952, p. 57) where a large proportion of the palms are also found. A familiar cultivated plant of this type is the papaya.

CACTUS:    members of the cactus family are notorious for their succulence and lack of leaves, which are replaced by sharp thorns. Natives of the Americas, the cacti are a large group and vary in form from a single barrel-shaped body through various small and bushy desert plants to many-branched trees that form woodlands or savannas and may even be constituents of a forest formation. Prostrate cacti inhabit sandy coastal soils at least as far northeast as New Jersey and shallow soils in pockets of granite outcrops in Georgia and nearby states. In Africa many species of *Euphorbia* closely parallel the succulent tree and shrub forms of cactus. The similarities are sometimes remarkable.

## CONCLUSION

An excursion among the specimens of taxonomic categories sometimes employed to represent vegetation formations has disclosed that by and large the intended meanings do not actually follow. When two particular plant assemblages are being compared, almost any designation, taxonomic or otherwise, will suggest their distinctions; but when the taxonomic usage is expanded into genetic proportions it is quite another matter. When any reasonably broad taxonomic unit is considered, the individual species within it must be different one from another, and one major differentiating factor for species is ecological isolation (Cain 1944, p. 367). Species in such a case are different because they have become adapted to different growing conditions, and there will tend to be morphological contrasts related to their ecological adaptations. But these morphological contrasts are just what is being illuminated in the selection of morphological characters to identify vegetation formations. The very success of major plant groups is a measure of the degree to which they have become established in the widest range of natural conditions. In this way the group is insured against disaster as a result of fluctuating stresses from the environment. By their very nature, then, major taxonomic groups cannot generally be categorized into any sort of consistent form character, and the difficulties encountered in using them this way are only to be expected. The use of taxonomic criteria for differentiating vegetation formations should, therefore, be avoided. On the other hand, the use of taxonomic designations in floristic regionalization and the identification of specific plant associations is inherent in the subjects involved. Should there be a significant form factor that correlates with some taxonomic unit, it would appear to be more reasonable to emphasize it rather than to infer it obliquely by reference to the taxonomic unit.

By removing taxonomic references from the classification of vegetation types the traditional list is reduced to *rainforest, evergreen seasonal forest, broadleaf deciduous forest, semi-deciduous forest, woodland, savanna, grassland, brush*, and *desert*. Logic would allow the replacement of the coniferous element by a needle-leaf element and thus add *needle-leaf forest* and *mixed broadleaf deciduous and needle-leaf evergreen forest*, alternate terms sometimes used. A major element, individual form, therefore emerges in the classification and will be considered next.

# 4

# Individual Form Factors
# Used in Vegetation Mapping

THE ELEMENTS OF INDIVIDUAL FORM, such as leaves and branching, are probably the most obvious form characteristics of plants and are widely used in schemes of vegetation formation types. In an earlier chapter we saw how attempts to avoid the use of external factors were made by emphasizing leaf qualities. Theoretically this could lead to a classification based entirely on the form details of the constituent plants, but this has never actually been achieved. The concept of cover, the subject to be examined in the next chapter, has always been involved in classifications where external factors have been excluded.

The facts of individual plant form can be organized into three major headings: *leaf*, *branches*, and *stature*. The leaf, being the normal locus of food manufacture, deserves primary consideration. Perhaps the permanence of the leaf is not precisely a form element, but it is associated with structural factors and it seems appropriate to consider it here along with variations in leaf shape. Together with leaves, a tree is composed of branches, whose function is to position the leaves. Although branches are wont to be overlooked, their importance is at least implied when certain distinctive plants are given attention, as the Parana pine (American Geographical Society 1933; James 1942, p. 21). Finally, the stature of plants, involving the difference between trees and bushes and other less gross distinctions, is of fundamental importance. In addition to leaf form, branching structure, and stature, a number of other special plant form factors were mentioned earlier. One of these more special factors is the presence of thorns, which tends to be associated with more depauperate vegetation produced either by difficult growing conditions or in early stages of succession. Another is the property of succulence, also associated with difficult growing conditions. No precise data are available concerning the geography of these special plant form factors, and so they will not be given any extensive attention here.

## LEAVES

A great deal has been said concerning leaf types and their relationships. Certain leaf types are well known among particular taxonomic groups (as the needle leaf for the conifers), while climatic correlations are regularly made with leaf form. Little may be known about the function of unusual leaf shapes, but the discussion of the importance of leaves points strongly to the two general characteristics, leaf tenure and leaf shape. At the same time some vegetation classifications such as those of Bartholomew and de Laubenfels have completely omitted any direct reference to leaf condition, while many others include such reference only within the terms *xerophytic* and *sclerophyllous*. Perhaps omission is a matter of terminology, subsuming leaf characteristics, but the possibility is suggested that leaf type may not be important in classifying vegetation as an indicator of general environmental conditions.

### Tenure

Leaves may endure the year around or they may be discarded as part of a mechanism of dormancy. Year-around leaves are here called *evergreen;* those discarded during dormancy are referred to as *deciduous\**. It is understood that rainforests are essentially evergreen, but certainly broadleaf evergreen forests, not all meriting the designation of rainforest, are to be found in many parts of the world with a pronounced dormant period. Other forests also of a decided seasonal stamp display a mixture of evergreen and

\*These terms are not always used in this way. Technically, any leaf is *deciduous* if eventually it dehisces from the branch. In the tropics it is common to refer to trees which discard one crop of leaves to grow another as *deciduous* even if they stand bare for but a few days or possibly not at all (Richards 1952, pp. 193-98).

deciduous trees or are dominated entirely by deciduous species. Evergreen trees are successfully cultivated among natural stands of deciduous trees and vice versa. We must, therefore, examine the question of the relationship between evergreenness and deciduousness in other than rainforest associations.

The frequency of occurrence of evergreen, mixed, or deciduous forests can easily be tested because the competition between trees normally narrows down to one or only a few dominants, and individual stands of seasonal forests are known by their few dominants. If these few dominants can be either evergreen or deciduous the chance that all are either evergreen or deciduous can be stated simply. It is 100 percent for one dominant, 50 percent for two dominants, 25 percent for three dominants, and in the probably not-too-common case of four dominants there is still one chance in eight. On the following page is listed as a sample a cross-section of major forest associations with winter dormancy, each followed by letters corresponding in order to each dominant (usually a genus): E for evergreen and D for deciduous (see Map 11 for locations).

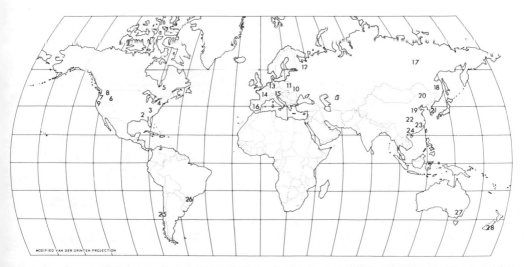

*Map 11.* Location of middle-latitude forest samples used in the text. The occurrence of deciduousness or evergreenness was scored for each sample.

## North America

|    |                                                           |       |
|----|-----------------------------------------------------------|-------|
| 1. | live oak-gum-hickory-magnolia                             | E D D E |
| 2. | oak-hickory-pine                                          | D D E |
| 3. | oak-tulip tree-basswood                                   | D D D |
| 4. | beech-maple-hemlock                                       | D D E |
| 5. | spruce-fir                                                | E E |
| 6. | yellow-pine                                               | E |
| 7. | Douglas fir                                               | E |
| 8. | Douglas fir-larch                                         | E D |
| 9. | oak-madrone                                               | D E |

## Europe

|     |                     |       |
|-----|---------------------|-------|
| 10. | oak-hornbeam        | D D |
| 11. | pine-oak            | E D |
| 12. | spruce              | E |
| 13. | oak-beech           | D D |
| 14. | oak-ash             | D D |
| 15. | beech-fir           | D E |
| 16. | evergreen oak       | E |

## Asia

|     |                                                           |         |
|-----|-----------------------------------------------------------|---------|
| 17. | larch                                                     | D |
| 18. | spruce-fir-larch                                          | E E D |
| 19. | oak                                                       | D |
| 20. | maple-basswood-birch                                      | D D D |
| 21. | oak-pine                                                  | D E |
| 22. | oak-gum-*Cunninghamia*                                    | D D E |
| 23. | evergreen oak-beech-etc.                                  | E D E D |
| 24. | evergreen oak-"laurels" *(Machilus, Magnolia)*           | E E E |

## South America

|     |                      |       |
|-----|----------------------|-------|
| 25. | roble-lingue-laurel  | D E E |
| 26. | Parana pine          | E |

## Australia-New Zealand

|     |             |   |
|-----|-------------|---|
| 27. | eucalyptus  | E |
| 28. | beech       | E |

The selection of examples for this list was based on a representative association from most major floristic regions with the choice based on available information. There is not always agreement on which tree types to emphasize, while combinations or segregates of the examples are also found. Combinations, especially the "mixed mesophytic forests" of North America and China (Braun 1950; Wang 1961), are almost certain to contain a mixture of deciduous and evergreen species, but questions arise as to which species are seral and whether some are edaphically specialized. The sample list includes nine single dominants, nine double dominants, eight triple dominants, and only two quadruple dominants. None of the single dominants can be mixed of course, but a ratio of 7-2 in favor of evergreen appears. With double dominants there is as close to an even split as is possible with an odd number, an even split being anticipated by chance, the larger number falling to the mixed category. This time the unmixed group favored deciduousness 3-1. The triple dominants would be expected to divide 6-2 in favor of mixed stands by chance, while a ratio of 5-3 obtained. The deciduous unmixed type exceeds the evergreen by 2-1. Both the quadruple dominants were evenly mixed. Taking the sample as a whole and adding up what would have been expected on the probability basis discussed previously, chances are that twelve of the examples would have been mixed, while in fact twelve were. Of the total of fifty-nine dominants, twenty-eight were evergreens, thirty-one were deciduous. The number of samples here is statistically small, but the close correspondence to a chance relationship strongly suggests the possibility that among these seasonal forests the occurrence of evergreenness or deciduousness or their combination is in each case to be explained as a product of chance.

Seasonal forests in the tropics yield similar relationships. Taking three major seasonal forest regions one finds that in Australia, where there is strong single dominance by eucalypts, the forests are evergreen; in Africa, where there are two very widespread dominants, *Isoberlinia* and *Brachystegia*, the forests are usually deciduous; in South America, where a larger number of dominants reign, the forests are characteristically mixed.

Perhaps, although in numbers there is a chance relationship between evergreenness and deciduousness, these two possibilities for dormancy nevertheless have different relationships to the kind or degree of dormancy. It has been observed in eastern North

America and in China that deciduousness reaches a maximum between the tropical rainforest on one side and the polar regions on the other (Braun 1950). These two floras are closely related, so their similarities are not to be wondered at greatly. There are two propositions here, that middle-latitude forests are deciduous and that polar forests are evergreen. The two most similar middle-latitude areas elsewhere are in southern Brazil and southeastern Australia, and in both the forests are strictly evergreen. The case of polar evergreenness with respect to China was never emphasized because the east Siberian forests are mainly made up of deciduous larch. Elsewhere the polar forests are a variable mixture of spruce, birch, poplar, fir, and pine as well as larch. Whereas evergreen spruce usually forms the tree line in west Siberia and North America, this honor goes to deciduous birch in northern Scandinavia (Polunin 1960, p. 344). The forests of the mild marine environment of western Europe are deciduous, but in similar areas in other parts of the world this is not true. The corresponding forests in New Zealand are evergreen, while those in North and South America are mixed. What then of the dry margins of the forest? In southern Europe the marginal forest is evergreen, in eastern Europe it is deciduous, while in the southwestern United States it tends to be mixed. Such forests in Australia are largely evergreen, but in Africa they are usually deciduous, while in western India both deciduous and evergreen trees can be demonstrated. It was mentioned earlier that a mixed pattern occurs in the Andes, while the forest margin in Patagonia is deciduous and that of the arid interior of North America (cf. pinyon-juniper) tends to be evergreen. There emerges here no generalization concerning the preponderance of evergreenness or of deciduousness under any particular set of conditions.

It must be accepted that deciduousness is an obvious physiognomic characteristic which can be readily detected by the untrained observer, especially during the period of plant dormancy (but not necessarily during the active plant period). It would appear, however, that because plants in seasonal areas can be either evergreen or deciduous, the dominance of the plant cover by only evergreen species or by only deciduous species merely represents special cases of the larger formation type which is a mixture of the two characteristics (Van Steenis 1958b, p. 79). As a matter of fact, there is no obvious reason why the distribution of evergreen plants should be different from deciduous plants with respect to the need for dormancy.* Whereas evergreen plants have their efficiency to photosynthesize impaired by the devices to protect the active tissue, such as a thick cuticle and the presence of wax, hairs, or other coating, deciduous plants also suffer from limitations in the form of the loss of investment when leaves are discarded and the delay necessitated by the time required to produce new leaves during a favorable period for activity. Either set of limitations is about as great as the other and obviously many other factors can become critical in the competition between plants for dominance in the regions of seasonal growth, while evergreenness or deciduousness are probably not determining factors at all. If the response to environment is to be illuminated by a study of the distribution of vegetation, the tenure of leaves does not appear to be an important consideration.†

## Leaf Form

Leaves vary tremendously in size and shape, from huge "elephant ears" to needles and scales. Some of the larger leaves are compound, the individual leaf unit or "leaflet" being of more normal size, while, for the most part, larger leaves of continuous lamina belong to herbaceous or aquatic plants. Still, tree leaves do vary considerably in size, more than is indicated by the division of broad versus needle (including scale) leaves. Raunkiaer (1905; 1934, pp. 368-78) devised six classes based on leaf surface area: *leptophyll* — less than 5 mm. squared (25 square mm.); *nanophyll* — 5 to 15 mm. squared; *microphyll* — 15 to 45 mm. squared; *mesophyll* — 45 to 135 mm. squared; *macrophyll* — 135 to 405

*Monk (1966) has argued for an edaphic relationship. His conclusions are based on one area and a relatively small group of species, some of which are evergreen and some deciduous. One could easily reverse his results by selecting certain other areas. See also Axelrod (1966).

†The significance of concentrated leaf fall is irrelevant here because many evergreen trees have such a leaf fall pattern. The effect of evergreen leaves on soil is through chemical composition, especially the concentration of silicates, which is not unique to evergreen leaves; post oak, for example, has very siliceous leaves. The effect of bare branches on evaporation of moisture and heating effects on the soil is complicated, and no simple relationship has been demonstrated. It is reasonable to assume that in some way deciduousness effects lesser components of the ecosystem differently than evergreenness, but, like the presence of nitrogenous root nodules, this is an effect of the vegetation and not a response by it, which is the concern here.

mm. squared; and *megaphyll* — more than 405 mm. (16 inches) squared. Clearly smaller leaves correlate with more difficult environments, but the difference between needle and broad shapes is more than one of surface area. A long needle may well have more surface area than a small flat oval leaf. The shape of leaves, therefore, involves a factor of surface-volume ratio as well as surface area. When leaves are appreciably flat, such a ratio is determined essentially by thickness. What is needed, therefore, besides an expression of size, is a descriptive system of surface-volume ratio such as *thin* (papery, flexible), *thick* (stiff), and *constricted* (needle and scale-like). Secondarily, when assessing leaf form, certain irregularities should be considered. Just as plants with very large leaves, such as palms and ferns, have achieved an approximation of smaller leaf sizes through division of the leaf blade (that is, compound leaves), so plants with very small leaves, especially the conifers, have approximated larger leaves through aggregated leaf-branch units that function much like individual leaves. Phyllodes and phylloclades are similar responses. Interestingly, needle leaves may become quite long in more favorable environments.

Evergreen-leaved plants occur under almost all natural conditions, but the leaf shape varies. Considering just those leaves growing in full sun, certain generalizations can be made. First, exposed leaves, even in the moistest tropics, are sclerophyllous (Richards 1952, p. 80). Second, such evergreen leaves are generally of the mesophyll (laurel) size or smaller (Richards 1952, pp. 80-85; Cain and Castro 1959, pp. 275-85). Finally, leaves are progressively smaller and more prone to constricted shapes in more severe environments. A number of examples should illustrate this last generalization. With regard to temperature, evergreen trees with laurel-like leaves are common in the subtropics, belonging especially to the laurel family itself (laurel from France to Yugoslavia, numerous species in south China, bay or myrtle in moist parts of California and Oregon), magnolia (southeastern United States, south China), winter's bark *(Drimys winteri)* in Chile and southern Brazil, rhododendron on the south and southeastern margins of the Himalaya and elsewhere, madrone *(Arbutus* sp.) in Arizona, along the Pacific coast of the United States, and in southwestern Europe and many others. Somewhat smaller leaves are characteristic of the evergreen oaks and their allies (*Lithocarpus* etc. of western North America and south China, *Nothofagus* of Chile and New Zealand) as well as holly (especially eastern United States), camphor of China and Japan, and podocarps (especially Brazil, China, and Japan). A few narrow but flat-leaved conifers also occur in moist subtropical regions, such as *Cunninghamia* in China, redwood in California, and certain podocarps of South Africa (yellow wood), Chile, and New Zealand. In colder areas more reduced leaves are found, as in the mild winter regions of southernmost South America, Tasmania, and New Zealand, where small-leaved beech *(Nothofagus)* and a few small-leaved and constricted-leaved conifers occur, or the severe winter parts of North America and China, where very small-leaved conifers (hemlock and arborvitae) or constricted-leaved conifers (pines and junipers) are common. Flat "needles" or slightly constricted leaves characterize the rainforest trees of the Pacific coast of Canada and parts of the United States. Finally, true needles characterize the leaves of evergreen trees of the cold boreal forests and woodlands. It is of interest to note that the evergreen trees (only three genera) of the very cold winter areas of the northeastern United States, eastern Europe, northern China, and northward are all conifers. That is, no evergreen non-coniferous trees, needle leaved or otherwise, have penetrated the exclusive group of three genera that have conquered these rigorous lands.

The sequence of evergreen leaf shapes in progressively arid environments is essentially similar to that of colder conditions. The sclerophyll type of dry summer areas has already been discussed. Small-leaved live oaks also occur from Arizona to Texas in semi-arid environments, and some of the eucalypts and acacias with phyllodes in Australia are similar. Even smaller leaves occur on such types as the pepper trees *(Schinus)* of South America, while constricted evergreen leaves are especially common among trees growing in such drier places as Mexico, the southwestern United States and inner Asia (pine, juniper, and tamarisk), and Australia *(Callitris, Casuarina,* etc.). Desert shrubs in general from the tropics to the polar regions are often evergreen and have very reduced and constricted leaves. Completely leafless plants (including trees) with green stems are common in the Americas and Africa (cactus and euphorbs). It should be noted that much the same plants associated with arid environments also turn up in humid areas on poor soils, especially sandy soils, and to a lesser extent as pioneer plants of the early stages of succession. Thus there are the pines and junipers of the southeastern United States and of central China.

Understory and shrubby plants, being less exposed, tend to

have leaves which resemble those of milder environments. For example, holly in England and western Europe extends the range of broad-leaved evergreens, and rhododendron does the same in eastern North America. The narrow-leaved yew penetrates even farther into cold winter environments, but the leaf here is similar to hemlock which as a canopy tree grows in some of the same regions.

Even deciduous trees have smaller leaves under the most severe conditions. Deciduousness allows leaves of the broader types to unfold in areas with harsh dormant seasons, but there is a limit. For example, the aspens and birches of the far northern forests have small leaves, and the trees of the coldest winter areas are larches with deciduous needles. Deciduous trees in dry areas also tend to have small leaves, as the blue oak in California or the elms of the Texas Cross Timbers. The legumes are noted for their compound leaves with small leaflets that are very prominent in the semi-arid and even arid areas throughout the world. Some desert plants not only have reduced or constricted leaves, but also are deciduous, like *Parkinsonia*.

There are exceptions to the generalizations about leaf size and shape. One reason why the broad-leaved evergreen rhododendrons are able to prosper in cold winter areas is because their leaves roll up from the sides during cold weather, thus reducing the exposed surface. Many eucalypts display unusually broad leaves in severely arid areas, and this is facilitated by the leaf habit of hanging vertically and thus reducing the exposure to the midday sun. They cast very little shade. On the other hand, small-leaved and con- stricted-leaved trees even penetrate the rainforest (as a minority, to be sure). Members of the mimosa family, with highly compound leaves but small leaflets, are important (usually successional) constituents of many rainforests, while needle-leaved dacrydiums are to be seen in the rainforests of the East Indies (Viet Nam to Fiji and New Zealand), and even some pines (i.e., *P. patula*) extend successfully a short distance into the rainforest in Mexico. When the leaves of any of these apparently misplaced dry climate forms are inspected, two characteristics can be seen. The leaf and branch growth is dense and it is unusually soft and flexible. What is seen here is the successful invasion by plants whose ancestry is else- where into a different (more favorable) environment, and, although they still reveal their antecedents in some aspects of form, they are yet able to compete because in other ways they make up for such limitations. This only shows that leaf form is but one of many factors in competition, even though it is both a visible and an important one.

*Summary*

The significance of leaf condition in terms of response of vegetation to the environment is a complex of factors. It is probably an oversimplification to speak of broad-leaf evergreen forest, broad-leaf deciduous forest, and needle-leaf evergreen forest, although particular examples can be found. One might as well identify oak forests, eucalyptus forests, or pine forests because particular examples of these can also be found. Each of these examples covers things which in themselves are quite variable and whose individual parts can be paralleled by different examples responding to similar environments. One can say that rainforests are characterized by broad-leaved evergreen trees. With a pronounced unfavorable season rainforests are replaced by a mixture of deciduous and evergreen trees, with the evergreen leaves tending to become reduced as the unfavorable season becomes more pronounced. Under even more severe conditions the deciduous leaves also become reduced, while the evergreen leaves at the same stress level are sharply reduced even to the point of disappearance. Enough variations or downright exceptions occur to make any possibility of sharp division doubtful.

## BRANCHING

The function of branches is to position the leaves, and this becomes important if there is competition for light. There are two ways to consider the geometry of branching. One is the different solutions to placing leaves in a particular way and the other is the different ways that leaves may be positioned. Secondarily, branches must respond to certain stress factors such as wind, the weight of snow, or the attacks of large animals and fire. Considerable variation in branching arrangement is possible and some aspects may be significant.

Each plant has its characteristic form, largely dictated by the

| OVERGROWN BUSH | WINE GLASS | DENDRITIC | TELEPHONE POLE | UMBRELLA |

*Figure 13.* Classes of tree branching diagrammed. In each case the leaves are displayed the same; it is only the structure of their support which varies.

branching structure. The usual crown of a tree or other plant growing in proximity to others is shaped more or less as a dome, with maximum vertical exposure. With this external shape, five classes of branching can be resolved (Figure 13). First, multiple stems can emerge as a clump from the ground. When such a plant is tall it may be referred to as an "overgrown bush." Second is the "wine glass" shape typical of an elm, where branching is well above the ground but where no distinct central leader appears among the branches. Next is the common "dendritic" branching form, with random dichotomies. A strong central leader may result in essentially horizontal branches resembling a "telephone pole." Finally, with branches concentrated at the apex of the tree, one has what might be called an "umbrella" effect.* But all five possibilities result in a similar placement of the leaves. Trees whose crowns are more horizontal display slight modifications of these five types. When adjacent formations are dominated by plants of rather different branching structure, one is tempted to use this as a basis for a major division of kind; yet the difference is probably not critical.

Several possibilities for relative advantage or disadvantage of the different classes of branching can be suggested. Obviously the plants with lower branching will require a greater volume of wood, a less efficient use of their energies than for other branching strategies. The structure of wood growth is such that dichotomous branching arrangements are notoriously vulnerable to splitting, a

---

*Note that vast differences in leaf size may produce the same effect. The umbrella form is characteristic of palms, with a crown of huge compound leaves and no true branches, but the same effect is produced by some araucarias with rather small leaves and very formal branching.

liability of the second type especially. On the other hand, too great a dominance of one leader and the concentration of branches into a small region increases the severity of damage, should it occur in the critical region of the tree (Richards 1952, p. 10). Many other factors than branching structure determine the success of a given plant, but these considerations suggest that the preponderance of the intermediate or "dendritic" branching type is a result of its optimal or compromise character with respect to the range of possibilities. Certainly no distributional distinctions have ever been assigned to branching form in general.

There are two possible basic alignments of leafy crowns which can be conceived. Crowns can be arranged with an emphasis on horizontal placement or with an emphasis on vertical placement. The more usual dome shape with a horizontal alignment has already been mentioned. But trees, especially in the higher latitudes, have a pronounced vertical form. The spire shape may have an advantage for shedding heavy snow where this is a hazard, but probably more important are considerations of illumination. A vertically elongated tree receives less light from an overhead sun. This may be a factor in columnar rainforest emergents, the araucarias of New Caledonia particularly (Figure 14), as the tropical noonday sun is intense. The same effect may be had by a vertical arrangement of the leaf surface, as for the eucalyptus. A vertically elongated tree also receives more light from a low sun and, in higher latitudes, that is the most that ever occurs. Many considerations of limiting temperatures and cloud cover along with lower sun angles make a precise determination of a latitude for equal efficiency of vertical vs. horizontal surfaces for accumulating sunlight impossible, but simple observation shows that beyond 45 degrees, the vertical form is very noticeable (Figure 15). Vertical tree crowns may not make a solid horizontal cover, and they inevitably will be periodically shaded as the sun moves behind their neighbors. There is no reason to expect a sharp gradient from horizontal to vertical crown shapes, but it is reasonable to expect the vertical form to be more important with increasing latitude.

Other than the positioning of leaves, animals and fire may have some effect on branching structure. Fewer lower branches might reduce vulnerability to animal pressure but might also be a result of the attack of animals. Fire might well operate on trees in the same way. Both effects are more obvious on open-growth plants than in a closed forest, and in the open areas the placement of

*Figure 14.* Columnar rainforest emergents in New Caledonia. The rainforest canopy is about thirty meters high and the emergents, *Araucaria bernieri*, are at least twice as tall.

leaves for gathering light does not matter. Characteristically, open-growth trees have more branches because lower branches are free from shading limitations. Therefore, the absence of lower branches would seem logically to be either a defense against or a result of disturbance. Thus it is that one of the characteristics of savannas (by no means universal) is free-standing trees without the skirt found on woodland trees.

Only a few generalizations can be made about the branching pattern of plants, even though the branching pattern is so obvious to the observer. The major differences amount to different ways of accomplishing the same purpose, with a most prevalent optimum form. Vertical trees have an advantage in gathering sunlight, and lower branches tend to disappear from disturbed trees growing in the open. No sharp transitions from place to place are indicated in these factors.

*Figure 15.* Columnar spruce and fir in the Cascade Mountains. Shedding snow is one advantage of this growth form which becomes progressively commoner in higher latitudes where the angle of the sun is always low.

## STATURE

It is not clear what emphasis should be placed upon stature in vegetation formations, but certainly height cannot be ignored as an element of physiognomy. A number of suggestions have been made, and there are several considerations. First, the possibility of any critical-height classes needs to be examined. Then the possibility of significant relative height can be explored.

### Critical Height

Various authors have used certain height classes in descriptive vegetation analysis. Raunkiaer (1905), for example, based these on the position of the perenniating bud, so that among the woody plants there are the *megaphanerophytes* (whose buds are at least 25 meters above the ground), the *mesophanerophytes* (10-25m), *microphanerophytes* (2-10m), *nanophanerophytes* (¼-2m) and *chamaephytes* (close to the ground). Du Rietz (1921, pp. 131-32) chose three height classes: *magnoligniden* — greater than 2 meters, *parvoligniden* — 0.8-2 meters, and *nanoligniden* — less than 0.8 meter. Dansereau (1957, p. 148), like many other authors, based his height classes on Raunkiaer's classes, but he added the distinction between trees and shrubs at 8 meters.

Küchler (1947a; 1966, pp. 120 and 126), after using many aspects of Raunkiaer's classes and dividing shrubs into two classes of more or less than one meter high, has rejected the idea that anything more than arbitrary height classes can be used, of which he supplies eight.

Logic suggests that there ought to be some very important relationships attached to height, and yet the specific heights of vegetation stands have so far eluded the determination of any meaning. Some examples will illustrate the problem. The coastal forests of Oregon and Washington are composed of magnificent trees, with both the pioneering Douglas fir and the succeeding hemlock being trees of more than two hundred feet in height. In Tasmania, with a very similar climate, the pioneering eucalypts are also over two hundred feet high, but the succeeding beech reach only half that height (Figure 16). In Chile, where Australian and North American trees have prospered when introduced, the native forest of mixed beech in all stages does not pass one hundred and fifty feet. In various parts of Australia, where local soils do not favor eucalypts, there grows a forest scarcely forty feet high but with scattered "emergents" in the form of bottle trees and wattles; but the eucalypts on other soils within the same zone are much taller. Where pines are mixed with broad-leaf deciduous trees, it is not uncommon for them to tower over the general canopy as, for example, the digger pine in California and the white pine in eastern North America. One could cite numerous examples where a taller tree species does not form a continuous or thick canopy sufficient to shade out shorter trees, and thus a two-level effect results. Clearly, where taller trees form a closed canopy, shorter trees will be excluded, unless they are shade tolerant or understory types. But the mature height of trees varies, and the ability of any particular species to become established in an area depends on much more than size. Particularly do tall sun-requiring pioneering

*Figure 16.* Two-layered rainforest in Southern Tasmania. Smaller trees of *Nothofagus cunninghamii* about thirty meters high form a continuous canopy. An open stand of *Eucalyptus obliqua* is twice as tall. Both layers are mature trees.

species lose the battle in the long run to shade-tolerating trees, no matter how small they may be. Apparently one must accept the conclusion that gross height of a vegetative cover cannot be made to yield any significance, and this would have to apply to shrubs as well as trees.

*Relative Height*

There is another aspect of height than measured values that appears significant: relative height. A vegetative cover can be divided vertically into major synusiae or layers, each of which has its own particular relationships (Richards 1952, pp. 19-21). Relative to the total body of vegetation three major positions can be identified: the *canopy* which is exposed to the sun and wind, the *understory* sheltered under the canopy, and the *ground cover* independent of vertical increments of growth. Other positions or layers have been identified but are of lesser importance. These others include *emergents*, a discontinuous layer of trees whose crown is above the canopy; divisions of the understory (whose existence is challenged; Richards 1952, pp. 22-39. Richards argues for several distinct layers but quotes some of the dissenters) or of the main canopy, and moss layers. The position of plants relative to each of these strata is significant.

The canopy or upper layer is the dominant part of a stand of vegetation. It is the part of a vegetative cover which absorbs the direct sunlight but which, on the other hand, is exposed to the full fury of the elements. There is a tendency to think of the canopy as a single continuous layer, but that is an oversimplification. Where it is dominated by one kind of plant or by more than one which achieves the same height in competition with each other, then it will indeed be a single continuous layer. But we have already seen that dominant trees do not necessarily form a continuous cover, thus leaving direct sunlight for trees of a lesser stature where the taller fail to coalesce. The more complex the vegetation the more likely is this to occur, and in the rainforest it is the rule. Not only are there the occasional trees of great height, but also there are the taller full-sun trees and the lesser or partial-sun trees, these two positions accounting for the first two strata usually identified. The term "partial-sun" may not only describe the amount of sun that the shorter trees get, but may also indicate the degree of sun which they can tolerate, a relationship that suggests a possible cause for the distinct height difference that has been claimed for this part of the rainforest. In any case, as long as competition for sunlight is critical, the canopy, simple or complex, will be continuous where allowed to develop. However tall the canopy may be, it is the uppermost part of a vegetative cover.

The understory is made up of the trees, larger and smaller, which have not, or must not reach the canopy. Under the canopy there is protection from wind, from most daily temperature fluctuation, and from the desiccating effect of direct sunlight. As a result, this is a habitat of moist, relatively isothermal conditions, but it is also relatively dark. Delicate plants can live here, but robust plants find the limited light a handicap or totally inadequate for survival. Three kinds of plants occupy the understory. The first kind is one whose life processes are adjusted to the conditions there and it cannot survive complete exposure. The second are suppressed trees which are able to tolerate the shade and are there only because they are poor competitors of the successful canopy trees. Finally, from few to many juveniles of canopy trees are present, often in their juvenile forms resembling the understory species and quite distinct thereby from their mature form. Juveniles and suppressed trees rush growth to fill any gap which may occur above them. The understory is the second stratum when the canopy is simple and the third when it is complex. Where the understory is continuous, additional strata of shorter trees and giant herbs may be identified but it is doubtful if these can ever be clearly distinguished as a definite layer.

Ground cover has certain special properties. Prominent in ground cover are herbaceous plants — plants that can and usually do die back to the ground seasonally. Often intermingled with herbs, or even growing to the exclusion of them, are woody shrubs which do not necessarily die back to the ground. Significantly, however, ground cover shrubs not only compete directly with herbaceous plants but also are quite capable, once established, of growing from ground level to their mature height in one growing season. Ground cover plants normally are partly covered by dead leaves or snow during the dormant season. The critical thing about them is that they do not depend on their aboveground parts for survival, and after desiccation, killing cold, fire, or even grazing, they can renew themselves in one season.* Naturally, there is a limit to what any plant can endure, and ground cover plants can be killed, but they can and do survive conditions that eliminate larger, more vulnerable plants. The ground cover is sharply divided into shade and sun varieties. Its stature might vary considerably just as does that of forest, and in the sun-growing variety there is the possibility of smaller understory shrubs and herbs.

The importance of relative height is clear, while, conversely, specific height appears to have little meaning. Vegetation therefore should be viewed relatively in terms of the plant distribution at the herb or ground level, between this level and the canopy, and in the canopy itself. To a limited extent one can think of the ground cover as subject to being walked on (if it is not so tall and

*Bamboo is a remarkable plant which can grow to tree size in some species directly from the ground in one season and therefore in such cases differs from ground cover plants only in terms of the level at which it competes, and, of course, a bamboo clump takes years to establish and is quite perennial.

thick as to defy walking), the understory to be walked among (because its lower parts, however thin, continue down to man-level), and the canopy a thing one walks under, as a rough measure of magnitude and position. As will be discussed in the next chapter, there are distinct differences from place to place in the degree of development and of relative development of the different layers of vegetation.

## CONCLUSION

Vegetation is made up of an aggregate of plants, and, therefore, vegetation formation obviously will involve the aggregation of individual plant forms. Surprisingly little can be made out of obvious individual form factors, however, and this is because so many of them are distributed merely as mixtures or mosaics with their alternatives. Thus, deciduous leaves in areas of distinct seasonal growth form mosaics with evergreen leaf distributions; the geometry of branching presents alternatives which vary around an optimum type to accomplish the same result; tallness appears to be governed by the chance characteristics of the dominant plants of an area. Nevertheless, certain generalizations can be made about the factors of individual form, especially as to certain kinds of gradient. Starting with rainforests, trees tend to be evergreen mesophytic, followed in drier areas by deciduous leaves mixed with reduced evergreen leaves. Eventually the deciduous leaves in severe environments become reduced also, but generally less so than the associated evergreens. In higher latitudes a vertical-growth form becomes prominent. Finally, the height of plants can be related to a measure of relative position within certain definite layers of vegetation. There emerges, then, the idea of a structure of vegetation as a whole, to which individual plant form is sub-ordinate. By eliminating or severely downgrading the use of in-dividual form factors in favor of an overall composite structure, a more rational view can be achieved of the significant variations in vegetation formation.

# 5

# Cover Types Used in
# Vegetation Mapping

A SPECTS OF PLANT COVERAGE have been widely involved in the classification of vegetation formations. The distinctions between forest, grassland, and desert imply differences in cover of an absolute character. Savannas and woodlands are set apart by degree, that is, by the spacing of a discontinuous cover of trees. The question of the importance of cover types rapidly resolves itself into the question of whether there are distinct recognizable types or whether vegetation is a continuum along which only certain kinds of gradients and their end points can be described. The proposition that vegetation formation is a continuum means, therefore, that any type that might be named is purely arbitrary, and the identification of types, as a matter of fact, is meaningless (Polunin 1960, p. 336).* On the other hand, the identification of types implies that there are distinctions.

As long as vegetation formation is felt to be linked to vegetation associations, the reality of formation types will be governed by the reality of vegetation associations (Küchler 1959, p. 7; Polunin 1960, p. 333). Ecologists argue long on this subject (Daubenmire 1966), but the weight of the evidence is that associations are in fact only arbitrarily selected overlaps of different species distributions (Whittaker 1962, pp. 78-101; McIntosh 1963, 1967). However, field observation constantly demonstrates that

---

*Offhand comments that vegetation forms a continuum are common in the literature. It is not always apparent whether flora or form is being referred to (Wells 1960; Poore 1962, p. 53; Goodall 1963).

species distributions do not correspond to formation patterns. Not only do species not extend throughout the formation of which they are a part (Major 1962), but also, as will be shown below, species may well overlap boundaries of formation types. It must be understood, therefore, that the question of the reality of formation is not the same as the question of the reality of association.

In order to test the proposition that there are recognizable vegetation formation types based on cover distinctions, the spatial and structural contrasts between a series of specific proposed types will be examined. The following sequence is suggested, corresponding to specified contrasts in cover characters: *rainforest* with a continuous understory, *seasonal forest* without a continuous understory but with a continuous canopy, *woodland* without a continuous canopy but with a continuous cover of plants, and *desert* without a continuous plant cover. *Continuous* means that the elements involved are in contact with their neighbors and that the intervening spaces are isolated or absent. An exact percentage cover is not specified (Küchler has suggested a lower value of 76 percent for continuous cover, 1966, p. 120). Some variation is to be expected in the percentage cover and marginal cases are inevitable. A corollary of the proposition is that marginal cases will not be important; that is, ordinarily a particular stand can be classified without question. The four formation types to be examined are all thought to be of an undisturbed structure, that is, such disturbance as may have occurred has not been sufficient to alter their basic structure, and they are essentially structurally stabilized. In order to study them, therefore, only samples of vegetation giving no significant evidence of structural distortion have been considered.

After examining the four proposed basic vegetation formation types there should be a consideration of other formation types. These others should be of two sorts if the above assumptions prove correct. One of these groupings will involve secondary types or subdivisions of the primary types, which will tend to emerge from the discussion of the primary types. The other sort of formation types is essentially those not accounted for by the primary types and their varieties. By testing the primary types against lack of evidence of disturbance, these remainders are strongly implied to be the result of disturbance, not a new idea.

## RAINFORESTS CONTRASTED WITH SEASONAL FORESTS

There is no clear generally accepted definition of rainforest in the literature (Richards 1952, p. 2). Descriptions suggest that it is characterized by a great many species and is structurally organized into various tree strata, but these are matters of degree. Some stands called rainforests are less well endowed with these qualities than are other stands not admitted to that label. The most complex stands of vegetation can be accepted by all as being rainforest, but it is not clear what the limits might be, if in fact any meaningful ones exist. Field observation and written references have been used to clarify the problem, with particular attention to the understory character. Essentially what is involved is an examination of the transition from rainforest to some other formation wherever a limit might be indicated. These limits can be divided into dry season limits and cool season limits.

### Dry Season Limits

The bulk of the rainforest terminates where dry seasons are severe. This is because most rainforest is well within the tropics. Boundaries can be identified in each of the various continents with rainforest and considered one by one.

The rainforests of Africa are almost entirely surrounded by a border of savanna (Keay 1959, p. 7). Further from the main body of rainforest but in contact with outliers are "woodlands" which endure periodic fire, as do the savannas (Keay 1959, p. 9). The mature rainforest is described as having several more or less distinct strata and being evergreen or partly evergreen. The woodland is dominated by a very few species, sometimes all of the same genus, under which grows a dense cover of tall grass. The boundary of the rainforest is particularly sharp and in the case of bordering savanna, may have a fringe about eighty feet wide of a sort of woodland (Hopkins 1965, pp. 62-63). What form of vegetation might border the rainforest in the drier zones in the absence of fire is entirely speculation. The mixed deciduous zone of the rainforest, where several months deficient in precipitation occur, includes trees which may become bare of leaves for several weeks some time during the dry season, but is not structurally distinct from the wet evergreen zone and probably should not be distinguished from it in terms of formation (Richards 1952, pp. 338-39).

Next to the rainforests of south and southeast Asia is a vegetation often called monsoon forest (Richards 1952, pp. 327-34; Davis 1964, pp. 11-17). As in Africa, the rainforests are said to contain deciduous species, but these are few among a multitude and generally are bare only briefly, if at all. Probably the closest to an undisturbed seasonal forest of the monsoon variety is the mixed or semi-evergreen forest of Burma. This forest has a simple structure and is dominated by the legume pyinkado *(Xylia dolabriformis)* and by teak *(Tectonia grandis)*. In India the sal forests *(Shorea robusta)* are more open and have more grass growth, being subject to regular burning (Chatterjee 1958, p. 64; Schweinfurth 1957, p. 294). In western India and Ceylon, next to the rainforest and subject to a more pronounced dry season, a semi-evergreen or dry evergreen forest has been described which has some of the characteristics of rainforest (Puri 1961, p. 99; Holmes 1958, pp. 108-13). The canopy of this is less complex than rainforest and includes deciduous trees, but the understory is well developed. In Ceylon it is argued that this is successional to rainforest, but in both areas disturbance is so great that its status is unclear.

The rainforest of Australia terminates abruptly where it meets the eucalypt forest (Webb 1959, p. 551; Richards 1952, p. 369). On the one side is typical complex rainforest while on the other is an open forest of uniform structure made up of a thin canopy of tall trees and a ground covering of grass and only occasional small trees and juveniles. The sharpness of the boundary results from the interplay of fire against the rainforest. Where fire has advanced, there are burned trunks of rainforest trees among the eucalypts and a virtual wall of green where the rainforest begins. Where rainforest has advanced there are mature eucalypts submerged in rainforest growth and pioneering rainforest species coming up beyond the rainforest edge. When these construct enough protection, a riot of understory plants soon appear. A few moisture-loving eucalypts are characteristically seen very near the rainforest zone and give warning of its proximity to the approaching forester. Such trees form magnificent stands where large swaths of rainforest have been eliminated. But not far from the rainforest, sometimes less than a mile, the monotonous sclerophyll forest is fully developed to extend seemingly endlessly into drier country. What would happen in the absence of fire to this open forest can

be seen in the suburban area of Sydney where the presence of
houses and roads has been associated with reduced fire frequency.
First there is an increase of bushes and the invasion of juvenile
trees from refugia. Gradually as the tree species grow the vegetation changes into a denser stand with a sparse undergrowth of more
shade-tolerating plants. Of course, where fire has been most frequent as in northern Queensland, a cessation of fire may result in
no change because the fire-sensitive and shade-loving plants may
have been totally eliminated.* It is doubtful that a fully developed
mesic seasonal forest exists anywhere in Australia. There is a
marginal form of rainforest called "dry rainforest" in some places
which undergoes a fairly severe dry season with progressive leaf fall
that is not total. The dry rainforest is lower and has fewer species
than the typical rainforest but is still complex in structure with
many understory trees and few or no herbs.

The rainforests of South America frequently terminate against
savanna, especially woodland (Soares 1953; Richards 1952, pp.
317-27), if they are not bordered by high mountains, although
there are extensive zones, including many poorly mapped interior
areas, where semi-deciduous forests border the rainforest. Inland
from the coastal escarpment of Brazil is the most accessible zone
of semi-deciduous forest-rainforest juxtaposition and the boundary
is said to be sharp (Hueck 1966, p. 168). Although the semi-
deciduous forest is the prime target for agricultural settlement
(James 1953, pp. 308-10), very little is known of the structure of
this forest (Hueck 1966, pp. 168-69). The general description,
rich in species with much undergrowth and sometimes numerous
tree ferns, is not too helpful. Perhaps some or all of it corresponds
to what would be called rainforest in Africa and Southeast Asia,
but forest remnants available for study are not necessarily typical,
and its status must remain uncertain. However, it appears to
represent, along with similar zones in northern South America, a
range of vegetation types from dense to sparse with much of it not
at all of a rainforest type (Hueck 1966, pp. 123-28, 167, 272-74).
It differs from the rainforest not only in the predominance of
deciduous trees, but by a well-developed ground cover of bushes
and herbaceous plants, implying not much understory tree cover.
There seems to be in some cases a rather open stand of taller trees

*For a description of the contrast between rainforest and monsoon forest
in New Guinea see Womersley and McAdam (1957), pp. 19-20.

so that many shorter trees are in evidence, possibly, but not necessarily, indicating disturbance. In northern South America, Beard
recognized a series of seasonal forests from evergreen to deciduous,
the first of which Richards equates with rainforest and others
which include edaphic as well as climatic types (Beard 1944, p.
135; Richards 1952, pp. 317-20). It is clear that forests distinct
from rainforests exist in South America, but how sharp a transition exists between the two is not explained in available sources,
probably because the forests themselves have not generally been
studied structurally in any detail.

Boundaries of the rainforest in Central America are likely to
be edaphic in part, as in the Miskito pine savanna (Parsons 1955)
or associated with disturbance, as for the pine forest-rainforest
boundary in the uplands (Denevan 1961). The forests of Central
Mexico are particularly disturbed with scarcely an acre of stabilized forest to be found. Nevertheless some field study of the
relationship of rainforest to other vegetation types shows a sharp
distinction. The rainforests of Mexico grow on the eastern mountain face and have a typical structure. On the inland side is a belt
of deciduous forest including such trees as alder, sweet gum, and
walnut or in places species of evergreen oak different from the oak
of drier areas. Rainforest first appears where the canopy is fairly
simple, but evergreen, with a mass of understory trees and vines.
On its lowland side the darker evergreen rainforest gives way rapidly to lighter colored legumes and a ground cover of herbs. The
transitions are sharp, partly because the moisture gradient is sharp,
but the existence of distinct vegetation formations is significant.

I studied the rainforest boundary on two large South Pacific
islands where still different floristic contrasts might obtain. Much
of the drier part of Fiji is maintained in grass, but there are some
introduced casuarina forests with a simple structure. Next to the
rainforest, or occasionally preserved elsewhere, there is a forest of
legumes (mimosa, etc.) with a light cover of grass and other herbs
underneath. The transition between this into classical rainforest is
almost abrupt. The transition can be seen clearly because of the
difference in tree color and because it often occurs on steep slopes.
In New Caledonia, the dry side is covered with niaouli *(Melaleuca
leucadendron)* savanna which is subject to regular burning (Sarlin
1954). The native dry forest is called gaiac *(Acacia spirorbis)* and
survives in protected places where fire is less of a possibility. The
abrupt margins of the rainforest appear where a few rainforest tree

species hold forth in ravines and sheltered spots, but behind them grows a fully developed rainforest (White 1926, p. 75). Because of the soil patterns of New Caledonia, there are numerous interruptions of "dry forest" in the rainforest where there is a ground cover of grass and brush. When hiking through the forest one attempts to walk around such places if they are small because the rainforest is easier to walk in.

*Cool Season Limits*

Very little information concerning the cool season limits of rainforest can be had for several reasons, not the least of which is that only a small part of the rainforest terminates in cool but not drier regions. Other reasons involve the broken terrain and abundant disturbance endemic where cool season limits occur, not to mention a lack of agreement as to just what the rainforest might be by those concerning themselves with vegetation in such reaches. In the section on latitudinal vegetation zonation the relationship of temperate and highland rainforest to rainforest in general was discussed. With that as a basis, an attempt can be made to examine the cool season limits of rainforest.

About the only subtropical lowland margin of the rainforest not markedly transitional to drier conditions is to be found in South China. Here the Southeast Asian rainforest extends into the lowlands in unaltered form where it meets an evergreen broad-leaf "sclerophyllous" forest of distinctive structure (Wang 1961, pp. 130, 133-34, 155-59). The rainforest is a complex of many tree species and abundant understory with normally but a scanty ground cover, while in the neighboring stands only a few tree species completely dominate the canopy and the understory is normally not dense. There does not appear to be a broad transition zone between these contrasting types except that in southern Yunnan and nearby Burma lowland rainforests gradually merge with elevation into a very moist cover of evergreen oak having many associated tree species and thick undergrowth as well as abundant moss and epiphytes clothing the tree trunks in the form of a *temperate rainforest* (Wang 1961, pp. 150-51; Davis 1964, pp. 30-31). Clearly the "sclerophyllous" forest corresponds to colder winter areas, but heavy rain in certain places counteracts, to a degree, the lower minimum temperatures. To the west along

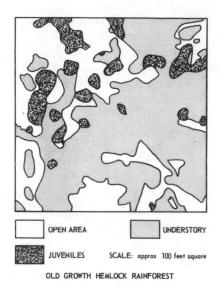

OLD GROWTH HEMLOCK RAINFOREST

*Figure 17.* Old growth hemlock rainforest understory pattern. Small understory trees form a continuous stand covering a majority of the area and are augmented by scattered juveniles.

the upper slopes of the Himalaya, mountain rainforests extend well up the mountains (Schweinfurth 1957, pp. 297-301).

The hemlock forests of the Olympic Peninsula northward into Alaska represent a higher-latitude occurrence of lowland rainforest. The hemlock forest grows particularly near the coast where it is exposed to the moderating influence of maritime air on temperature extremes and where humidities and rainfall are high, even though forests further inland are also rather moist. Careful study of a sample of hemlock forest showed an understory of many broad-leaved trees of small stature covering about 60 percent of the surface and continuously interconnected (Figures 17 and 18). Another 15 percent of the stand was covered by juveniles, leaving openings in the understory accounting for one quarter of the area. The forest floor was everywhere covered with moss, and there was only a scattering of herbs. By contrast the most luxuriant stand found of old-growth fir in the Cascades had but a 20 percent understory cover of just the one plant, yew. An additional 5 percent of the surface was covered by juveniles, while the forest floor was covered sparsely by herbs with considerable bare areas. With the exception of juveniles obviously growing in response to in-

*Figure 18.* View of the area diagrammed in Figure 17. A mature closed canopy covers this dense understory growth on the Olympic Peninsula of Washington.

creased sunlight, other stands of fir investigated had less of an understory. Although the generally accessible areas of forest are either sporadic or associated with very broken terrain, there seems to be a fairly consistent contrast between the hemlock forest and its continuous understory on the one hand and fir forests on the other.*

The more northern part of the coastal hemlock forest in Alaska is described by Sigafoos (1958) in terms comparable to that above. Inland it is replaced by a forest of white spruce and white birch which, when they form a dense canopy, have a sparse understory. However, for the most part, hemlock forests are bordered inland

*Hemlock often also grows with fir as in the examples of fir forest cited, while fir forest includes Douglas fir with true fir in the Northwest. The same description of fir forest applies to spruce and fir stands within the Rocky Mountain chain or to redwood areas (usually involving Douglas fir), all of which were studied. Arguments about possible succession in Douglas fir probably have no bearing on the factors described here.

by high mountains. The forest is reduced at higher elevations to noncommercial stands mixed with other tree species next to the timberline.

Elsewhere middle-latitude candidates for rainforest, as in Tasmania, New Zealand, and southern Chile, border mountains in much the same way as do the hemlock forests, but inland conditions are unquestionably drier. In Tasmania the insular position appears to be related to a somewhat depauperate flora, while virtually no completely stabilized rainforest is to be found. Potential rainforest areas are represented at one extreme by a "wet sclerophyll forest" of giant eucalypts of a rather open crown and a solid lower layer of trees of various species and a sparse ground cover of herbs. The increase of myrtle *(Nothofagus cunninghamii)* gradually crowds out most other tree species and the herbs. A robust understory, largely of tree ferns, can develop, particularly in the absence of the successional eucalypts (Walter 1962, pp. 139-41; Williams 1955, p. 7; and personal observation). The transition from "wet sclerophyll forest" to "dry sclerophyll forest," although seldom encountered because of the widespread and frequent fires, appears to be sharp. That is to say, intermediate forms are essentially lacking. "Dry sclerophyll forest" has an open understory of small trees (to fifteen feet) and different species of dominant eucalypts. Most of the forest of New Zealand is reckoned as rainforest varying from "podocarp-mixed hardwood" in warmer areas to "beech-podocarp" in the south, all in very dynamic adjustment (McLintock 1960, pp. 23-24; Holloway 1954; Cockayne and Turner 1958, pp. 11-26; Cumberland 1941, pp. 531-32). Yet, in the South Island east of the high mountain divide is a strip of monotonous beech forest bordering the tussock grasslands and enduring not only colder temperatures, but distinctly drier conditions. Although surprisingly little information is available concerning areal variations in New Zealand forest structure, the "dry beech forest" is definitely less dense than the rainforests and probably should be clearly distinguished from them. The Chilean rainforest is much like the more southern parts of New Zealand forest and survives almost entirely in rugged mountainous terrain (Corporación de Fomento de Producción 1950, pp. 398-408; Butland 1957, pp. 29-33; Hueck 1966, pp. 333-81). East of the mountains is a drier forest of deciduous beech with a considerable ground cover of bushes. To the north, rainforest is replaced by a semi-deciduous forest, but no information is available concerning the nature of the transition between the two, other than that they are quite distinct forms, the one with abundant understory tree species and the other rather open underneath.

Rainforest limits with elevation can be divided between low latitude, with no important seasonal temperature variations, and higher latitudes, where seasonal temperatures unfavorable for growth intrude with elevation into the course of a year. In both cases effects of exposure and erosion characteristic of many high-elevation areas will complicate the structure of the vegetation. The low-latitude *montane rainforest*, nevertheless, can pass directly into treeless mountain meadow and shrub, although usually it is slowly reduced to a dense stunted forest before the treeline is reached (Womersley and McAdam 1957, pp. 25-27). In higher latitudes the rainforest is bordered at higher elevations by a less dense forest generally with a thick surface growth of shrubs (Sigafoos 1958). The transition can be sharp but it is not clear what the usual form of the change might be.

*Summary*

The available evidence consistently shows that a rainforest type of vegetation contrasts sharply with adjacent forest formations. Examined with particular reference to the understory density, it appears that a continuous growth of understory is a highly consistent characteristic of those stands called rainforest, and in this they differ from neighboring forests. It is significant that in field observations and available references, intermediate or equivocal cases can scarcely be found. It was earlier developed that other presumed rainforest distinctions, such as lack of clearcut dominance among canopy species, cannot be considered as distinguishing rainforests, even while rainforest is almost universally accepted as a distinct type. Thus it can be concluded that it is the understory that sets the rainforest apart (Figure 19). Where wilting drought or killing cold can penetrate within the shady forest, the delicate shade-enduring plants are largely eliminated. But if these perils are even barely escaped the forest interior can nurture a rich array of understory trees. One can propose that the rainforest is that vegetation formation where deleterious conditions do not significantly affect the abundant understory tree cover; seasonal forest by contrast has no more than scattered trees below the canopy.

*Figure 19.* Interior of a rainforest in northern Queensland. The continuous character of the understory is evident. Walking through such a rainforest is not difficult, however.

## SEASONAL FORESTS CONTRASTED WITH WOODLANDS

*Woodland* is here taken to involve a discontinuous cover of trees whereas *forest* has a continuous tree canopy, a distinction generally understood between these two kinds of vegetation formation. The question concerning the relationship between them therefore resolves itself into how sharp a division can be made and to what degree do secondary characteristics correspond. Woodland in anything like an undisturbed condition is so scattered that transects from forest to woodland are difficult to find and the literature has little to say about this transition. The problem has been studied in the field in North America, where several transects in hilly terrain were identified, while numerous stands were observed to ascertain the degree with which they could be divided between forest on the one hand or woodland on the other. The existence of a broad spectrum of intermediate types would demonstrate that the woodland-forest distinction is not a sharp one; a clear dichotomy would confirm their separate reality.

*The Forest-Woodland Boundary*

By searching in the general vicinity where apparent woodland approaches apparent forest, places can be found where these two formations meet with a minimum of disturbance evident within the individual structures. In such places the tree canopy will be continuous and the openings discontinuous in the part called forest, but the tree canopy will be discontinuous while the open areas are continuous where the term woodland is to be applied. The actual percentage of tree cover dividing the two categories may vary somewhat depending on the shape of the tree crowns and in any case is particularly difficult to measure accurately, because considerations of varying angles of the sun are relevant but highly complicating. Rather, observations of secondary plant growth, including lower tree branches, merit particular attention in the neighborhood of the boundary in question. However, the possibility also exists that crown itself divides in a distinct way along the boundary. The following examples (all based on field work by the author in the latter half of 1964) should clarify the situation.

1. Twenty miles northeast of Helena, Montana, an extensive woodland of juniper meets a yellow pine-Douglas fir forest in hilly terrain. A gradually turning slope was selected where the western part faced the afternoon sun, being clothed with woodland, whereas to the east the slope faced southeast having a continuous forest cover. Tree canopy in the woodland, where essentially undisturbed, amounted to about 40 percent coverage or less, and only occasional tree trunks were not imbedded in foliage, their own lower branches, or that of smaller plants. The forest canopy ranged between 85 and 100 percent coverage. At a level above the ground cover and below the tree canopy (three to six feet), coverage in the forest was generally about 5 percent, while that in the woodland reached a maximum of 40 percent, being mostly bushy trees (Figure 20). At the contact between woodland and forest, the forest edge was irregular in shape, beyond which extended the typical woodland of small clumps and isolated bushy trees. The

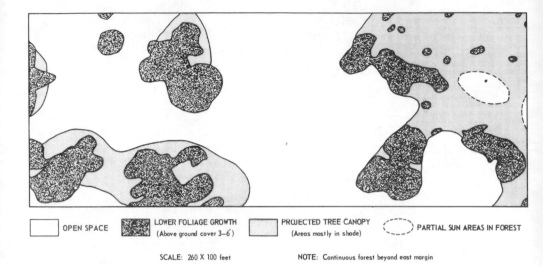

OPEN SPACE          LOWER FOLIAGE GROWTH          PROJECTED TREE CANOPY
                    (Above ground cover 3–6′)      (Areas mostly in shade)          PARTIAL SUN AREAS IN FOREST

SCALE:  260 X 100 feet                    NOTE: Continuous forest beyond east margin

*Figure 20.* Cover pattern at a forest-woodland boundary near Helena, Montana. Forest continues to the right of the diagram for many miles and woodland continues equally to the left. Lower foliage growth in the forest is understory but in the woodland it is edge. The forest has an edge and the woodland is essentially all edge.

exposed edge of the forest consisted of a mass of bushes and lower branches directly above the ground cover and about fifteen to thirty feet in depth measured NNE from the open side. Conversely, the woodland was, in effect, all edge (Figure 21). Qualitatively the woodland and the forest edge were of the same composition. Inside the forest, however, the sparse (5 percent) understory was mostly forest tree juveniles and the junipers became rare. Forest tree species occasionally rose above the large woodland junipers but within a mile became sporadic. Small openings in the forest did not have an edge structure but did carry numerous tree seedlings. The ground cover was entirely lacking in shady areas both within the forest and under woodland bushes. A sparse cover of grass occupied partly sunny areas in the woodland, along the forest edge, and under the small forest openings. A meadow of grass, other herbs, and small cactus grew in the mostly sunny areas of the woodland. The entire area was well stocked with mature and old plants, whereas the juveniles were fewer in number and similarly distributed to the adults, which suggests that the area

*Figure 21.* View in woodland near the forest boundary of Figure 20. The forest is yellow pine *(Pinus ponderosa)* and the pines mix with junipers *(Juniperus scopulorum)* in the woodland clumps close to the forest. A short distance away the pines disappear. The ground cover is mostly grass.

was generally stabilized. That is, there was no evidence that would indicate an advancing forest into a degraded forest zone. Here is a forest-woodland boundary that is discrete, with the two entities being aboslutely different in structure right up to the boundary.

2. East of the Cascade Mountains in Oregon a belt of yellow pine forest is bordered on the east by a juniper woodland, with the transition occurring in a short distance of less than half a mile, the correlation between species and formations being strong. The pine forest which extends for many miles to the west is made up of columnar trees over one hundred feet high, with old growth specimens up to 125 feet. The tree crowns do not in general touch, but, because of their shape, direct sunlight does not reach the ground except briefly in small exposures. This must be considered a continuous canopy so far as direct sunlight is concerned, but indirect sunlight rather than deep shade is available at the ground

level, where a low bush cover of the bitterbrush type occupies up to 20 percent of the surface, otherwise covered with somewhat sparse grass. The woodland to the east, which also extends for many miles, consists of a cover of up to 40 percent which rises above the sunbathed grass and brush. Old-growth trees may be up to fifty feet high; younger plants are horizontally of the same extent but more bushy in stature. An area where pine and juniper were about equal in importance was selected for study. Here occasional unusually large junipers up to one hundred feet high were encountered among the pines, where in general the shade at the ground level was continuous. In openings caused by the death of pines (or where a few large pines were cut many years before) a thicket of junipers had sprung up. Characteristically on the NNE side of the juniper thickets and the single large old junipers, younger pine trees were found. In shady areas, the bulk of the surface, juvenile pines were clearly dominant over juniper. The area studied was unquestionably forest, but the juniper has penetrated where suitable openings have occurred from time to time (Figure 22). Within a quarter of a mile to the east, mature pine trees were greatly outnumbered by mature junipers which grew separately from one another with branches in clear sunlight down to the ground. Although the transition to woodland was rapid, the lack of a sharp edge as in the first example appears to be related to the lack of a sharp contrast between sunny and shady areas, resulting from the fact that the columnar pines do not produce a deep shade underneath.

3. With the help of the California State Cooperative Soil-Vegetation Survey, an area was selected south of Shingletown in the northern part of Sacramento Valley, where a south-facing slope had a transition from forest to woodland without any complicating soil factors (Pacific Southwest Forest and Range Experiment Station 1958). The woodland consisted predominately of blue oak with scattered digger pine and somewhat bushy live oak. The pines, which grow up to 125 feet, can be nearly overlooked because their growth is so sparse they cast hardly noticeable shade. Large oak to seventy-five feet were to be found, but forty to fifty feet was more usual. Here, as in other areas of oak-digger pine woodland sampled, the tree crowns covered approximately 40 percent of the surface and the trees showed a strong tendency to clump, several together. Lower branches down to the level of the bushes were much less extensive than the tree crowns and an

*Figure 22.* Yellow pine forest east of Sisters, Oregon, close to the woodland boundary. The forest here forms a continuous canopy with small openings as in the right foreground. A few hundred yards away there is typical woodland. An unusually large juniper *(J. occidentalis)* survives in the forest on the left probably antedating the establishment of the current stand of forest trees.

occasional tree was actually open underneath, although smaller trees were more or less of a haystack shape. Brush formed an irregular cover of about a quarter of the area while everywhere the ground was clothed with grass. Occasional juvenile blue oaks and digger pines were scattered about, usually at the edge of a bush or tree. The forest up to its margin was made up of yellow pine and black oak, having the same vertical dimensions as the pine and oak of the woodland but forming a thick canopy with dense shade underneath. Shrubs and juveniles of the canopy trees occupied less than 10 percent of the space under the canopy and the ground was nearly bare of herbaceous growth. Although the woodland and forest boundary formed a mosaic, the edge of the forest was as sharp as the area under the branches of the last tree. Near the forest manzanita grew unusually large and thick, and under manzanita bushes forest trees became established, while just inside the forest large dead and dying manzanita were common. The whole change from typical woodland to continuous forest occurred in a distance of two-tenths of a mile. Obviously the forest edge was a tension zone, but the contrast here between the two formations was remarkably strong.

4. The same transition between pine-oak forest and pine-oak woodland was observed north of Igo, California, but because of broken terrain the change could not be so clearly described. However, the same contrast between closed crown yellow pine-black oak forest on the one hand, and open digger pine-blue oak woodland on the other could be identified over a distance of less than two miles, whereas in either direction the respective formations extend for many a mile with no significant discernible change in form.

5. In an attempt to study intermediate conditions between forests and woodland, sites with from about 40 to 80 percent tree cover were looked for. In the case of the yellow pine zone from South Dakota to the Cascade Mountains such places, if they did not show evidence of recent fire or of destructively heavy grazing, had crowds of young pines coming up in the openings. In the oak and pine forests, particularly in southern Oregon and northern California, such a tree cover was sometimes found where an oak savanna graded into a denser oak stand or where an oak forest bordered on more open country. Whether observed samples were studied in detail or not, it was invariably apparent that the area was in a state of dynamic succession and with no true woodland anywhere in the vicinity. Fire has historically burned over large areas of forest in this zone, and few forest trees have been able to reclaim the open grass cover. With the aid of shrubs, particularly manzanita, young trees could be seen establishing themselves.

6. A transition from Jeffrey pine forest to sage brush was found in a rare essentially undisturbed state about eight miles south of Reno, Nevada (local residents were almost pathologically afraid of the possibility of fire). As in the yellow pine forest margin described above for Oregon, the forest here did not have a sharp edge, but the change from closed crown forest on this east-facing slope to open woodland required no more than a quarter of a mile. Pine, mostly with a skirt of lower branches, extended for about half a mile beyond the forest proper among small bushy trees of a species of bitter brush and sage brush (Figure 23). To-

*Figure 23.* Woodland of bitter brush *(Purshia tridentata)* near a forest of Jeffrey Pine near Reno, Nevada. Scattered pines grow in the woodland which is quite open while a few hundred yards away there is a closed crown forest. In the other direction the pines soon disappear.

gether the pines (twenty to sixty feet high) and the bitter brush (about twelve feet high) had a crown cover of not more than 30 percent. Low sage brush to the extent of 40 percent of the surface alternated with the bitter brush but became only sporadic in the shade of the pines. The ground was everywhere covered with grass. Out on the flats there was nothing but sage brush and grass. There is a hint that juniper could grow in the area if it were locally available, because it grows in similar areas some distance away.

7. In the southern Sierra Nevada the margin of forest with woodland generally is found in very steep and broken terrain; more level areas are often given over to grassland and savanna. Observations were made on both sides of a forest zone in which Alta Sierra is located. The forest near its limits consists of yellow pine, black oak, and incense cedar, with little or no ground cover. The woodland is live oak and digger pine with some blue oak, under all

of which is a continuous cover of grass. The change from forest to woodland in both cases was rather sharp (not over a quarter of a mile) with individual specimens of incense cedar for a short distance in the woodland and a few digger pines within the forest.

8. The woodland boundary with forest in the Pinoleña Mountains in southeastern Arizona was studied as an example in the flora which extends from there far south into Mexico, where marked disturbance is almost impossible to avoid (See Whittaker and Niering 1965. They speak of a physiognomic continuum — in terms of individual species growth forms — but identify associations and such cover categories as forest, woodland, grassland, and desert scrub). Even in the study area, the sporadic cutting of trees, so ubiquitous in Mexico, was evident. The forest at its lower levels was mostly Arizona pine, but other pine, white oak, and madrone were seen. The well-developed pine forest had little or no ground cover. The woodland was made up of short oaks, twenty feet high, and in warmer areas included alligator juniper. Abundant large coarse bunch grasses grew among the woodland trees. Near the forest and within it, Chihuahua pines grew, possibly being able to invade the forest zone with the help of disturbance to the forest. Detailed observations were made just beyond the forest. Here the trees were mostly oak in a series of small thickets that occupied about half the area (Figure 24). Several Arizona pines had at one time grown in the area, their cut-off trunks now lying on the ground. Compared to less dense woodland areas, the ground itself was rather bare, and the oak, in spite of the loss of the pine, did not seem to be expanding, although a few young junipers had invaded the area. Possibly in good years more pine and oak could become established. Nearby upslope the oak thickets merged and there Arizona pine directly became abundant; together these marked the beginning of the forest. A few hundred feet downslope grew a typical woodland of oak and juniper.

9. The forest-woodland boundary was observed in a variety of places in Mexico, despite the fact that nowhere could the vegetative cover be considered stabilized. Broad areas of forest on the one hand and woodland on the other could be identified. In western Chihuahua there was a pine forest, with a secondary admixture of oak, madrone, and juniper, under which grew a sparse ground cover of herbaceous plants and sometimes a scattering of shrubs. Large trees had been for the most part removed, but numerous juveniles were present. The woodland was dominated

*Figure 24.* Oak woodland in the Pinoleña Mountains, Arizona, at the forest margin. The view lies in the transition with typical woodland a stone's throw in one direction and closed crown forest as close in the other direction. Openings as in the foreground alternate with stands of trees.

by various species of oak, with pinyon pine, Chihuahua pine, and juniper (locally any one type of tree may predominate). Because of fire and much other disturbances, the woodland was largely confined to broken country, where between the trees there was much grass, small cactus, and many juveniles. The transition from forest to woodland was brief, the edge of the pine forest being marked by diminished tree size, fewer trees and increased grass. Where the forest opened up, about half of the forest species were absent, and woodland species began to appear.

10. In Durango near the forest boundary the woodland was very disturbed by chopping, grazing, and fire. Between the woodland pines and oaks there was a brush of juveniles and manzanita scrub, possibly maintained as woodland over forest by the disturbance. Nevertheless, the change in species and form to forest was rapid. The forest, here of lutea pine, formed a continuous

canopy, with grass and a kind of prostrate oak everywhere on the ground. In places, forest tree oaks were mixed with pine and the cover of grass and juveniles under the trees was in indirect proportion to the density of the canopy. In central Mexico the vegetation, particularly the woodland part, was hopelessly disturbed.

11. In the vicinity of Ciudad Victoria in northeastern Mexico a rough contrast can be made between woodland and forest in spite of continued disturbance of the vegetation cover. In this area the soil is generally sandy and poor, forest and woodland alike having a stunted effect. Mile after mile of low forest ten to twenty feet high was observed, with scattered larger trees suggesting that most of the trees were immature. Under the trees there was a ground cover of herbs, grass not being important. The woodland consisted of trees at least ten feet high in most cases, with grass and other herbs everywhere on the ground but thicker under the trees. Although the woodland tree species were different from the forest tree species, their general appearance (color, leaf size, and branching pattern) was so similar that the change from one to the other was difficult to observe. Nevertheless, the transition, in spite of disturbance, was narrow compared to the extent of forest on the one side and woodland on the other.

12. In southeastern Texas the relationship between forest and woodland was marked by farming and by soil distinction. On sandy soils grew grasslands reverting to mesquite, which is essentially a continuation of Mexican coastal woodland. The non-sand soils are sufficiently better that, at this point, forest could become established. Northwest of LaGrange and Carmine, Texas, an area of apparent forest-woodland transition was found. On the woodland side there was a discontinuous canopy of oak with juniper and holly (Figure 25). Grass covered the ground everywhere, with bushes and regeneration mostly under the trees. At the forest boundary was a mosaic of open and closed canopy areas with little or no undergrowth in the closed canopy areas. To the east, beyond a cropped area and in better soil, was a well-developed forest of oak and hickory. Because soil boundaries generally can account for the observed vegetation distinctions in southeastern Texas, not much can be said here concerning the other aspects of the forest-woodland boundary.

In spite of the widespread lack of stability attending woodlands in general and forests near their boundary, the relationship between the two formation types can be observed. Where the

*Figure 25.* Oak woodland east of Giddings, Texas, close to the forest margin. The trees here are large for a woodland, and this may be a successional woodland that could revert to forest with the suppression of fire.

vegetation cover appears to be fairly stabilized, rather distinct boundaries are to be found. Using the criteria for forest and for woodland as stated above, the zone of transition is generally less than a mile and can be an abrupt edge. That is, field observation indicates that a continuum does not exist.

## Forest-Woodland Distinctions

The distinctions between forest and woodland, or the equivalent with a different terminology, has long been made in the literature. Schimper (1903, p. 162; 1898, p. 176), using the term "woodland" *(Geholz)* for all formations with trees, distinguished *forest (Wald)* with a closed cover of trees from *bushwood (Buschwald* or *Gebüsch)* with trees separated by shrubs. He gives little attention to bushwood as a type, and it is evident that his *sclerophyllous woodland* and probably some of his thorn forests belong to this general type. Dansereau (1957, pp. 84-93) has a general category of *forest* characterized by a dense formation of trees and contrasted with formations of widely spaced trees (this is largely based on van Faber's revision of Schimper's work). Among the latter are *savanna woodland* and *thorn forest* both of which have a considerable tree cover, luxuriant herbaceous growth, and possibly shrubs. Eyre (1963, pp. 12 and 125) also divides vegetation into *forest* and *non-forest*, defined only by implication. Among the non-forest "communities" is woodland "composed of small trees forming a more or less open canopy." Further reference to such differentiations has already been made in Chapter I where I have reviewed systems of classification. It is remarkable how often such vegetation categories are used in texts or on maps without recourse to any firm definition. By and large the difference between forest and woodland then is acknowledged if not sharply defined.

Numerous samples were made in North America of forest and of woodland to test the proposed distinguishing characters and to encompass the range of variations that exists. Observation, as was specified earlier, was limited to vegetation cover showing a minimum of disturbance, particularly by chopping, by heavy grazing, and by fire. Conversely, the vegetation was evaluated in terms of stability: mature trees, a balance between juveniles and adults, and general uniformity. These observations were extensively supplemented by examination of photographs of other parts of the world and by less rigorous field notes in various other areas, particularly Australia. It should be immediately admitted, as was stated before, that woodlands in apparently undisturbed condition are generally sporadic, but large areas do occur. Several woodland formations have already been described above in terms of woodland-forest boundaries. These include a juniper woodland in Montana *(Juniperus scopulorum)* and in Oregon *(J. occidentalis)*, two pine-oak woodlands in California, a bitter brush (and sage) woodland in Nevada, and an oak woodland in Arizona. In addition the somewhat disturbed woodlands of Mexico, including the oak-pine-juniper woodlands of the northwest and the mesquite woodlands of the northeast and into Texas, were covered.

Several additional types of woodland can be described. In the southern part of the Sierra Nevada of California there are pinyon-juniper woodlands that can be used to represent this type. A stand of single-leaf pinyon and California juniper sampled had a tree cover of about 40 percent with trees to a maximum of thirty feet high. The herbaceous cover of annual grasses and some forbs was poorly developed, with about 15 percent of the ground in open sunshine and completely bare. In addition a low cover of bushes, mostly sage but with other types such as scrub oak, between the trees, occupied about one-third of the area. Under the trees the herbaceous growth was better developed. Some tendency for clumping of the trees was evident and a few juveniles were found.

Another stand of pinyon and juniper was studied, this one in eastern Arizona, different species being involved (Utah juniper and two-leaved pinyon) with a secondary mixture of oak. Again the tree cover amounted to about 40 percent with a definite tendency toward clumping. Small trees either formed a cluster or crowded around the edges of the few large trees. Grass and other herbs covered the ground everywhere, while juveniles and bushes such as evergreen scrub oak, although well represented in numbers of individuals, occupied hardly 10 percent of the surface and prospered mostly near established trees. This pinyon-juniper stand was relatively close to yellow pine forest whereas the one described previously was relatively close to the desert boundary.

In several places on dry slopes a yellow pine woodland was observed, although yellow pine only occasionally in fact forms a woodland. Junipers *(J. scopulorum)* were present in such areas, while in the vicinity the vegetation was largely highly disturbed. A few miles inside Wyoming west of the Black Hills such a woodland consisted of clumps of small pines up to fifty feet tall with smaller junipers about ten feet tall. Possibly one-fifth of the area was covered by trees, while a scattering of juveniles and of yucca plants were present. Not very dense grass with small cactus grew everywhere. Thirty-five miles southwest of Missoula, Montana, was an area of dispersed and scrubby pines occupying about 20 percent of the surface accompanied by a very sparse scattering of yucca and juveniles. Grass with other herbs and cactus grew everywhere but markedly better in areas of midday shade.

Southwest of Guadalajara (east of Ayutla), Mexico, a low-elevation woodland was selected for study. Quite a few kinds of trees up to fifteen feet high were present, the most prominent being a mimosa, a prickly pear cactus, and a locust-type tree. Nearly 40 percent of the area was covered by tree crowns with a definite tendency toward clumping. Grass and occasional other herbs were everywhere, whereas bushes consisting of juveniles and many other things, although numerous, covered no more than 15 percent of the surface and were mostly clustered near or under the trees.

Each of these samples described was compared in the field to extensive areas nearby, and except as noted they appeared to be quite representative. The fact that a great deal of similarity exists among them as well as with other areas more cursorily observed has led to the conclusions that there is something definite that can be referred to as woodland. Bringing the various factors together, the woodlands studied have a discontinuous cover of trees, seldom over 40 percent, except on the very margin with forest,* but also not often greatly below 40 percent of cover in stabilized stands even close to the desert margin. One might guess that there is an uninterrupted stratum of tree roots. The extent of low woody plants, both bushes and juveniles, not significantly taller than the herbaceous plants (or than growth in a single season) in the detailed observations was always less than and often markedly less than the area covered by trees. Significantly, where any appreciable number of juveniles was at hand, they showed a strong tendency to locate under the shady edge of larger plants. The ground cover of grass and other herbaceous plants was generally continuous although near the forest boundary it was sometimes absent under dense evergreen bushes while in seemingly severe environments, as near the desert margin, thinner areas or even bare places occurred in the open. Normally the woodland trees tended to form clumps — two or more trees growing against one another. However, each tree, even where clumps were common, was exposed on at least one side to the full sun. In effect, woodland trees are all edge. The presence of juveniles or of bushes around a tree

*Keith L. White (1966) studied blue oak "woodland" south of Monterrey Bay in California close to forest stands and found an average canopy coverage of 49.5 percent. Actually his woodland is essentially savanna, but he rejected the more open areas in his samples. Lower branches in his study area are almost completely browsed off while bushes and juveniles are only sporadic. Evidence was presented for severe browsing on seedlings, and it is suggested that fire at least used to be common in the area. With the widespread stocking of cattle in the region one might suppose that natural predators for the deer are rare or absent. Thus tree reproduction in the face of deer and cattle pressure must be sporadic. There is no reason to assume that this area cannot become a closed crown community and probably eventually will if no new pressures are applied to it. Such savannas are widespread from southern Oregon to the Mexican border, and there is every reason to believe that they are maintained by fire or by unnaturally heavy browsing. In density they vary from open grassland to closed forest.

often, at least in part, replaced lower branches, and woodland trees seldom presented a bare trunk to the open sun.

The description of forest, or more specifically seasonal forest, is much simpler than that of woodland and many more examples were available. Whether quadrant maps were made or not, the forests observed all over North America and elsewhere consisted of a continuous tree canopy with only tree trunks connecting the tree growth to the ground cover. Understory trees of juveniles and shade-growing species were very discontinuous (see the early part of this chapter for a discussion of understory density near the rainforest boundary). The ground cover of the forest was generally continuous but sometimes randomly variable in thickness and even in some cases absent. A reasonable explanation of no ground cover is that the forest may represent a recently reestablished cover and shade-growing ground cover plants may simply have been previously eliminated in the area. There may also be special factors of toxic leaf litter or edaphic conditions that preclude available ground cover plants as well. Openings in the forest canopy are generally accompanied by a thicket of juveniles or are surrounded by an edge of sun-growing plants in which juveniles grow. Otherwise juveniles are randomly located within the forest.

Forest can be distinguished from woodland in the following tabular form (see also Figure 26):

| FOREST | WOODLAND |
|---|---|
| 1. continuous canopy (only sporadic openings). | 1. discontinuous canopy (rarely more than 40 percent cover). |
| 2. open underneath (crown not in contact with ground cover). | 2. crowns everywhere in contact with ground cover. |
| 3. juveniles randomly distributed or concentrated where openings occur. | 3. juveniles avoiding open areas. |

Field evidence has shown that woodlands and seasonal forests each have their own more or less consistent characteristics by which they can be distinguished and that intermediate types essentially do not exist. Specifically, the generally assumed distinction between continuous canopy and discontinuous canopy has

*Figure 26.* Profile of forest (left) and woodland (right) to illustrate their distinguishing characteristics.

been shown to be pronounced, with marginal cases in stabilized growth areas virtually absent. In effect, where a cover much exceeds 40 percent it would appear that inadequate light is available for the hardy woodland tree species while apparently there is at the same time sufficient shade to encourage the general growth of forest tree species. Thus it becomes unnecessary to define carefully what continuous canopy as opposed to discontinuous canopy means. Either it is definitely the one or it is unquestionably the other. Forest areas are seen to be actively closing up such openings as may occur — woodlands have their surface divided into tree islands surrounded by sunny spaces which are continuous in time as well as space. Disturbance can reduce the trees in either case, of course. It can be proposed that woodland is that vegetation formation where conditions will not support a continuous cover of trees so that only those trees can grow that can endure general exposure in all stages (except perhaps the very small seedling) to sun from the side as well as from above. In a seasonal forest, by contrast, the trees must survive shade in the juvenile form or rely on disturbance in order to become established.

## WOODLANDS CONTRASTED WITH DESERTS

Desert is everywhere in the literature accepted as a major vegetation formation, but the boundary tends to be elusive. Desert is characterized by continuous bare ground, but near its margins, unfortunately, the amount of bare ground fluctuates from year to year or even seasonally during the year. The same problem addressed earlier for distinguishing formation types is repeated here in greater relief. How can one tell where the desert begins? To answer this question, desert boundaries in various parts of North America were examined. The high arctic desert, however, was not included in the study.

An example of the difficulty of distinguishing the desert margins can be given concerning the southwestern corner of New Mexico. In 1954 I evaluated this area as desert throughout the lowlands, but in 1964 in the same area, all but a small part was clearly a grassland. The first examination was during a severe dry period when a few scattered bushes and some miserable tufts of grass were all the vegetation to be seen; whereas the second view took place when conditions were moist, so that a robust cover of grass dominated the surface, relieved here and there by an occasional small bush. Actually the area has the potential to become a woodland particularly with mesquite, in the absence of fire, as was implied by a sequential study in a nearby area (Buffington and Herbel 1965; Harris 1966). But the effects of drought, particularly on the herbaceous content of the vegetation in a marginal area, can obviously temporarily convert a continuous cover into a distinctly discontinuous stand.

In this same area, however, other observations were quite helpful in understanding the long-term relationships between the various plant formations at hand. As the desert was approached the grassland gave way to a thicket of mesquite with a minor constituent of other bushes. This thicket was only a few miles wide, in some areas forming a mosaic with grassland. The far side of the thicket rapidly opened up with desert plants becoming dominant and mesquite becoming subordinate as bare ground predominated, and from here, the rather uniform desert continued for many a mile. The same transition was seen time and again in southeastern Arizona and southward through Chihuahua, Durango, and even as far as the state of Hidalgo. Whatever it is that produces grassland did not seem to be effective at the very desert margin, and mesquite, which is a minor competitor in the desert, had been enabled to prosper right at the edge. It can be suggested that in dry years the grassland is seared out allowing the mesquite to take over just where there is enough moisture in some years for effective competition with desert plants. Surely the climatic boundary is not as sharp as the vegetative boundary, however, and the actual boundary represents a partly stabilized front between the fluctuating interplay of desert plants and the alternatives (grassland and mesquite).

Where the desert margin reached up onto the lower slopes of the islands of rough country in the same region, as on the northeastern side of the Pinoleña Mountains in southeastern Arizona, the situation was slightly different. Scrub oak and pinyon-juniper woodlands clothed the broken land, and patches of desert plants appeared on dry sites. The change from woodland species to desert species, among which ocotillo and various types of cactus were conspicuous, was almost abrupt, with the complete disappearance of the non-desert plants that grow throughout the woodland zone. In the woodland the ground cover of herbaceous plants is essentially continuous while it is only sporadic within the desert, but this factor changes only gradually in space and, obviously, varies considerably with the fluctuations in rainfall.

Elsewhere marker plants announce the desert margin in the same way. In southern California and nearby areas, the California juniper forms a narrow belt just at the edge of the desert, being partly in woodland and partly in desert. (It also grows on dry sites, generally more or less desert, on the inner side of the Coast Range and occasionally elsewhere. See Vasek 1966, map on p. 367.) On one side extends oak woodland or chaparral for large distances while on the other opens out the great expanse of the desert. In the same area the joshua tree also is an inhabitant of the desert margin only sometimes mixing with the junipers. Presumably these plants cannot compete effectively in a community with continuous cover nor can they endure full desert aridity. Therefore they find their place where the environmental factors involved alternate with both being common.

Marker plants are not always present on the desert margin. For example, the shadscale desert in the Great Basin sometimes borders on grassland as in the area east of Reno, Nevada. The transition here occupied a distance of several miles (fully developed grassland and undoubted desert were not more than twelve miles apart). The herbaceous growth increased among the desert bushes as the grassland was approached and where the overall cover began to be continuous, the desert plants became reduced and soon were not to be found. Shadscale is associated with salt, of course, and variations in salt content of the soil presumably produce the vegetation transition. More commonly the shadscale desert borders sage brush or pinyon and juniper woodland, usually on the slopes of

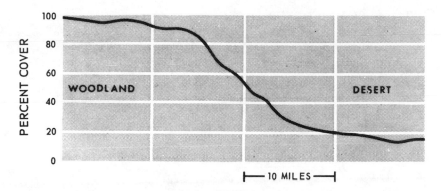

*Figure 27.* Generalized profile of total plant cover between woodland and desert. This is a composite of many observations to show the character of the transition.

the many ranges which rim the desert basins (Billings 1949). The change along these slopes in species composition and in cover can be abrupt, perhaps in response to sharp soil boundaries.

Samples of the areal coverage of plants near the desert margins emphasize the contrasts qualitatively described so far. In the desert, virtually up to its limit, plants occupy a maximum of one-third of the total surface. In the woodland close to the desert, patches of bare ground were not found amounting to more than 15 percent of the cover. Intermediate values of bare ground as a proportion of the total area were essentially confined to the immediate zone of transition. This can be illustrated by a composite and somewhat schematic profile in Figure 27.

Field observation in western North America has supported the idea that desert is a distinct vegetation cover type contrasting clearly with woodland (and grassland). There is really no question as to what desert is, while in the areas studied it appears that, in spite of short-term variations, a definite boundary zone, much narrower than the formations involved, can be identified. Desert is a vegetation cover where bare ground predominates (occasionally perhaps filled with desert ephemerals), and woodland has an emphatically continuous cover (that may be shrivelled back to more or less desertic conditions during major drought). These two can normally be distinguished by their characteristic plant constituents, except rather near their mutual boundary.

## OTHER COVER TYPES

In the literature and in various places above, other cover types than the four just analyzed in their relationships and characteristics have been touched upon. In some cases their origins or even reality has been challenged, in other cases only qualitative differences have been suggested. These other cover types will be grouped into secondary types and disturbed types for discussion.

*Secondary Cover Types*

Within each of the vegetation formations so far examined, various phases have been suggested descriptively. For most, and perhaps all, of these phases no sharp division exists between them and other aspects of the same formation. Rather, as far as the available evidence indicates, a gradual transition unites each phase with the rest of its formation and each of the phases have all of the general characters of the formation of which it is a part.

Three zonal phases of the rainforest can be recognized. All rainforests have a continuous understory as well as canopy. The bulk of the rainforests, which can be called *typical rainforest* or the rainforest proper, is the ultimate in vegetation luxuriance without significant mechanisms for enduring prolonged environmental stress. On the dry margins of the typical rainforest is found the *seasonal rainforest* in which a marked seasonal rhythm of growth of the vegetation system as a whole occurs. This phase, sometimes called monsoon rainforest, is seen generally as discontinuous lobes or a marginal fringe, rarely as a broad belt beside the rainforest proper. It is somewhat reduced in luxuriance but in my experience contains many of the same species as the fully developed rainforest. When the rainforest is reduced by disturbance, it is the seasonal rainforest that takes the brunt of attack. On the cool margin of the typical rainforest there is a gradual reduction of leaf size and canopy variety resulting in the *sclerophyll rainforest* which has been variously called temperate rainforest and mountain rainforest. This phase is the only type of rainforest seen outside of the tropics (Figure 28). It forms forests of limited extent in tropical highland areas and along some moderate marine middle-latitude coasts.

Seasonal forest can be divided into two recognizable phases.

*Figure 28.* Rainforest in western Tasmania. Composed mostly of *Nothofagus* with a well-developed bushy understory. The uniformity of the stand is characteristic of cool sclerophyll rainforests.

The most extensive such forests display a dense canopy which produces deep shade underneath, suggesting the name *dense seasonal forest* for this phase (Figure 29). The drier parts of the seasonal forest generally have a tree canopy which allows a great deal of indirect light to reach the ground cover, a difference of degree for which the name *light seasonal forest* can be applied (Figure 22). The same basic structure of a continuous canopy and discontinuous understory characterizes both forest phases, but more shade-tolerant trees can frequently be seen invading the light phase. In fact, the light seasonal forest obviously is enabled to expand through disturbance as a successional form at the expense of the dense seasonal forest and is also characteristic of droughty soil areas. Virtually the entire extent of seasonal forest fragments in the tropics is of light phase. The vast disturbances within the seasonal tropics make it almost impossible to know whether the dense phase can exist there. In the middle latitude the dense seasonal forest does sometimes, on the other hand, meet the

*Figure 29.* Dense seasonal forest of mountain hemlock and alpine fir near Santiam Pass in Oregon. Despite the moist environment and dense tree growth, the understory is quite open and nowhere like the rainforest understory. A fallen tree has opened the canopy on the left.

woodland, as was seen above. Perhaps the difference between these two seasonal forest phases is the result entirely of disturbance, or perhaps the denser phase correlates with the lack of a severe dry season.

Woodland can be said to have two phases, the distinction between which is probably not very significant. In all woodlands the plant growth above the seasonally renewable ground cover is quite discontinuous. For woodland one ordinarily thinks of the larger plants as trees or a *tree woodland* (Figure 30). Among these trees and above the ground cover but yet of rather low stature grow plants which are popularly called bushes. Toward the desert margin but in cool areas only, these "bushes" alone grow above the ground cover, as in sage brush areas, so that one could speak

*Figure 30.* Tree woodland of legumes in westernmost Jalisco state, Mexico. Because this is the end of the wet season the ground cover is particularly robust.

of *brush woodland* (Figure 31). It is not clear that this brush woodland would not become tree woodland in the absence of all disturbance, for trees do advance into the brush areas. It is probably only that plants of lesser stature are more able to survive the vicissitudes so often present than are plants of greater stature. The relationship of high-latitude woodland to other types has not been investigated here (See Hare 1959, 1950).

There are three phases into which desert can be divided. Two of these parallel the division made above in the woodland. *Tree desert* is of limited extent near the desert margins in warmer areas, as in the attractive stands of saguaro cactus and palo verde trees of Arizona and Mexico (Figure 32) (Nichol 1952). *Brush desert*, or semi-desert of some authors, is the usual aspect of the desert, where scattered small bushes and clumps of bunch grass cling to an

*Figure 31.* Sage brush as a brush woodland in central Washington. The sage brushes here reach almost two meters high and are surrounded by grass and a few low shrubs. Sage does not form a continuous cover of the type known as chaparral.

existence (Figure 33). All deserts have continuous bare ground and under more extreme conditions the plant content of the area becomes so sparse that one begins to talk about *barren desert,* a condition not achieved in every desert region (Figure 34). Some essentially barren areas have been produced, of course, by goats and other factors of disturbance.

The various secondary cover types discussed have two kinds of position. Generally, they represent qualitative phases within the major categories, involving denser or larger growth forms. There is some suggestion in the case of dense seasonal forest and brush woodland of a relationship to temperature stress as well. A diagram (Figure 35) shows how these divisions are related to one another with respect to the two gradients, moisture and temperature.

*Figure 32.* Desert with trees near Phoenix, Arizona. In spite of the size of the picturesque plants here the bare ground is continuous. Such growth lies near the wet limits of desert and in areas of mild winters and summer rains.

## Disturbed Cover Types

In addition to the four vegetation formations or cover types and their phases treated here, there are some others commonly mentioned, particularly *grassland,* *savanna,* and *brush.* Clearly many areas cannot be accounted for by the other formations so far considered. There is an extensive literature concerning the nature and origin of these formations, especially grassland and savanna (See International Congress of Geography 1956; Blydenstein 1967; Thornthwaite 1952; Sauer 1950; Cole 1960, 1963). An argument rages as to whether they owe their existence to disturbance, an argument that this study has not undertaken to supplement. Clearly a great deal of disturbance, particularly fire, occurs within these formations, a fact which eliminated them from the study of essentially undisturbed vegetation. Which, then, came first — grassland, savanna, and brush or the disturbance? Undoubtedly

*Figure 33.* Brush desert in western Texas. Creosote brush here is more typical of deserts around the world than the display shown in Figure 32.

the more severely disturbed areas tend to have natural conditions of climate and soil that mitigate against rapid recovery, while some disturbance is a natural if sporadic part of the environment without the help of man. The position taken here, not without evidence, is that grassland, savanna, and brush (except perhaps under special local conditions) are essentially the result of disturbance and, in the presence of alternatives, are not stable formations. Even so, it is admitted that grassland, savanna, and brush are a normal part of the world's vegetation cover.

If grassland, savanna, and brush result from disturbance, then each could vary, depending on the effective amount of disturbance, from little different from undisturbed cover types to extremely different. That is, there ought logically to be a continuum varying with the degree of disturbance, and these types could only be marked off by evidence of the modifying disturbance. To be sure, sharp boundaries for each of these can and do occur where sharp limits to disturbance have obtained, but my experience, coupled with the essential lack in the literature of conflicting

*Figure 34.* Barren desert near Antofagasta, Chile. Nothing whatever grows in this area.

evidence, indicates that these formations are distinguished only by degree. One is perplexed to know where a woodland changes into a savanna or brush and where a savanna becomes a grassland.* Grassland is the extreme where woody plants are unimportant. True brush, as opposed to brush woodland, is a continuous cover of bushes and in this sense is of rather limited and sporadic occurrence. Savanna is a scattered cover of trees or bushes and differs from woodland in that the woody plants are so far apart that their roots do not touch continuously. Clearly, any more luxuriant cover type could be reduced by disturbance to a lesser cover type, but the forms being considered here are additional types. Even if undisturbed examples indeed exist, these three differ from rainforest, forest, woodland, and desert in lacking consistent boundaries where they can be specifically distinguished from other cover types.

*Eiten (1963) suggests a limit of 25 percent cover for the boundary between savanna and woodland, with forest having more than 50 percent cover.

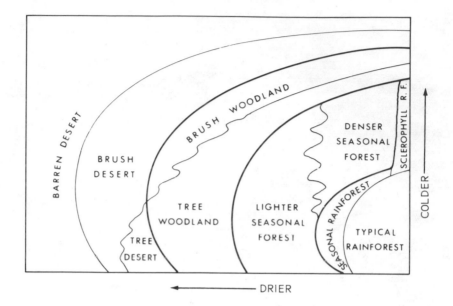

*Figure 35.* Diagram of the relative position of the various primary and secondary vegetation types with respect to moisture and temperature gradients. These are all fully developed vegetation formations. Grasslands and savanna often replace many of them over large areas.

## CONCLUSION

From the evidence accumulated here concerning the spatial and structural contrasts between a series of specified undisturbed vegetation formations, the conclusion emerges that the four *(rainforest, seasonal forest, woodland,* and *desert)* are distinct in kind and not arbitrary points on a continuum. In field experience, vegetation stands selected for lack of evidence of significant physiognomic disturbance could be assigned in the vast majority of cases to one of the four without hesitation. Areally each of the four was divided from any other by brief transition zones or even abrupt boundaries. In support of the idea that one is dealing here with real entities is the fact that in the literature (see the first chapter for an extended discussion) each of these formation categories is repeatedly identified as a type (or group of types subdivided by other kinds of criteria). It would appear that the distinctions being discussed here have been widely recognized but not heretofore tested. Other recognized distinctions have been tested and found wanting, but for those utilized here, field support has been presented.

The sharpness of boundaries sometimes found merits special consideration. Where abrupt boundaries coincide with breaks in terrain or changes in soil, an adequate explanation is at hand. But abrupt boundaries frequently occur in the absence of such correlations, and these edges tend to show signs of disturbance. The more complex of the adjacent vegetation formations either has been destroyed back to its edge or it can be seen to be aggressively advancing. Such frontiers are commonplace between disturbed vegetation and a vegetation formation unmodified by disturbance; the gradient from more elaborate to less elaborate vegetation cover might well also be sharpened by disturbance. The significant fact here is that on either side of such boundaries the same basic formation types are consistently found. If sharp boundaries were caused by random disturbance within a continuum, then, although distinct formation regions might occur locally, these regions as units would still fall randomly on a larger continuum. Such is not the case, and therefore these several systems of vegetation formation must have reality. Given these physiognomic systems, it is reasonable to conceive of each tending to advance toward areas of marginal conditions where it would naturally be vulnerable to stress even in the form of rather minor disturbance. Thus, its boundary with lesser formations would be a tension zone with the balance at any time as likely to be in its favor as against it. Sharp boundaries are a logical characteristic of the interplay of distinct systems.

That grassland, savanna, and brush lack consistent boundaries puts them in a different category from the above sequence. There is, in effect, a continuous gradient from the four types dominated by woody plants toward a grassland extreme. Savanna or brush (as well as a woodland which is a degraded forest rather than a stable formation) occupy intermediate positions. It is suggested that disturbance tends to reduce the woody content of vegetation formations and to create a more open condition. The definition of these formations remains qualitative.

In summary, it has been demonstrated that certain aspects of plant coverage correspond to real natural systems of vegetation formations. These can be used effectively in mapping world patterns of vegetation, particularly when the intention is to illuminate the broad pattern of vegetation response to the natural environment. To the four basic undisturbed formations can be added the open areas resulting, as is taken here, from disturbance, and the major habitat choices in terms of plant cover have been illuminated. The use of elements of cover distribution can form the basis of a significant and rational classification of vegetation.

# 6

# The World Patterns of Vegetation Formations

WITH THIS CRITICAL ANALYSIS of the significance of characteristics used to map the vegetation of the world there naturally arises the question, what world patterns of vegetation logically result from an application of the conclusions reached? One immediately encounters here the problem of data — its multiplicity of forms and variations in coverage. Nevertheless, a reasonable attempt can be made to order the information in terms of the ideas developed above and to produce such a map. The distribution of each category on the resulting map deserves comment, together with a consideration of the categories not used. World maps of each category separately will be included here rather than a single composite generalized map.

## THE MAJOR VEGETATION FORMATIONS

The thrust of this study has involved those broad vegetation formations that can effectively be considered on a small scale and for the whole world at one time. Special emphasis has been given to four undisturbed types of formation — *rainforest, seasonal forest, woodland,* and *desert* — which can be considered as a zonal sequence. Two disturbed types — *savanna* and *grassland* — must also be included on a world map, even though their distinction from one another and from other vegetation types is sometimes but a matter of degree, because they are widespread, involve distinct aspects of cover, and cannot be equated specifically with the undisturbed forms. There are thus six major vegetation formations. The recognized subdivisions of these are not easily mapped at the world scale and, for the most part, have never been so mapped nor will they be included here.

## Rainforest

Rainforest has a continuous canopy and a continuous understory. There are three great rainforest regions — in South and Central America, in Africa, and in Southeast Asia-southwestern Pacific (Map 12). These are the world's reservoir of plant species *par excellence*, with many hundred in every square mile. On the other hand, the larger uniformity of each of the three regions is remarkable, for same species are found over ranges as vast as from Mexico to central Brazil or from Nepal to the Fiji Islands. The bulk of the rainforest lies near the equator in the Amazon Basin, in the Congo Basin, and in the East Indies. However, arms of the rainforest spread even beyond the tropic circles in five areas — Mexico, Brazil, Madagascar, Southeast Asia, and Australia, along mountain barriers facing persistent winds from the sea. Lesser arms can be seen on the eastern side of the Andes both north and south. Several such strips of rainforest are thus rather isolated from the main masses, particularly on the east coast of Brazil, on Madagascar, and on the western side of peninsular India. Incursions into the Amazon forest occur where savannas extend along certain sandstone plateaus, while the edge of the rainforest appears to have been drastically cut back in Africa, probably from native cultivation.

Additional rainforests occur in the higher latitudes on certain west coasts. The rainforests of Tasmania, New Zealand, and Chile have a great deal in common with one another and with the highland rainforests of the East Indies and of South America, in particular, but also with the attenuated highland rainforests of Africa. In both America and Asia-East Indies the highland rainforests also have elements related to the northern hemisphere flora. The rainforest along the west coast of Canada and adjacent parts of Alaska and Washington stands as the most isolated rainforest region, except perhaps for the small areas on distant Pacific Islands such as Hawaii. In Alaska the luxuriant coastal forest reaches slightly beyond sixty degrees in latitude.

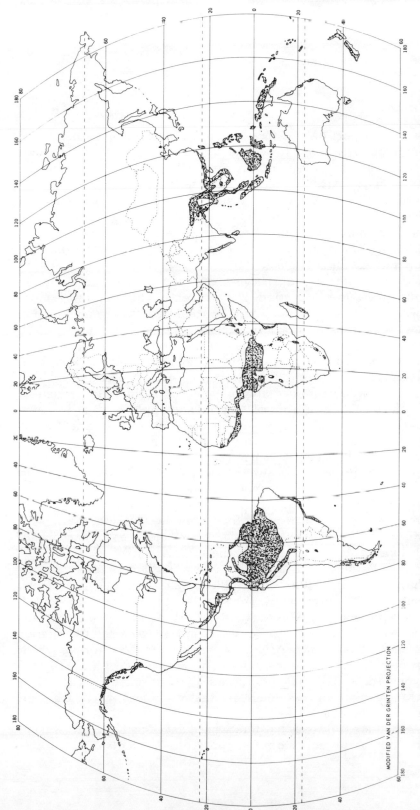

*Map 12.* Rainforest regions of the world. There are three major tropical regions. The scattered areas include various coasts in the tradewind zone, certain tropical highlands, and several rather isolated middle-latitude west coasts.

MODIFIED VAN DER GRINTEN PROJECTION

*Seasonal Forest*

Seasonal forests do not have a continuous understory below the continuous tree canopy. Such areas are extraordinarily extensive, perhaps the commonest of any class of vegetation formation but also a major target for agricultural settlement (Map 13). Three broad northern hemisphere regions occur — in eastern North America, in Europe, and in East Asia. These regions have a great deal in common, with many pairs of closely related species being represented between any two regions. In the far north they are more or less interconnected by the so-called boreal forests, in which a limited range of species forms monotonous stands stretching in an east-west direction. The areal extent of the forest is more fragmented to the south where scattered patches (remnants perhaps of more extensive interglacial stands) connect the western United States, Mexico, and the southeastern United States in the western hemisphere, and a string of mountain forests lead from the Balkan area across the Caucasus, Persia, and northern India to China. As was mentioned above, elements of these forests extend into the highlands of tropical America and Southeast Asia.

Tropical seasonal forests are in some areas so fragmentary as not to be mappable on a world scale. Elements of these forests, particularly the legumes such as acacia and mimosa, are practically worldwide (probably because of their effective seed dispersal in recent times), but several more or less unique blocks of seasonal forest can be identified within the tropics. Rather large areas of forest, at least until recent times, grew in southern Brazil with outliers in Paraguay and Bolivia. These are the so-called semi-deciduous forests and contain the greatest variety of species of any low-latitude seasonal forest area. The largest forest area in Africa outside of the Congo Basin rainforest lies in Angola, Zambia, and nearby areas, the so-called myombo "woodlands." These appear to be extensively disturbed and are often erroneously mapped as "scrub forest" or woodland. In India and the interior lowlands of Southeast Asia grow the sal and teak forests which resemble the African seasonal forest. Both well within and well beyond the tropics extends the eucalypt or sclerophyll forest of Australia, more or less encircling that continent, particularly on the north and east.

Small areas of seasonal forest have developed in New Zealand and Chile as variants from the rainforest. Elements of this forest

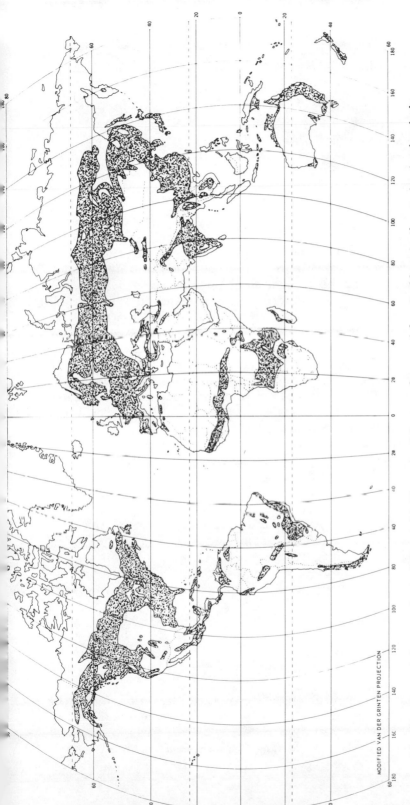

*Map 13.* Seasonal forest regions of the world. The potential areas of seasonal forest add up to the most extensive single vegetation category. A high percentage of the area is reduced to forest remnants within agricultural and stock raising regions. A small part is actually grassland. The Atlantic, the Sahara, and the Malesian rainforests separate seasonal forests into four discontinuous regions while North and South America are nearly unconnected.

MODIFIED VAN DER GRINTEN PROJECTION

are also found in southern Brazil. The limited southern extent of seasonal forest is, of course, a function of the limited areas available for its development.


## Woodland

Woodland lacks a continuous tree canopy, but the total coverage of the vegetation is continuous. Characteristically, woodlands are scattered in patches beside the deserts or as islands rising above the desert or grassland, remnants after widespread disturbance. Several regions can be recognized (Map 14). The pine, oak, and juniper woodlands of western North America in their various forms are well known and have their counterparts in the Mediterranean Basin and central Asia. These overlap with a more southern flora of mesquite and cactus woodland which as a generalized type extends from Texas to Chile. Two extensive areas of woodland in South America have regional names — the Chaco and the Caatinga. Woodlands south of the Sahara are not differentiated from savannas on most available sources except for the small but unique area in Cape Province of South Africa. Most of the widespread eucalypt woodlands of Australia are called mallees, and attention is called to the massive underground woody growth that sometimes develops in various plant species.

The northern or boreal woodland has not been studied here. This is a circumpolar formation containing much the same species of trees as found in the closed crown forest on its southern edge.* This woodland gives way on the northern side to grasslands strong with sedges intermixed with woody shrubs, the classic tundra. Perhaps the trees have not had time to make the necessary adjustments to invade these areas of abundant plant growth, only recently released from the grip of glaciers (Griggs 1946, 1937; Sigafoos 1958, p. 175; Larson 1965; Tikhomirov 1963).


## Desert

Deserts have a discontinuous cover of total plant growth. For the most part they occur in distinct blocks and have names (Map 15).

*There seems to be a specific floral element present; see Norin (1965).

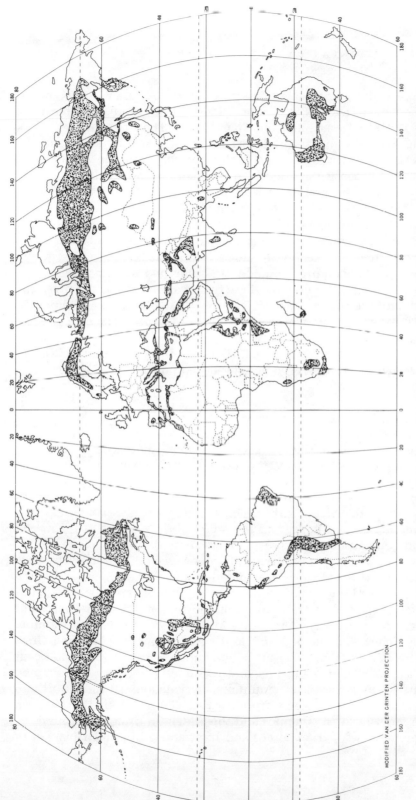

MODIFIED VAN DER GRINTEN PROJECTION

*Map 14.* Woodland regions of the world. Even more than seasonal forest, woodland is broken into patches often separated by open grassland. At least half a dozen middle- and lower-latitude regions can be recognized along with a great strip of boreal woodland. Most of the localized areas where brush occurs are subsumed into this map of woodland.

There is the pair of small deserts in North America, Sonoran and Chihuahuan Deserts, the vast Sahara Desert and its extensions, the Arabian Desert, and the Thar Desert. The Atacama Desert is a long narrow strip, the Kalahari Desert is a smaller strip, and the Great Australian Desert is actually not very large. In cooler areas there are extensive deserts on the Iranian Plateau and across Russia and Chinese Turkestan, with a strip called the Gobi Desert extending through Mongolia. Only a small area of desert occurs in the Great Basin of the United States, but a larger area apparently occupies Patagonia. An isolated small bit of desert is found at the very northern tip of South America and bits of what is essentially desert are located in high mountain basins and on bleak peaks.

Not well known is the fact that real desert characterizes the high-latitude barrens, particularly in Canada but also in many cold areas where glacial ice has not persisted. The surface of glaciers and bare rock exposures are also technically deserts so far as plant growth is concerned, although there are places where a soil cover and even forest have become established on the top of a glacier.

*Grassland*

Grassland is a continuous ground cover of herbaceous plants (of which grass is normally the predominant form). By definition grassland differs sharply from the four formations discussed above, and where they are adjacent there is characteristically a sharp boundary or edge. With savanna, however, grassland does not form any sort of consistent boundary in time as well as space, and such boundaries as are shown are essentially arbitrary (Map 16).

The world's grasslands are open sweeps of relatively level land. In this category are included the Great Plains of North America and the steppes of Inner Asia, the two greatest grasslands. Somewhat smaller areas are included in the so-called Pampas of Argentina and nearby Uruguay and Brazil, The Llanos of Colombia and Venezuela, the Veld of South Africa, and the Mitchell Grass plains of Australia. Other more interrupted areas of grassland occur in the high rolling uplands of the Andes (the Puna and Páramo grasses) in strips near mountains in Patagonia, Chile, northern Mexico, California, and from British Colombia to the Mexican border, within the Campos and the Sudan, in Ethiopia, around the mountains of Turkey, Iraq, and Iran, and on the high plateau of

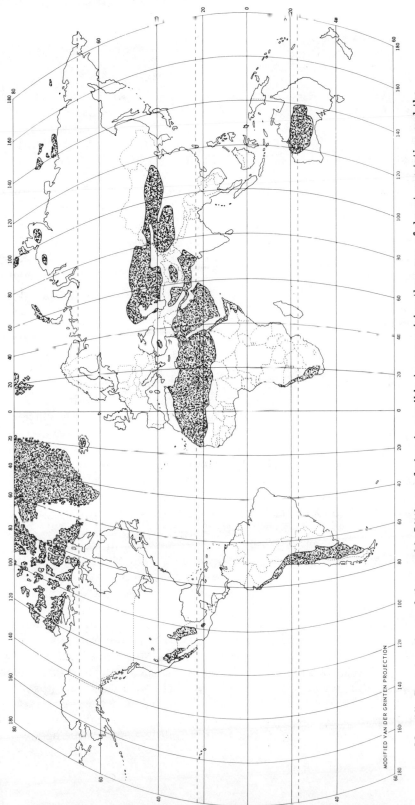

*Map 15.* Desert regions of the world. Little confusion is possible in recognizing the areas of desert vegetation and the well-known desert regions of the world. The polar deserts can be extended to include ice-covered land masses.

MODIFIED VAN DER GRINTEN PROJECTION

Tibet. Rather broad sweeps of grassland, finally, stretch across the Arctic Tundra. Locally there grows many a meadow or pocket of grass within forests and woodlands. In any grassland area, bluffs and isolated hills are likely to be clothed with trees (Wells 1965). Grasslands seldom cover broken country and steep slopes, this terrain correlation being rather suggestive (Wood 1958).

Grassland is sometimes divided into short and tall phases (sparse and dense), perforce an arbitrary separation. When this is done, however subjectively, it does become apparent that the short or sparse grasslands are interspersed with woodlands and they border deserts while the more luxuriant grasses border forests, as might be expected.

*Savanna*

The definition of savanna is elusive (Hills 1965; Hills and Randall 1968). It involves a discontinuous canopy of trees and a continuous ground cover of herbaceous plants. The boundary with forest can be abrupt, as was mentioned earlier, but the distinction from woodland and grassland is only a matter of degree (Map 16). The questions of how many trees make a savanna and how few woody plants between the trees no longer is a woodland cannot at this time be answered. The typical savanna is distinct enough, but this grades into woodland savannas and parklands on the one hand and into open grassland on the other. If savanna is regarded as a disturbed formation, perhaps a consistent distinction should not be expected.

Savannas are widespread in the tropics, so much so that a climatic zone is sometimes named for them. The classic savanna is in Africa, where most of the zone between rainforest and desert can be said to be savanna. Isolated patches of open grassland and forest do grow in that continent, but savannas dominate the scene. Maps of African vegetation, however, group forest and savanna together in zones, because there is an intricate intergradation and interdigitation between them (Keay 1959). Much the same thing occurs in Brazil in the Campos where there is a greater importance of woodland savanna or cerrado, strongly correlated with soil conditions (Eiten 1972; Ferri 1955). Although much of the heart of the Llanos is open grassland, the margins gradually become savanna. Australia is not noted for savanna because of the aggres-

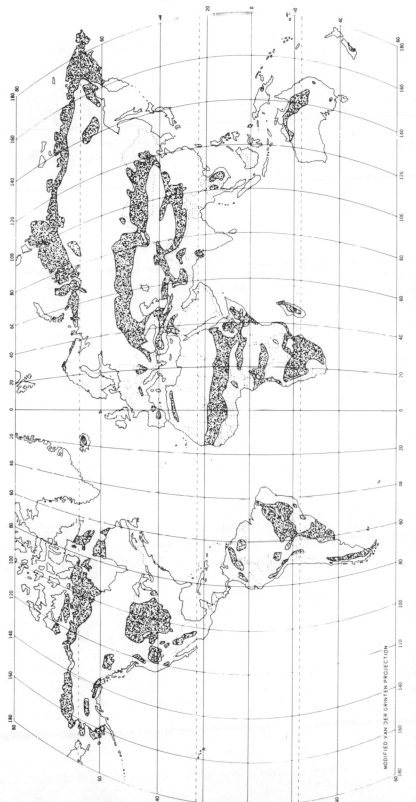

MODIFIED VAN DER GRINTEN PROJECTION

*Map 16.* Grassland and savanna regions of the world. There is no way to decide how many trees makes a savanna. The areas shown here tend to overlap the areas of other vegetation categories, particularly woodland. Large areas are in reality mosaics. Many continuous grasslands have well-known regional names, and such terms as *steppe* and *tundra* are at least in part synonomous.

sive eucalypts which grow more vigorously than herbaceous plants. In some areas apparently related to soil conditions grasslands do prevail in Australia, but seldom are they totally devoid of trees, and along bluffs and islands of upland they clearly become savanna, while on the margins there is a gradual gradation through denser savannas into forest. Even the high-elevation grasslands of the Andes over large areas are in fact a "bush" savanna.

It is a mistake to assume that savannas are confined to the low latitudes. In the first place the great grasslands are usually separated from the adjacent forest by a parkland "transition," much if not all of which fits any definition of savanna available. More than that, vast areas of the western United States support yellow pine savanna, various pinyon and juniper savannas, or oak savanna of a classical form in California. The same thing is true in the Mediterranean Basin and in Inner Asia; the Argentine Pampa has a well-known grassland-monte "transition." Man-made and intentionally maintained grasslands and savannas can, of course, be omitted here.

## OTHER VEGETATION FORMATIONS AND CATEGORIES

There exist other distinct kinds of vegetation formation which are not extensive. For this reason they cannot be treated on a world scale and have not been closely analyzed here. Sharp boundaries do, at least in some cases, exist, but these are generally related to sharp edaphic contrasts. Essentially these local formations are related to severe local conditions, particularly of the soil, but also climatic. Some may in time develop into more general formations, as through the filling in of a bog, while brush may in part represent a disturbed woodland or forest. Many other local areas may also contrast with their surroundings because of local edaphic conditions or isolation but support a common type of vegetation formation simply remote from other similar areas. The more prominent sorts of local formations include brush and thicket, elfin woodland, and bog.

A continuous cover of woody plants directly in contact with the ground cover or the ground itself may be called *brush* or *thicket*. The term *brush* is used generally when a standing man's head rises above the plant level. By and large *brush* and *thicket*

*Figure 36.* Chamise *(Adenostoma fasciculatum)* chaparral west of Redding, California. Serpentine soils here discourage the growth of trees. Manzanita is scattered in the chamise in this particular view.

seem to be associated with certain poor soils, around which on better soils other vegetation formations grow. For example, part of the so-called chaparral of California grows in serpentine soils and is covered by almost impenetrable chamise (Figure 36). Fire, at least sometimes, seems to be a factor here and trees can be seen raising their crowns above the brush where there has been enough time for growth (Figure 37). A similar sort of thicket in New Caledonia, also on serpentine soils, borders areas of rainforest (Figure 7) (Sarlin 1954). Apparently as a result of soil nutrient deficiencies, the usual trees do not grow well or at all in some places where the climate admits abundant plant growth. Stunting and the exclusive growth of certain short, hardy plants results in brush or thicket. There is also the situation, generally omitted in vegetation mapping, where thickets or other formations obviously represent a brief successional stage in some more advanced formation area.

*Figure 37.* Trees growing out of chaparral in the Santa Lucia Mountains, California. The conditions which maintain brush usually eliminate trees so that this combination is unusual. The trees are knobcone pine *(Pinus attenuata)* whose cones will not open without fire.

The elfin woodland, a low growth of trees on wet exposed ridges, has been mentioned before. Where mechanical effects reduce the stature, perhaps one is again dealing with a thicket, but the elfin woodland is also characterized by abundant epiphytic growth, particularly moss (Figure 38) (Grubb and Whitmore 1966). Such a plant cover can be delightful to behold along a level ridge where a path has been established among the festoons of moss enveloping everything in the shade and with all manner of delicate fern-like plants emerging from the moss, a dense canopy growing directly overhead. But the mossy forest can be a formidable foe to penetration along a broken ridge without a trail where a jungle of tree trunks and fallen branches and a jumble of rocks all covered with slippery moss hides many a hole for the unwary. By its very nature, elfin woodland is local.

Various aspects of vegetation growth related to shallow surface

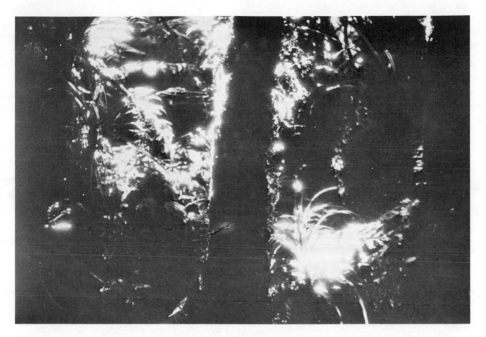

*Figure 38.* Interior of an elfin woodland in New Caledonia. Shafts of light illuminate parts of this fantastic tangle of plants and moss.

water have special names. To a considerable degree the vegetation cover itself, if the drainage factor be overlooked, is not really unique. *Marsh* is an herbaceous cover in stagnant or in brackish water. It can be equated with grassland. *Swamp* is a forest in flooded areas, often in a drier zone with the structure of rainforest. *Mangrove,* where allowed to develop fully, is a forest in tidal areas, particularly, but not exclusively, in salty water. *Bog* perhaps merits special distinction. Bog is a peat-covered or peat-filled area associated with poorly drained conditions (Heinselman 1963, p. 373). Some impressions of the tundra actually refer to bog because there can be so much of it there. Bog grades into swamp as trees invade. Occasional areas of poor drainage can be extensive enough to map at least at intermediate scales and they can show up as small areas on a world map.

A world map with as much detail as is usually included in maps at relatively small scales can be drawn with the six formation categories used here. The division of the forest and woodland into tropical and non-tropical types would create more categories but would not convey any more information, besides being inconsistent and misleading. The further addition of tundra is likewise inconsistent and misleading if the map is to portray the nature of the vegetative cover. Thus do six categories more accurately describe what nine traditional categories are used for and with no loss of information. Doubt has been cast on the general significance of contrasting evergreen forest with deciduous forest, and this is certainly not properly handled by reference to conifers. If it is felt that deciduousness ought to be identified, this would further elaborate the map and require the addition of a new dimension to the system of classification. Consistency would require that evergreen, mixed, and deciduous woodlands and deserts also be identified. By leaving leaf tenure out of the classification, there is, nevertheless, produced what ought to be a significant world map of vegetation.

## CONCLUSION

Analysis has shown that the world's cover of vegetation is not a continuum in the undisturbed state but that certain significant boundaries exist. In response to the natural environment, several distinct types of vegetation cover have developed, each of which is clearly divided from the others in a consistent way. It would appear that certain levels of environmental conditions must be reached before the various elements of cover can fill in, that is, become continuous. The first closed cover is the simple cover of the ground. The second closed cover is of the tree canopy and the final cover closed is the tree understory. After a certain cover density is reached, one which is nearly half of the total area, the respective cover rapidly closes over. If plants can cover as much as half the total area they can just as well cover all of it at a particular level.

Many factors widely used to distinguish types of vegetation are not properly employed for this purpose either because they involve aspects of the environment or because they portray little or no real information about the vegetation itself. Climate, landform, and soil should be purged from vegetation maps. Flora and form are not the same thing and should not be confused. Even individual form factors, as physically obvious as they may be, may yield only a meaningless random pattern which frustrates the purpose for drawing the map, particularly where that purpose is to illuminate the significant variations in habitat from place to place. To do so it would be useful to correlate the other elements of that habitat with vegetation patterns independently derived, which has not really been possible with the approach used until now for world-wide mapping of vegetation. Perhaps the ideas and the maps developed here will increase the understanding of the interrelationships between vegetation and other aspects of the natural environment.

# PART TWO

# *Floristic Realms and Subrealms*

# 7

# The Evolution of World Floristic Maps

PLANT GEOGRAPHERS have long come to accept the notion that the flora of the world can be divided geographically into about half a dozen distinct units, often called floristic realms, and that these can be further subdivided in various ways. There has developed a high level of agreement, furthermore, as to how the major divisions should be made, even though their subdivisions are subject to diverse interpretations. It is therefore remarkable how cursory are the justifications given for the differentiation of these realms, while next to nothing is offered by way of accounting for them. The reality of the prime divisions of flora has, to be sure, been tested over the years by innumerable local observations which appear scattered through the literature, and there is really only mild disagreement as to the relative importance between the several major divisions. But if there are such real contrasts in the plant content of world land space, there must be definite reasons. The objective of this chapter is an attempt to supply some possible explanations.

Up to seven floristic realms are usually presented in works on plant geography today, based on only a few sources which themselves stem in large part from a limited number of nineteenth-century works. It is therefore appropriate first to examine the development of these ideas in order to understand, if possible, how current ideas evolved. The major regions will then be examined in some detail to illuminate the nature of the divisions being considered. This examination has, in fact, led to some reorganization of the presentation — that is, a slight reinterpretation of the emphasis to be granted to different regions.

The development of concepts of floristic regionalization reached a peak in the latter part of the nineteenth century, although undoubtedly any observer who had visited diverse regions must have realized that differences from place to place existed. The organization effected by Linnaeus in the middle of the eighteenth century, more than anything else, probably stimulated the thinking concerning the plant content of area. The first ideas about distribution made no clear distinction between flora, form, and the environment. Slowly the study of the different aspects of plants diverged until each was considered independently, although their interrelationships do continue to be recognized and referred to, from time to time. Today the regions of flora are thought of as distinct from the patterns of formation and environment; a whole set of regions and their designations have been developed for the world and its parts.

Carl Willdenow is generally credited as the first to enunciate a general basis for plant geography antedating by a few years the famous works of Humboldt. In his books on herbs in 1792, Willdenow (pp. 345-80) included a chapter on the history of plants wherein he recognized how plants differed for each distinct habitat (Engler 1899, pp. 6-7; Graebner 1929, pp. 3-4; Wulff 1950, p. 10). He proposed five major floras for Europe, and in later editions of his work he called attention to similarities between northern Asia and America and between South Africa and Australia. More than any earlier botanist, Willdenow understood and offered explanations for the distribution of plants in the world.

Because of his many contributions concerning plants in space, Alexander von Humboldt is usually considered the father of plant geography, and yet, despite the great amount of information he supplied which related to the question of flora, he never quite came to grips with this particular idea. In his *Prolegomena* to the work describing the plants that he and Bonpland collected in tropical America, Humboldt (Bonpland and Humboldt 1815; Humboldt 1817) developed a number of important ideas, among which are the latitudinal variation in species variety and the correlation of physiognomic features to environmental zones (Grisebach 1880; Drude 1884, pp. 9-11; Engler 1899, pp. 7-9; Graebner 1929, pp. 4-6). To be sure, he compared the assembled plants of Europe and of North America, of Virginia and Germany, and of Japan and South Europe to show that widely separated regions, even with similar climates, do not share the same plants. This is a floristic idea, but he did not pursue it in that way; rather he turned to the even greater differences manifested between environmental zones, tropical to polar and lowland to highland. He found tropical mountain species which were allied to species of higher latitude, but he was puzzled by also finding mountain species which were closely related to nearby lowland species. Humboldt even busied himself in relating important plant groups to the total plant content of a region by calculating ratios of the number of species. Again the focus fell not on defining a flora, but on an understanding of a plant group. As a result of his efforts, however, he assembled a great store of data that was widely used by later workers, including those who developed the concepts of flora.

A detailed account of the flora of Australia and its distinctness was presented at an early date by R. Brown (1814) who, in later years, continued to add significantly to knowledge of flora in different parts of the world. Most of his efforts, however, were directed toward taxonomy and the individual plant.

The elder de Candolle (1820, pp. 411-12) divided the world into twenty general regions characterized by numerous, sometimes endemic, plant species and bounded by natural barriers such as mountains, deserts, and oceans. The idea of flora was taking form here, although de Candolle was more interested in identifying the natural (habitat) divisions of the earth than in the flora in particular.

The work of Schouw (1822, 1823, 1824, 1833, 1838, plate 1) is generally recognized as the first to classify the world's flora and to present the regions cartographically (Drude 1884, pp. 12-14; Engler 1899, pp. 22-23; Good 1953, pp. 24-25). He divided the world into twenty-two realms, later expanded to twenty-five, based on the predominance of certain prominent plant groups (Map 17). He presented a series of map plates showing the distribution of important wild and cultivated plants such as pines and palms, cactus and beech, and even wine grapes. These were manipulated along with other evidence to discover the world's regional groupings of flora, the plant realms. Schouw held that in order to qualify as a realm, a region must have at least half of its plant species unique, a quarter of the genera, and even some whole families. The emphasis here is clearly on flora, but the result is not greatly different from what Humboldt or de Candolle presented. The

*Map 17.* Floristic regions according to Schouw (1823). The first map of floristic regions. The fact that it is partly incomplete is not surprising. Later

dominant plants can be considered in terms of their physiognomy as a response to environment, and Schouw's regions are, indeed, more or less climatic regions.

By this time many investigators were engaged in assembling the facts on the plant content of particular parts of the world, a task which is by no means completed today. It must not be sup-

XII.
*Eintheilung der oberfläche.*

editions filled in some of the gaps and increased the number of regions identified.

posed that all such endeavors were based on or attempted to delimit a discreet flora. In fact, perhaps the majority were addressed to particular political units. Others encompassed convenient land areas surrounded by water or other distinct barriers. Nevertheless, now and then attention was directed to floristic regionalization, particularly through the percentage of species shared with each distinct nearby region. Such a view, of course, also implies the percentage not shared, and therefrom a notion of the relative distinctness of each division of flora. Bentham (1832-36) divided the world into no fewer than sixty-one regions grouped into nine plant geographic zones circling the world. He was later to become one of the giants of taxonomic botany. In numerous taxonomic publications Bentham's associate, J. D. Hooker, considered the origin of particular floras and offered explanations.

During the middle of the nineteenth century additional world treatments of plants appeared from time to time. Failing to illuminate the character of flora was a text by Meyen (1836) in which the emphasis was on physiognomic zones and climatic relationship. Numerous regions were set apart by two workers with an emphasis on degrees of endemism. One of these was the younger de Candolle (1837, pp. 382-90), who recognized forty-five regions, and the other Martius (1831-50), who established fifty-one realms. Later, de Candolle (1855, chapter 25: De la division des surfaces terrestres en régions naturelles) emphasized that, in order to achieve a satisfactory plant geographic division of the world, the major regions must be subdivided and re-subdivided ultimately into "districts," the smallest units having their own floristic character. Even later, de Candolle (1874) proposed his famous physiological classification of plants with four temperature and four moisture categories. No map was presented, but, if applied to the world, it would logically produce at least a dozen and perhaps as many as twenty regions. Even though the floristic merit of this classification is somewhat limited, it would correspond, with little adjustment, to the scheme put forth by Schouw after various mountain and insular categories are removed.

The work of Grisebach was quite influential in the progression of ideas concerning the regionalization of plant growth. Over the years he carefully assembled every pertinent reference he could find, including those of untrained travellers, and he collected where he could or studied the plant collections of others (Engler 1899, pp. 24-25). All this was brought together in his well-known world map published in 1866 (reprinted in slightly modified form in 1872) which he regarded as having the same conceptual basis as that of Schouw, being further refined more than modified (Map 1). The regions were not, of course, in every case corresponding, but their definitions and boundaries were based nearly always on physiognomic and climatic criteria. In only a few cases did he call attention to strong endemism, and he expressly rejected a dependence thereupon because of the great variations in degree to be found between the different regions. It was just this which led to a system of flora presented by later authors, but Grisebach's twenty-four regions were each treated independently as far as flora is concerned. As a matter of fact, by color coding his map, he called attention to physiognomic-climatic similarities and it was precisely this which stimulated Köppen (1900, p. 593) to develop a system of world climates. Clearly Grisebach felt that flora divided between different major plant formations, particularly forest, woodland, and treeless, thus the distinction between flora and physiognomy had not yet been made.

Two other authors made an attempt to cope with world patterns of plants not long after the work of Grisebach. One of these was Pickering (1876), who divided the world into eleven primary divisions or clusters formed by grouping 150 local regions (Drude 1884, pp. 19-20; Engler 1899, p. 25). The emphasis was on environmental adaptation as in "polar," "wintry," and "temperate" as well as division by continent, and is floristically trivial. The other attempt by Thiselton-Dyer (1898) was more pertinent if quite general (Engler 1899, pp. 25-26). He divided the world into three zones — northern, tropical, and southern. The northern was subdivided into arctic-alpine, temperate, and Mediterranean-Caucasian categories; the tropics yielded Asian, African, and American regions; and the southern was made up of Australian, South African, temperate South American, and antarctic-alpine parts. There is a suggestion here of floristic system foreshadowing the much more detailed treatment proposed soon thereafter by Engler.

The foundation for modern understanding of the geography of flora was presented less than a century ago by Engler (1879 and 1882) in a study emphasizing the developmental history of flora (Engler 1899, p. 26; Drude 1884, pp. 20-21). Thus he identified four distinct floristic elements in the world — the arcto-tertiary, the palaeotropical, the neotropical, and the ancient-ocean — each of which he traced through earlier geologic periods. These then are mapped as four floral realms, each of which is subdivided into regions of which there are a total of thirty-two, including ten local island regions (Map 18). For the most part the individual regions correspond rather closely to those of Grisebach and

*Map 18.* Vegetation regions according to Engler (1882). For the first time a floristic system is enunciated by this rather complex map which was pub-

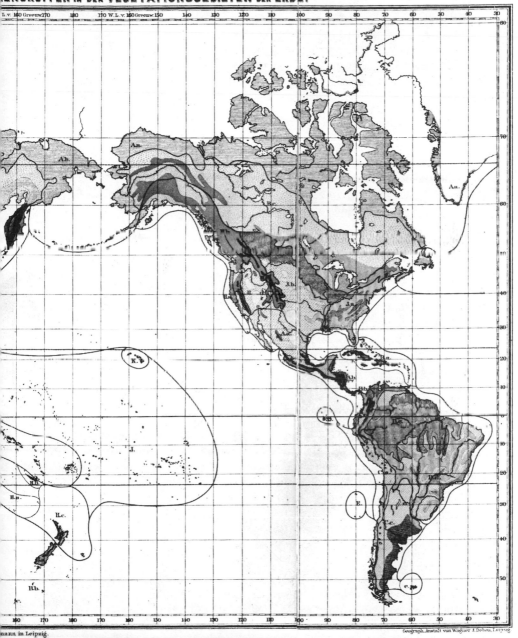

mann in Leipzig.

Geograph.Anstalt von Wagner & Debes,Leipzig

lished along with a set of confusing categories probing other characteristics of vegetation.

Schouw, but, for the first time, major floristic elements were recognized, grouping the more local regions which were themselves based on floristic-systematic studies.

From a geographic point of view, it is interesting to analyze the differentiation of Engler's realms and regions. He recognized that the boundaries are not necessarily sharp, although the body of his work makes it clear that he regarded the regions as quite distinct. He also regarded his framework of a hierarchy of regions and the definitions of realms to be based on the 1874 treatise of de Candolle, that is, physiological-climatically determined. For the subdivisions he recognized physiognomic factors, particularly *forest*, but also *brush* and *grass* to a lesser extent. Some clearly expressed areas were admittedly suppressed where they were "geographically inconvenient." He was, as he said, only giving an overview. The insistence on the recognition of developmental history was thus honored more in discussion than in the actual differentiation of regions.

A comparison of the three effectuated world divisions of flora shows clearly the nature of their differences. Schouw, being the earliest, lacks many distinctions later made, resulting, admittedly, from lack of information. In fact, some divisions were added by him, after his first attempt. One curious character is the luxuriance of regions in tropical America, which can be traced directly to the influence of Humboldt, who had gathered much data in that area. The main changes on the map of Grisebach involve subdivisions based on physiognomy. These were not continued by Engler, who also brought tropical America into balance with the rest of the world. Engler made a number of new subdivisions, breaking up some of the larger regions. Several innovations by Engler, such as the division of African steppe into a northern and a southern region or the grouping of the Andes with the Pampa, were later dropped in the outline of the floral regions in his Syllabus of many editions (1898). He was the first, of course, to identify several major floral elements, the factor which dominates current thinking on world flora.

The leading contemporary of Engler was Drude who was, in a way, the successor of Grisebach, whereas Engler claimed to look back to de Candolle. Drude (1884, 1887, 1890) asserted that his maps were based on current conditions rather than pretending to be derived from historical trends, a difference he felt was more a point of view than a significant contrast in results. Drude recognized the importance of a hierarchy and did not claim his work represented any major innovation over that of Engler or other predecessors (Engler's map having appeared before any by Drude). In fact, for the most part, he repeated boundaries used earlier, emphasizing that the transition between regions was gradual and the boundary just an expediency.

Drude distinguished fourteen "realms" in his works, giving long lists of characteristic plants and providing maps showing the distribution of important plant groups, as did Schouw and Engler before him (Map 19). These fourteen realms correspond to the regions of Engler but are somewhat fewer than had been generally recognized. The differences, however, are slight. Drude eliminated a few questionable categories and made some combinations. Gone, at this level, are the Arctic, the Sahara, and the oceanic islands, as well as the Mexican highlands. India is combined with the tropical Pacific, and central Europe is included in the northern (forest) realm.

Although his major emphasis is on the realms, Drude does combine these into seven groups for which his criteria seem to be more distinct. There are three Boreal groups — northern, Mediter-ranean-southwest (inner) Asia, and middle-latitude East Asia-North America; two tropical groups — palaeotropics and neotropics; and two Austral groups — southern South America and South Africa-Australia. He asserted that these groups are distinguished by im-portant, unique or nearly unique families or, in some cases, sub-families. Across a group boundary, he said, most families will be different and sometimes not even analogous. By contrast, the realms display only a few distinct families, but most subfamilies and genera will be unique. He made further subdivisions for which it is primarily the species that would be distinct. He rejected the use of any rigid formula, because the proportions of endemism vary in different directions and because one must also consider the existence of unique forms and systematic relationships. His group of realms, in fact, correspond largely to Engler's realms, the main difference being the division of the Boreal element.

In presenting his version of the geography of flora, Drude made several contributions. In contrast to Engler, he placed the emphasis on present-day assemblages, and, in contrast particularly to Grise-bach, he distinctly separated flora from formation, although he also treated formation in his works (without developing any regional system of formation other than zones from north to

Entw. v. H Berghaus 1886, mit Hinzufügungen v. O. Drude. Ausg. 1887

GOTHA: JUSTUS PERT

*Map 19.* Floristic realms according to Drude (1884). In two ways Drude demonstrated that his boundaries were not to be taken seriously. Each category had a color and a pattern. All over the map the patterns were bled into other regions overlapping other patterns. The main map was accompanied by a smaller world map on which the fourteen realms are combined into seven groups. The boundaries for the groups usually differ from the boundaries given on the main map for the realms.

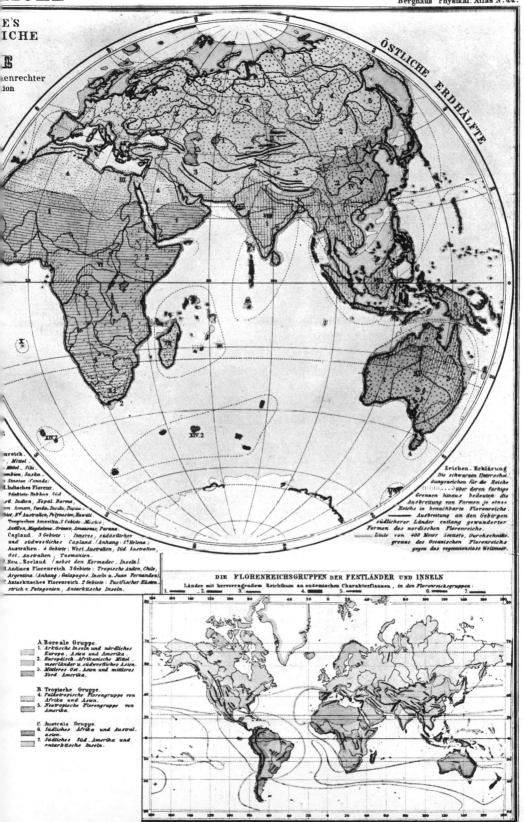

ÖSTLICHE ERDHÄLFTE

DIE FLORENREICHSGRUPPEN DER FESTLÄNDER UND INSELN
Länder mit hervorragendem Reichthum an endemischen Charakterpflanzen, in den Florenreichsgruppen:

A. Boreale Gruppe.
1. Arktische Inseln und nördliches Europa, Asien und Amerika.
2. Europäisch-Afrikanische Mittelmeerländer u. südwestliches Asien.
3. Mittleres Ost-Asien und mittleres Nord Amerika.

B. Tropische Gruppe.
4. Paläotropische Florengruppe von Afrika und Asien.
5. Neotropische Florengruppe von Amerika.

C. Australe Gruppe.
6. Südliches Afrika und Australasien.
7. Südliches Süd-Amerika und antarktische Inseln.

south). Although he felt boundaries were hardly more than a convenience, Drude seems clearly convinced of the objective reality of his regions. Thus, he reinforced the conclusion that definite regionalization of flora can be effected, and he sharpened the understanding of these regions. Together with Engler in subsequent years (1896), he sponsored a series of studies by local experts on the vegetation of different segments of the world.

By the end of the nineteenth century the study of plant geography had reached a level of maturity suggesting a summing up. This was done quite well in the 1884 treatise by Drude (see above), but the grand summary was produced by Engler himself at the end of the century (1899) on the occasion of the hundredth anniversary of Humboldt's famous excursion. Engler concluded that the art had progressed to the point where no more than minor changes could be expected to be added to the understanding of the floristic divisions of the earth. A survey of subsequent works reveals nearly unanimous agreement so far as the major divisions of world flora are concerned.

Among the later authors to treat the floral realms was Diels (1908), whose modification of Engler's concepts was not profound. Essentially he subdivided the "ancient ocean" realm into three parts which were, after all, already separated by vast stretches of ocean. The southern tip of South America together with the austral islands became the Antarctic realm; the tip of South Africa became the Cape realm; and Australia stood apart as a third realm. New Zealand went to the palaeotropics. A few suggestions to explain floristic regionalization are offered with the observation that further investigation is necessary in order to comprehend the factors which produce distinct flora. It is this Diels organization which is most often repeated today, particularly in German publications.

After some years, a fresh if not profound treatment was presented by Newbigin (1936). The main feature is a latitudinal division into northern lands, inter-tropical, and southern parts of southern continents. Intruded into this are the Mediterranean belt and a zone of Old World warm deserts. Except for a parochial reorganization, this adds little to our understanding of plant geography.

Perhaps the last important analysis of floristic regionalization is the widely quoted work by Good (1947, reproduced here as Map 20). For realms (kingdoms) he follows the system of Diels with

Map of the World showing Floristic Regions. Original.

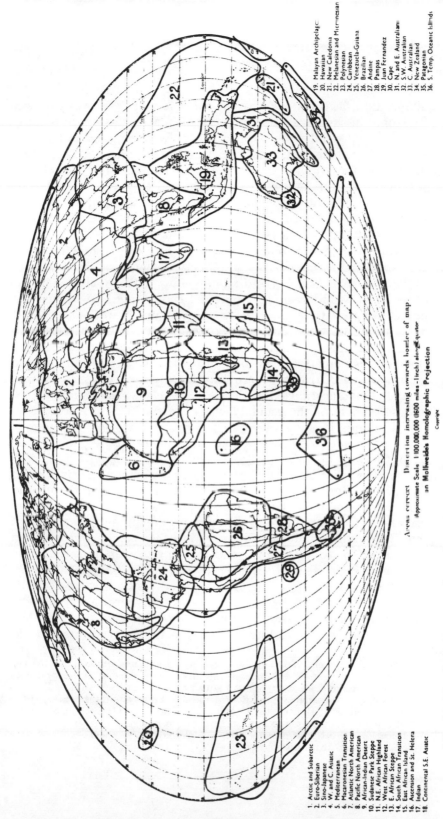

Area correct   Distortion increasing towards border of map.

Approximate Scale 1:100,000,000 (1600 miles = 1 inch) along Equator

an Mollweide's Homolographic Projection

Copyright

1. Arctic and Subarctic
2. Euro-Siberian
3. Sino-Japanese
4. W. and C. Asiatic
5. Mediterranean
6. Macaronesian Transition
7. Atlantic North American
8. Pacific North American
9. African-Indian Desert
10. Sudanese Park Steppe
11. N.E. African Highland
12. West African Forest
13. E. African Transition
14. South African Transition
15. East African Steppe
16. Ascension and St. Helena
17. Indian
18. Continental S.E. Asiatic
19. Malayan Archipelago
20. Hawaiian
21. New Caledonia
22. Melanesian and Micronesian
23. Polynesian
24. Caribbean
25. Venezuela-Guiana
26. Brazilian
27. Andine
28. Pampas
29. Juan Fernandez
30. Cape
31. N. and E. Australian
32. S.W. Australian
33. C. Australian
34. New Zealand
35. Patagonian
36. S. Temp. Oceanic Islands

*Map 20.* The floristic regions from Good (1947). The grouping of the 37 regions into kingdoms was given in the text but not on the map published by Good.

minor modifications such as the inclusion of New Zealand and Patagonia in the Antarctic kingdom. Also, the palaeotropical kingdom is divided into the African, Indo-Malaysian, and Polynesian sub-kingdoms. He emphasizes thirty-seven regions, each of which displays a flora of its own — that is, one that has largely developed within the region. This number is achieved by recognizing almost all of the divisions previously reported, including Central Asia, Pacific North America, and the group consisting of India, Southeast Asia, and Malaysia. Tropical Africa is divided into five parts, tropical America into four, and Australia into three, these divisions corresponding in many cases to climatic differences. Not only are there two large Pacific Island regions, but there are also some six other local island regions. Whereas Drude sought to reduce the number of regions, Good inclines toward a maximum.

Although Good admits to investing much care and attention to his floristic classification, he allocates little space for its explanation and demarcation. The book is organized around taxonomic groups whose distributions are only loosely related to the regions, if at all. Good acknowledges the use of Engler's system and others, and he points out the general lack of agreement as to where many of the boundaries should be drawn. Finally, he insists that the map being presented is small and that questions of pure convenience cannot always be ignored. Good invokes the "demarcation knots" of van Steenis (1950), places where there are comparatively sudden changes in floristic composition, as being particularly useful in defining boundaries. Good envisions advancing fronts of more aggressive flora or retarding barriers producing such sharp lines, but also admits gradual infiltration in other places. Actually van Steenis refers to two straits and an isthmus, far more isolation than most regional boundaries enjoy. As to the definition of individual regional types, Good gives the impression that no formula can be justified and, by omitting definitions almost completely, that the regional selection must be largely subjective.*

In recent texts relating to the geography of plants, a clear

*Since the system of Good there has been published one original map of flora by Lemee (1967). His map is actually a very general compromise of flora and fauna and, as such, is not really new. The latest version of Engler's Syllabus displays a slightly modified form of Good's system (Melchior, 1964; the map itself is attributed to F. Mattick). Takhtajan (1969) has also published a map based on Good and on Mattick (in Engler) but with many small modifications mostly improving the location of boundaries. As usual very little factual justification is given.

distinction is consistently made between flora and formation (sometimes called vegetation). Only a perfunctory treatment is given to flora if it is included at all. Strangely, texts that purport to cover biogeography are nearly pure plant ecology; titles involving vegetation geography or plant geography are also much the same in coverage, and a geographer may well be perplexed as to the significance of the word *geography* in the title. The slighting of floral distributions is consistent with the general slighting of geographic questions and shows that ecologists are not currently preoccupied with differences from place to place and what they can illuminate.

By way of summary, the idea that there are floral realms and subrealms has been generally accepted, even though the boundaries are treated with considerable diffidence. Boundaries are drawn, and their existence is critical to the concept of distinct floral groupings because, were flora a continuum, particular groupings would be utterly arbitrary and meaningless. Certainly flora is more than a regional gradient, and the nature of regional discontinuities merits careful investigation. The literature deals repeatedly with isolation and climatic conditions as differentiating forces. Intuitively a relation was suggested with formation in many early works, but it is well known that similar formations occur with floristically unrelated assemblages; today flora is detached from formation. Climate, of course, is a primary factor in the genesis of formation, but its role in the differentiation of flora is not very clear. A closer look at the nature and boundaries of floral regions, particularly the primary divisions of realms, would appear to be needed.

# 8

# Floristic Regionalization

THE BASIC ASSUMPTION that there is an inherent regionalization of the flora of the world needs to be examined carefully. All of the literature discussed above is weak on specific differentiation and even on description. What is the nature of the major regions and what sort of boundaries, if any, can be discerned? In order to answer these questions the different regions and their boundaries will be analyzed. As a first step, we present a review of how broadly the various plant groups are distributed.

## THE GEOGRAPHY OF PLANT TAXONOMIC GROUPINGS

Clearly the various plants growing together are not everywhere the same, but how local are plants, taxonomically speaking? This question has been extensively covered, especially by Good, and only a summary is necessary here (Good 1947; Walter and Straka 1954. Takhtajan 1969, in particular, lists endemics for his set of regions). The answer depends on the level of taxonomic aggregation to be addressed. The *order* and higher levels involve relationships too broad to be useful in the regionalization of plants. In effect, most orders originated so long ago that their members have had ample opportunity to adjust and migrate to all parts of the earth. Below the order is the *family*, of which there are close to four-hundred among the land plants. Each family is represented by one or more *genus* which is made up in turn by one or more *species*, a single kind of plant. Not only are the well over 200,000 plant species too numerous to contend with in a broad division of world flora, but the vast majority are distinctly local, so that few or no species are shared between major or even secondary floristic regions. Significant for world floristic regionalization, then, are the *genus*, a group of closely related species, and the *family*, a grouping of genera whose common origin is rarely in doubt.

The primary unit for world regionalization of flora is the family. Only a few families are common in most parts of the world. Those which are include, often, weedy herbs, such as grass and composites, or highly specialized plants such as cattails and mistletoe. Other very widespread families are nevertheless rather rare in some parts of the world, such as orchids, euphorbias, and the sedges.* In fact, only about 15 percent of the families can reasonably be considered world wide in distribution (cosmopolitan), and of these a wide majority are yet concentrated in some part of the world, especially the tropics or the extra-tropical areas or occasionally the eastern or western hemisphere. The few elements which stray beyond are likely to be quite atypical, such as in Verbenaceae, Oxalidaceae, and Violaceae.

Size of family plays an obvious role in overall range. It is not surprising that the small families are not widespread. About one family in three has fewer than twenty species and, with the exception of highly specialized groups such as aquatics (*i.e.*, Juncaginaceae), are almost exclusively local in distribution. Even the middle third of the families, ranging between about twenty and two-hundred species, include few widespread families almost all of which are conspicuously specialized (Droseraceae, insectivorous; Nymphaeaceae, water lilies; Cuscutaceae, parasitic; and many aquatic families). Only a few families of this size extend significantly across more than one region such as two or three tropical areas. It is only in the larger families that any sort of cosmopolitanness is important, and even here, as indicated above, most are either emphatically or distinctly zonal while a few are strictly local.

If the range of whole families is clearly limited, it follows that genera must be more limited. In fact, the truly widespread genus, such as *Celtis* or *Hibiscus*, is almost a curiosity. Even when a tropi-

---

*Most of the groups are well known. Family names include Graminaceae for grass, Compositae, Typhaceae (cattail), Loranthaceae (mistletoe), Orchidaceae, Euphorbiaceae, and, for the sedges, Cyperaceae.

cal genus is shared between the Old World and the New World *(Ficus, Acacia)* the chances are that there are clear subgeneric distinctions.

There can be no doubt that not only individual plant species, but also the more obvious groupings of genera and families, are overwhelmingly unevenly distributed over the land surfaces of the world. It follows that the plants in widely separated parts of the world will differ markedly one from the other. What does not follow is that there will be distinct floristic regionalization. Given variations in size of different taxonomic units, their distributions could well be essentially randomly related. Curiously, in the summarizing works discussed above little or no evidence supporting such regionalization has been offered; they hardly more than assert that such regions exist. It may well be that the floristic groupings suggested largely reflect land mass isolation. A closer look is required.

## THE MAJOR REGIONAL FLORAS

Whatever may be the significance to be attached to regional floras, there certainly are differences between the associations of plants in the various major land regions of the world. This can be illuminated by an account of the important genera and families of different regions. Without yet commenting on the reality of floristic divisions, the major regions widely accepted can be used as a framework. Rather than try to cover every plant group for every part of the world, particularly the humid tropics, this can be done by a process of elimination. What is and what is not widely developed in certain regions can be offered so that by analogy the remainder must be concentrated elsewhere. Thus the holarctic and the antarctic can be differentiated. The three tropical regions, being separated by oceans, can be contrasted without difficulty. The arid-humid dichotomies of the warmer parts of the world also merit consideration.

What constitutes importance for a plant group within a flora is rather subjective. Included are such factors as size, abundance, dominance, fidelity, and exclusivity. Trees easily stand out and can be given primary attention. Weeds and other widespread specialized herbs, on the other hand, are not important, and rare plants cannot be given much attention. Unfortunately, information on all of these factors is scanty and uneven, and one is generally reduced to discussing groups in terms of their number of species and predominant form.


*Holarctic Plant Groups*

Far more than any other part of the world the holarctic is known to scholars. Thus it is particularly effective to survey what is and what is not to be found within this domain. Quite a few whole plant families are essentially limited to the holarctic. Where this is not so, the genera often divide within the family between those of the holarctic and others.

The tree families of the holarctic are dominated in species and individuals by Pinaceae and Fagaceae. The first of these, which includes pine, spruce, fir, larch, and hemlock, is an example of the group of families essentially limited to the northern hemisphere. Other important examples are Aceraceae (maple), Betulaceae (birch, alder, hazel, hornbeam), Salicaceae (willow, poplar), and Juglandaceae (walnut, hickory). All of these enter the tropical highlands, and a few may sparingly penetrate tropical lowlands, particularly after disturbance. These tree families number their species in a few hundreds or less. In addition there are more than a dozen very small families of which Nyssaceae (tupelo) and Platanaceae (sycamore) are the only ones that are truly widespread. Most of the others are in eastern Asia.

Fagaceae is an example of a tree family well established in both the holarctic and the antarctic flora. This family includes oak, beech, chinquapin, and chestnut. Several species enter into tropical forests, particularly in somewhat cooler mountain elevations, but a large majority are non-tropical. Other similar families are Oleaceae (ash, lilac, forsythia, privet, olive, jasmine), Cupressaceae (cypress, cedar, arborvitae, juniper), and Taxodiaceae (redwood, sequoia, bald cypress), this last being a small relict family.

Some generally smaller families of trees and shrubs also have widespread and important holarctic species although the family extends into the tropical highlands or sometimes beyond. Included are Magnoliaceae (magnolia, tulip tree) with two tropical genera, Hamamelidaceae (sweet gum, witch hazel) with two genera in

Africa, Hippocastanaceae (horse chestnut, buckeye), Taxaceae (yew), Staphyleaceae (mostly Asian), Myricaceae (sweet gale, sweet fern), and Cornaceae (dogwood). The largest of these counts about two hundred species, the smallest barely a dozen.

There are several large families of primarily shrubs (but which may include trees or herbs) which are principally found in the holarctic and antarctic floras. Outstanding among these is Rosaceae, with more than a hundred genera and three thousand species, including such groups as apple, cherry, peach, hawthorn, mountain ash, rose, spirea, blackberry, and strawberry. Others, all numbered in hundreds of species, are Ericaceae (rhododendron, madrone, blueberry, heath), Berberidaceae (barberry), Hydrangeaceae (hydrangea, philadelphus), and Caprifoliaceae (elder, viburnum, honeysuckle).

Four very large families consisting of herbs and a few woody plants are rare within tropical areas. The third largest family in the world is Papilionaceae (sometimes grouped with two smaller tropical families into Leguminosae, beans). This family embraces many important extra-tropical herbs such as clover, pea, soy bean, lupine, vetch, and lentil, but also includes the locust and a few other trees. The other three are Gentianaceae (gentian), Polygonaceae (buckwheat, rhubarb, many weeds), and Saxifragaceae (saxifrage, currant), the smallest in the group with seven hundred species.

Of the many families of herbs only a few of the large ones are essentially limited to the holarctic, but quite a few others have reached the antarctic while largely avoiding the tropics. Campanulaceae (bellflower, lobelia) is the most clearly holarctic large herb family. Primulaceae includes one widespread genus. Two smaller families (only a few hundred species) belong to the holarctic for the most part, Hydrophyllaceae and Valerianaceae. Another family, Polemoniaceae (phlox) is mostly in North America. The large herb families which appear in the north and the south include Cruciferae (cabbage, mustard, radish, alyssum, and various weeds), Umbelliferae (carrot, celery, parsley, dill, anise, caraway, poison hemlock, and many others), Ranunculaceae (buttercup, delphinium, anemone, and many others), and Caryophyllaceae (pinks), all with at least two thousand species. Some smaller families are Onagraceae (evening primrose, fuchsia), Portulacaceae, Papaveraceae, Fumariaceae, Plantaginaceae, Orobanchaceae, and Juncaceae (rushes). There are various other small (fewer than one hundred species) and not very important herb families in the holarctic, including local endemics and totaling about two dozen, if small families with at least some shrubs are added in.

Some holarctic plant families are more or less restricted to arid areas. There is one large family of succulent herbs, particularly in holarctic arid areas and South Africa: Crassulaceae (sedum), with fourteen hundred species. Other families of arid regions involve mostly shrubs and find their greatest area for development around the Mediterranean and the nearby areas of Central Asia. Among these are Plumbaginaceae, Globulariaceae, Cistaceae, Tamaricaceae (tamarix), Dipsacaceae (teasel), and a number of smaller families of fewer than one hundred species each.

With the addition of cosmopolitan families, the vast majority of the plants of the holarctic have been accounted for. It is of interest to notice that the most cosmopolitan families divide mainly into herbaceous families and into mixed families whose holarctic representatives are herbs. The first group includes Orchidaceae, Compositae, Graminaceae, Liliaceae, Cyperaceae, Labiatae, Scrophulariaceae, and Dridaceae. The latter includes Euphorbiaceae, Rubiaceae, Boraginaceae, as well as the primarily tropical Verbenaceae, Apocynaceae, Loranthaceae, Oxalidaceae, Violaceae, Polygalaceae, and Linaceae. In some of those there are a few holarctic shrubs or small trees or, for Vitaceae (grape) woody vines. There are, in addition, about a dozen small- to medium-sized (a few hundred species) families of cosmopolitan aquatics and a few other small cosmopolitan families of specialized habitats.

The few remaining holarctic plants belong to tropical families of which only a few members have strayed. In some cases a holarctic tree genus has its relatives in the tropics, while in others a tropical tree genus actually crosses substantially into the holarctic realm. Together the invading tree families amount to more than three dozen. Another two dozen tropical families, most of them quite large, send only a few herbaceous representatives into the holarctic. There are also several largely tropical families of vines, including Cucurbitaceae (melons) and Dioscoreaceae (yams).

To complete the allocation of plant families, there are those not to be found within the holarctic at all. Not surprisingly, only a few really large families like Piperaceae, Proteaceae, Zingiberaceae, and Myrsinaceae, have nothing to do with the holarctic. Still, about three dozen families of over two-hundred species each are excluded from the holarctic along with a slightly larger number of smaller but widespread families and, of course, numerous (more than three score) endemic families. The lack of precision in the census of families derives from the compelling fact that every category is somewhat imprecise and many allocations are marginal.* Nevertheless, it is clear that at the family level the vast majority are either to be identified with the holarctic or outside of the holarctic, another way of saying that there are few truly cosmopolitan families. On the other hand, among the larger families there is usually some overlap across the holarctic boundaries. As was indicated earlier, few small families are widespread.

At the generic level holarctic distinctions are much more profound. There are far too many genera to present a complete division by genus, but some examples can make clear how they segregate.

Among the primarily holarctic families, few genera transcend the boundaries. Only pines among the Pinaceae, for example, overstep the limits in any way. Less than half a dozen species can be found in the lowland tropics and then in restricted areas not far removed from their usual domain and generally in difficult soils where fires have destroyed a more complex cover. Willows sometimes are found along the banks of tropical streams and have been widely introduced by man far from their natural habitat. Oaks are common in tropical highlands, and I have seen a near solid canopy of oaks in rainforest at intermediate elevations in both Mexico and New Guinea. Invasion following disturbance seems to be indicated for this unusual rainforest canopy purity, and certainly oaks are not a part of widespread lowland tropical forests. In this family, the antarctic beeches are of a distinct genus. The cypress family, though well developed in the holarctic, has several important southern hemisphere genera, none shared with the holarctic. Although a few junipers and *Libocedrus* inhabit tropical highlands, only one rare species of the latter genus reaches the lowland tropics in New Caledonia. In the redwood family, *Glyptostrobus* is found only in swamps on the margins of the tropics and *Athrotaxis* is in Tasmania. Otherwise the genera are clearly within the holarctic realm.

*The sum of the families covered here is short by a number of complex and of controversial families. A few families such as Nelumbonaceae have such peculiar distributions as to defy classification. Quite a few families are not widely recognized and often represent controversial, poorly understood elements for which reliable distributional data are not available. Prudence suggests that such families be omitted from enumeration by regions.

Extension of holarctic genera into tropical highlands is common but cannot really be considered a violation of the limits. Important examples include maple and yew which extend into Malesian mountains and walnut and alder widely distributed along the Andes chain. Most of these have several related genera which are more conservative. Of course, the smaller and more endemic families present no challenge in distribution.

There are families in which the majority of genera are holarctic; but some genera are excluded. For example, although ash is widespread in north temperate areas, extending only beyond to Cuba and Java, the related jasmine and *Forestiera* genera are largely tropical. Magnolia and its relatives are most abundant in the highlands of southern China and southeast Asia extending into Indonesia but also far north as well, while the related genus *Talauma* is scattered across the humid tropics.

The reverse is also common. Tropical families such as Anacardiaceae have largely holarctic genera as *Rhus* (sumac), *Pistacia*, and *Cotinus*. Other families with this sort of division include Tiliaceae with *Tilia* (basswood), Bignoniaceae with *Catalpa* and *Paulownia*, and Buxaceae with *Buxus*. It is interesting that such important tropical families are often named for their aberrant holarctic representative. There are many more examples.

In fact, what is rare is the genus which transcends the boundaries more than slightly. Certain cosmopolitan weeds have followed man and his settlements around the world. A few tree genera are at home in the holarctic and in the tropics. The most prominent example is *Celtis*, which we know as hackberry. Others are *Ilex* (holly), *Persea* (bay, avocado), *Rhamnus* (buckthorn), *Diospyros* (persimmon, ebony), *Euonymus*, and even *Ficus* (fig). There is always the question how far into (or out of) the holarctic qualifies for membership in both floral realms, but there certainly are more than a dozen more examples, mostly in eastern Asia, of tree genera alone. Still, this is a paltry list when measured against the vast number of genera which are restricted to the holarctic. Herb and bush genera conform in general to the pattern here illustrated with trees. To travel out of the holarctic is to confront a phalanx of unfamiliar plants.

## Antarctic Plant Groups

The antarctic realm is much smaller than the holarctic and is quite discontinuous. Nevertheless it displays a remarkable degree of distinctiveness particularly at the generic level.

Unique antarctic families are not numerous. Possibly a few endemic families might be considered purely antarctic. There are several important families, however, that are strong in the antarctic together with the Asian tropics. One of these is the Cunoniaceae which is largely found in the humid parts of Australia and New Guinea but with a few genera extending to Indonesia and Fiji as well as to New Zealand and other antarctic regions plus one genus (*Weinmannia*) which covers tropical highlands as far as the Philippines, Madagascar, and Mexico. A similar situation accrues for Winteraceae with *Drimys* (winter's bark) being the widespread genus. In the family Pittosporaceae the Americas are excluded and the widespread *Pittosporum* penetrates tropical lowlands and parts of China. The type genus of Stylidiaceae extends into the Asiatic tropical highlands while the remainder are strictly in cool antarctic regions. Somewhat similar is Restionaceae which, however, is also represented in the southern parts of Africa.

Several important families are based in the antarctic realm but extend widely into the tropics. Podocarpaceae is equally important in the cool antarctic and eastern Malesia but extends throughout the Asian tropics and into the tropical highlands of Africa and the Americas. The family Proteaceae is strongest in South Africa and the humid parts of Australia but has representatives throughout the tropical regions of the world. Monimiaceae is strong in Australia and other antarctic areas but also extends into the tropics. Haemodoraceae is apparently similar. Sometimes the Philesiaceae are separated from the vast lily family and are strictly southern, extending into the Andes and highland New Guinea. While all of the foregoing families number from about one hundred to several hundred species, the few species of the family Eucryphiaceae are also shared between southeastern Australia and Chile.

In the discussion above, the families shared between the holarctic and the antarctic were delineated. Few if any of these are primarily antarctic and many are of only secondary importance there.

From the discussion of the families it can already be seen that there are a number of clearly antarctic genera. Antarctic forests

are strongly dominated by trees of the genus *Nothofagus*
(Fagaceae) which extends into the highlands of New Guinea. Al-
ready alluded to are *Drimys*, *Weinmannia*, *Podocarpus*, and
*Eucryphia*. Other important genera are *Laurelia* (Monimiaceae),
*Prumnopitys* (Podocarpaceae), *Libocedrus* (Cupressaceae), *Gunnera*
(Haloragaceae), and *Fuchsia* (Onagraceae). There are some antarc-
tic genera whose relationships belong in tropical or cosmopolitan
families. Examples are the legume genus *Sophora*, the genus
*Aristotelia* (Elaeocarpaceae), and a number of herbs and shrub
groups such as in Compositae.

The widely separated elements of the antarctic flora, Tasmania,
New Zealand, Chile, and, to a lesser extent, South Africa are
remarkable for the fact that many important genera and families
recur in more than one and not infrequently most areal units.
Thus it is no surprise that endemic genera exist, particularly in the
characteristic families. Proteaceae has many examples such as
*Guevina* in Chile and *Knightia* in New Zealand as well as many in
South Africa. In Podocarpaceae there is *Saxegothaea* in Chile and
*Phyllocladus* in New Zealand, extending to the highlands of
Malesia. *Beilschmedia* and *Litsaea* represent Lauraceae in Australia
and New Zealand, *Cryptocarya* appears in Chile. Most of these
examples represent important forest trees, but there are many
other examples.

There are some examples in the antarctic of genera which are
primarily developed elsewhere. *Persea* penetrates antarctic Chile,
*Myrtus* appears in most parts of the antarctic as well as many
other regions including southern Europe. *Ribes* and *Berberis*,
temperate groups, are at home in Chile. *Dacrycarpus* (Podocarpaceae), a tropical genus, is important in New Zealand. The case of
*Araucaria* is interesting. Except for a special endemic development
in New Caledonia, most species are marginally tropical, often
spreading into disturbed and frost-prone areas to produce the
protective cover which allows rainforest to become reestablished.
One species in Chile, however, is completely removed from the
tropics. Among less important (in the antarctic) plants, there is
a long list of genera and families which can be found in only one
region.

It would appear that the antarctic flora as an assemblage has
much the same kinds of characterization as for the holarctic.
Most of the important genera are distinct, and a large part of the
families are not widely shared with the bordering warmer plant
realms. Sharing does occur, however, and it is more than sporadic.

## Tropical Flora

The character of each tropical realm can be easily summarized at this point. So far as extra-tropical relationships are concerned, these are already implicit in the discussion above of the holarctic and antarctic realms. The three tropical land regions are clearly separated by expanses of water, particularly the neotropical realm of America. Tenuous relationships exist across southern Asia between Africa and Malesia.

A great many families are found throughout the tropics. More than three quarters of all the families with more than five hundred species qualify, as do more than half of those numbering between two and five hundred. Yet among the smaller families almost all of the few wide tropical examples involve markedly specialized plants. It is also true that few of the pantropical families are totally absent from some extra-tropical region, north or south, and a significant number of these are more or less cosmopolitan as has been detailed above. There are perhaps two dozen families in the tropics which are incompletely distributed but not restricted to one region. Finally, about half of the endemic families in the world occur within the tropics where all but a few of these are small. Thus, among the important families, the tropics are certainly not regionally divided; on the other hand, because there are few truly cosmopolitan families, it can be said that the vast majority of the important tropical families are strongly identified with the tropics.

With genera the story is quite different. Among the many thousand plant genera within the tropics fewer than three hundred are found in all three subregions, only a few percent. Prominent among these are the legumes and grasses as well as many weeds. Some of these such as *Hibiscus*, *Eugenia*, *Ficus*, and *Diospyros* have been mentioned above. Well-known legumes include *Acacia*, *Bauhinia*, *Dalbergia*, *Mimosa*, *Caesalpinia*, and others. There are genera within which economic plants are found, such as *Piper* (pepper), *Ipomoea* (sweet potato), *Dioscorea* (yam), *Mimusops*, and *Strychnos*.

A somewhat larger number of tropical genera extend into two of the three regions, particularly between Africa and Malesia. Some of these, of course, are poorly represented in one of the two regions. Still, only a small percentage of the total number of genera are thus encompassed. At the generic level the three tropical regions have little in common and are as distinct as are the non-tropical regions already distinguished here.

## Arid Divisions of the Tropics

The drier parts of the lower latitudes can be floristically distinguished from the more complex wet parts. The segregation of Australian flora is widely accepted, but less has been done to distinguish the drier parts of the Americas and of Africa. One reason for this is obvious: Australian arid areas form a compact unit, and this is not true in the other two.

Australia is not strongly distinguished at the family level. Casuarinaceae is the most important family uniquely associated with Australia, and it characteristically extends into Southeast Asia, mostly in drier climates. An important concentration of Proteaceae centers on Australia as does one of the two major divisions of Myrtaceae. There are nearly a score of small endemic families associated with Australia.

No census of Australian genera which excludes the small, rich, floristically distinct wet forest areas is readily available, but the total must be upwards of a thousand, of which more than half are endemic to Australia or do not range far beyond. It may be much more than half. The genus *Eucalyptus* completely dominates the flora of Australia and drier parts of nearby New Guinea and Timor. Only two or three species range beyond this region, one reaching the Philippines. There are other myrtaceous genera, some only technically different from *Eucalyptus*, but also *Melaleuca* and *Leptospermum*. In Australia *Acacia* is also an important tree represented mainly by the phylloidous group which ranges as far as Hawaii. Prominent are *Casuarina* (see above), *Callitris* (Cupressaceae, this genus is also in New Caledonia), *Banksia* (Proteaceae), and *Brachychiton* (bottle tree, Sterculiaceae) which is reminiscent of the African baobab. Smaller plants include both species of some of the above along with *Xanthorrhoea* (grass tree, the type genus of an endemic family often separated from the lily family), *Cycas* (Cycadaceae) which extends into Malesia, and the related endemic *Macrozamia*.

Although considerable distinction can be adumbrated for Australian genera, there is a clear relationship to the moist tropical Malesian flora. The larger families in Australia either range into

Malesia for those few which are predominantly Australian, or, in the more usual case, Australia is an outpost for Malesian families. Moving from the Australian realm into neighboring realms means a substantial change in the genera of plants to be seen with only a few common to both sides along any part of the perimeter.

The flora of the drier parts of tropical America is every bit as distinct as that of Australia, even though the area involved is not compact or contiguous. There are several characteristic families the most obvious of which is the Cactaceae. Along with the Agavaceae (often separated from the vast lily family), these two families dominate, particularly in the visual sense, the dry flora; both involve conspicuous or even bizarre forms. On the other hand, both do extend beyond the arid tropics with a few generally inconspicuous species in sandy or rocky soils as far as eastern North America and south central Chile. Several families of arid areas around the world are well represented such as Chenopodiaceae, Ephedraceae, and Zygophyllaceae. Both legumes and composites contribute numerous elements and Anacardiaceae is also important along with the mostly American Solanaceae. There are several small endemic families, an outstanding example of which is Fouquieriaceae (ocotillo) of the Sonoran Desert. As in previously discussed realms, many foreign families have contributed one or two elements, but when summed these probably amount to a distinct minority of the total.

In genera, arid tropical America is strongly distinguished, not only by most of the cactus genera and the lily-like *Agave* and *Yucca*, but also many more. The mesquite, *Prosopis* (Mimosaceae), is almost everywhere, extending as far as Oklahoma in disturbed conditions, and the pepper tree, *Schinus* (Anacardiaceae), although widespread, has undoubtedly been expanded by man. Both of these are accompanied by less conspicuous relatives. To be sure, some very widespread shrub and herb genera, such as *Acacia*, *Atriplex*, *Ephedra*, *Oxalis*, *Euphorbia*, and *Senecio*, are shared with other mostly distant realms. Thus, passing into the neighboring humid associations means leaving behind practically all the resident genera and encountering a whole new assemblage.

The drier parts of Africa can be distinguished from the more humid parts even though there are no important families concentrated there, but granted there are a few small endemic families. Arid Africa is characterized by a remarkable development of arborescent legumes and of cactus-like euphorbs. The baobob tree

(*Adansonia*, Bombacaceae) is almost a trademark.

Arid African genera are, as in any area, more distinct, particularly if one admits the arid areas of Southern Asia which are a continuation of the African realm. Legume trees such as *Brachystegia* and *Isoberlinia* dominate large areas along with *Julbernardia* and *Albizzia*. Many species (often with heroic thorns) of *Acacia* are widespread in Africa, although this genus has great development elsewhere as well. The physiognomic resemblance of the euphorbs to cactus is paralleled by the *Aloe* species resembling the American *Agave* which, in this case, is in a closely related family. The genera of world-wide families of arid regions continue their importance here, and other widespread families such as Sterculiaceae, Anacardiaceae, Combretaceae, and Bignoniaceae are well represented. Some better-known endemic genera are *Boswelia* (frankincense), *Commiphora* (myrrh, both Burseraceae), *Encephalartos* (Cycadaceae), and the peculiar *Welwitchia* which stands in a family alone. As always, isolated representatives of many families are present.

The unusual case of South African flora merits notice. More specifically interest focuses on the small southwest part of Cape Province commonly known as the Cape region. Here are preserved thousands of endemic plant species, and there are more than a thousand genera found only here or not beyond South Africa. On the other hand, there are only about a dozen small and unimportant endemic plant families. Clearly climatic changes have crowded a once more-widespread flora into a narrow refuge. For its size, the diversity of endemism has few parallels, and the region has been designated by many authorities to the same rank as the holarctic, a conclusion which seems somewhat excessive. The families of the Cape region, for the most part, are either those important in the Australian flora, of which it can be considered to a degree an outpost, or they belong to the adjacent African flora.

Considering the generally accepted primary divisions of world flora, the floristic realms and possibly certain of their subdivisions, a fairly consistent picture emerges. Most families have a clear regional identification which is rarely pure when the small insignificant endemic families are omitted. For the most part, plant genera cleave to a particular region with only the rare genus transcending the boundaries. But many genera may not even approach the boundaries, whatever these may be, because available treatments of most groups are not based on any precise system of boundaries but are related to vague divisions such as the tropics or arid areas.

9

Major Floristic Boundaries

IN THE LITERATURE DISCUSSED in the previous chapter, what little is said of boundaries implies that they are indistinct and sometimes chosen for convenience. Yet a series of maps with rather detailed boundaries has been presented over the years. The nature of the floral realms depends, in part, on the reality of these boundaries. For all the justification in the literature, they might be imaginary. In order to elucidate this problem, several examples will be carefully considered.

## THE NORTH AMERICAN HOLARCTIC-NEOTROPICAL BOUNDARY

A full range of holarctic plants dominates to the southern fringes of the United States where it meets a neotropical flora (Map 21). It also reappears in the higher parts of a mountain chain from Chihuahua to Panama. Nearly everywhere the boundary of the holarctic in North America has one or more of the genera *Quercus*, *Pinus*, or *Juniperus* in dominance, while many members of the bean family appear in the neighboring neotropical area. The boundary zone can be described in segments.

In California, including Baja California, the boundary is nearly always on a mountain slope, with the holarctic plants upslope. Oak and pine species characteristic of large areas in California are stationed right up to the boundary, while the California juniper *(J. californica)* most commonly appears in a restricted zone along

*Map 21.* Holarctic boundary in North America. The dashed line on this and the following maps indicates where the boundary passes through grassland and is therefore not fixed. In Mexico the holarctic is confined to highland areas.

the boundary itself. Widespread associated shrubs are chamise *(Adenostoma fasciculatum,* Rosaceae), manzanita *(Arctostaphylos sp.,* Ericaceae), *Ceanothus* (Rhamnaceae), mountain mahogany *(Cercocarpus sp.,* Rosaceae), sage *(Artemesia sp.,* Compositae), and buckwheat *(Eriogonum fasciculatum,* Polygonaceae) (Hanes 1971). Also important are yucca (shrub form) and *Ephedra,* which are widely associated with the neotropical flora, as well as various small cactus plants *(Opuntia).* While the holarctic at the boundary is presented in the form of a woodland, the neotropical here is no more than a desert formation with a rather restricted flora. Near the desert boundary is often found the fascinating Joshua-tree *(Yucca brevifolia)* or in some areas, mesquite *(Prosopis)*. Most holarctic species completely disappear beyond a stone's throw into the desert, but sage extends farther from its primary associations in some colder areas. Cactus and *Ephedra* mingle with the dominant creosote bush *(Larrea tridentata,* Zygophyllaceae). The desert palm *(Washingtonia filamentosa)* marks springs scattered along the desert margin. Bur sage *(Franseria dumosa,* Compositae) is widely associated with the creosote bush and represents a tropical American genus which has one species in the central United States. Brittle bush *(Encelia farinosa,* Compositae) and various species of *Lycium* (Solanaceae) are other important shrubs of tropical affinities.

The holarctic-neotropical boundary in Arizona is very much like its counterpart in California. Nearly always it is along a mountain slope with the holarctic plants upslope, but in this case the holarctic woodland flora is more limited while the neotropical desert flora is robust. The woodland is dominated by oak and juniper with mesquite sometimes common near the desert boundary. Many holarctic plants are important associates in the woodland including pine, manzanita, *Ceanothus, Rhus,* mountain mahogany, *Rhamnus,* etc. (Nichol 1952; Küchler 1964; Whittaker and Niering 1965 — the emphasis here is on a continuum but a floristic change is still evident). Neotropical representatives which penetrate the woodland include small cactus plants *(Opuntia),* yucca, and agave, while in some areas *Acacia* is important.

The woodland desert boundary is often quite abrupt and is marked by the virtually complete termination of holarctic plants and the appearance of a wide representation of neotropical plants. Here on better soils is found the striking saguaro cactus *(Cereus giganteus)* along with the ever so spiny cholla *(Opuntia sp.),* palo verde *(Cercidium microphyllum,* Caesalpinaceae), and ocotillo *(Fouquieria splendens,* Fouquieriaceae, an endemic family), as well as large prickly pear (also *Opuntia sp.*), the endemic canotia *(Canotia holocantha,* Celastraceae), and various thorny species of *Acacia*. Particularly along washes are found mesquite, *Parkinsonia* (Caesalpinaceae), ironwood *(Olneya tesota,* Papilionaceae), desert willow *(Chilopsis linearis,* an endemic genus of Bignoniaceae), and desert hackberry *(Celtis pallida,* a world-wide genus of the Ulmaceae). Yucca, agave, and *Ephedra* as well as several of the above do extend from the desert into the woodland, while several less common genera such as *Vauquelinia* (Rosaceae), *Dalea* (Papilionaceae), *Bursera* (Burseraceae), and two more cactus genera *(Echinocereus* and barrel cactus, *Ferrocactus)* reach their northerly limits here without becoming a part of the holarctic flora. The inconspicuous creosote bush and bur sage are actually more widespread than all the others. To the east tarbush *(Fluorensia cernua,* Compositae), yet another tropical composite genus, also becomes important.

The tropical desert flora extends into southern Nevada and the extreme southwestern corner of Utah with a reduced content, meeting pinyon-juniper woodland on the lower slopes of the numerous small mountain ranges. In several places between these mountains the desert encounters sage brush on the flats rising to the north. In spite of often being called desert, the sage brush is a bush woodland often invaded by pinyon and juniper and sometimes mountain mahogany or oak, or is replaced by grassland. The desert boundary of sage brush comes where higher rates of evaporation from higher temperatures at lower elevations make the valleys too dry. Creosote bush and sage overlap, and the boundary is usually drawn where the creosote bush ends. If there is any desert north of the creosote bush range it is on alkaline flats where saltbush or shadscale *(Atriplex sp.)* and greasewood *(Sarcobatus vermiculatus)* grow, both of the world-wide family Chenopodiaceae which favors alkaline habitats.

From southeasternmost Arizona to central Mexico, southern New Mexico, and western Texas there is a different sort of floristic boundary. Here there are broad flat areas with tropical desert on one side and holarctic woodland on the other, species similar to those already discussed being involved for the most part. Between them lies grassland *(Bouteloua, Hilarea).* Outliers of the woodland often cling to hills and broken terrain, but oak or juniper savannas are common and one often sees uprooted trees where ranchers attempt to preserve the more valuable grasslands against invading woodland. The desert boundary is frequently marked by a thicket of mesquite clinging to the interval between grass fire on one side and drought on the other. But mesquite savannas and cactus savannas and even yucca and agave savannas are widely distributed, and I have seen extensive mesquite woodland where old-timers and old accounts say only grassland grew before. The ranchers fight the aggressive mesquite, but the cattle do eat the bean pods and that has something to do with its spread. Notice that the tropical plants which invade the grassland are also the ones which invade the holarctic woodland in Arizona.

Starting in eastern Sonora and continuing south to Central America the neotropical and holarctic floras meet on very steep mountain slopes facing the Pacific. Neotropical woodland gives way to grassland for the most part before it reaches the base of the mountains. Near Arizona the western mountain slopes have holarctic woodland surrounded by a sea of grass but soon to the south forest appears first with holarctic trees on the upper slopes followed by a tropical forest on the lower slopes. The upper forest is made up of pine, oak, and juniper with madrone *(Arbutus,* Ericaceae) and sometimes Douglas-fir *(Pseudotsuga)* or cypress *(Cupressus).* This is a familiar forest that reappears in northern California without the juniper, with outposts as far north as Vancouver, British Columbia, or is found from northern Arizona to Montana without the oak, madrone, and cypress. South of Guatemala the variety of species diminishes as well. Downslope there is a rapid transition where tropical plants first appear, with the holarctic plants disappearing just as abruptly. Most prominent among the many tropical trees are the legumes *(Lysiloma, Leucaena, Acacia,* Mimosaceae) (Pennington and Sarukan 1968). Other common genera are *Bursera, Ceiba* (Bombacaceae), *Heliocarpus* (Tiliaceae), *Pistacia* (Anacardiaceae), etc. Occasionally one meets palms, banyans, tree cactus, or even mahogany *(Swietenia,* Meliaceae). *Celtis* occurs here; otherwise virtually all the many genera are unknown in the holarctic. Along streams willow *(Salix)* and Montezuma cypress *(Taxodium)* are found. Where more level ground occurs, as in basins, the vegetation is highly disturbed and the boundary is not distinct. Second growth and a sort of rotation savanna are predominant.

On the eastern side of Mexico and southward again into Central America the situation is similar but wetter. In this case tropical rainforest clings to the mountain slopes, while oak and pine forest border it inland where the rainfall is lower. The forest resembles more that of the southeastern United States, including sweet gum *(Liquidambar,* Hamamelidaceae), walnut *(Juglans),* hornbeam *(Carpinus),* hop hornbeam *(Ostrya),* dogwood *(Cornus),* black gum *(Nyssa),* and sycamore *(Platanus).* Less common plants include other holarctic genera and some tropical invaders. The rainforest understory comes in under a canopy of holarctic trees such as oak, suggesting the tension along this boundary, but it is remarkable how distinct the flora of the two formations are. Northward toward Monterrey the rainforest gives way to tropical seasonal forest and the relationship with the holarctic forest is the same as along the western mountain slopes. Beyond the forests are woodlands, and inland there is desert. In broken terrain around Monterrey, the northern end of the Cordillera Oriental, holarctic woodland meets tropical woodland, with oak and pinyon pine appearing generally as islands on higher ground within a sea of mesquite. The area involved is not extensive.

The holarctic flora dominates eastern Texas but is absent in southernmost Texas. Along the lower Rio Grande and a little to the north is found the last outpost of many tropical woodland and desert plants. This is the eastern limit of creosote bush along with palo verde, horse bean *(Parkinsonia)*, desert willow, tarbush, and ocotillo. The Mexican genus *Leucophyllum* (Scrophulariaceae) is important here (ceniza shrub). Woodland trees which find their northern limit just inside Texas include *Pithecolobium*, and *Leucaena* (Mimosaceae), *Eysenhardtia* (Papilionaceae), *Amyris* (Rutaceae), *Pistacia* (Anacardiaceae, this genus in Eurasia is part of the holarctic), and *Ehretia* and *Cordia* (Borraginaceae). The endemic *Koeberlinia* (sometimes put in the Capparidaceae) is also here. As many tropical species drop out, the woodland becomes almost a pure stand of mesquite; that is, grasslands of southern Texas are aggressively invaded by this plant and today form woodland and savanna. There are associates, one of which is log wood *(Condalia obovata*, Rhamnaceae). The ubiquitous *Yucca* and *Opuntia* are here too, and closer to the border *Acacia* sometimes joins the mesquite. The first holarctic woody plants north of the lower Rio Grande are live oaks, generally found as island-like thickets and later in groves in lowland areas, only occasionally mixing with the mesquite. This is an oak forest, probably maintaining outposts on better soil within the mesquite woodland, which is characteristically found on poor sandy soils. As the oak becomes more common so does cultivation, and the mesquite clings to a few unused patches near its eastern limits. The more extensive forest is not just live oak but also other species of oak together with hickory, including pecan, cedar *(Juniperus)*, ash *(Fraxinus)*, holly *(Ilex)*, elm, plum *(Prunus)*, and an increasing variety the further east one goes. Westward the forest terminates along the heavily cultivated calcarious Black Prairie.

Directly west of the Black Prairie and north of the broad flat mesquite woodlands of southern Texas rises the Balcones Escarpment of the Edwards Plateau. Here grow extensive "cedar brakes," juniper-oak woodlands which are a variety of the type found southward into central Mexico and westward to southeast Arizona. Prickly pear cactus is widespread, and mesquite has established a foothold here and there. This formation grades northward gradually into the "Cross Timbers" woodlands with post oak *(Quercus stellata)*, blackjack oak *(Q. marilandica)*, and cedar elm *(Ulmus crassifolia)* becoming dominant. Other trees include ash *(Fraxinus texensis)*, red bud *(Cercis texensis)*, hackberry *(Celtis)*, and osage orange *(Maclura pomifera,* an endemic genus of Moraceae). Patches of mesquite on poor soil and on abandoned fields are found well into Oklahoma. Westward, patches of juniper cling to bluffs surrounded by mesquite woodland on what at one time was grassland. Finally further west, the High Plains remain largely grassland where they are not farmed.

It can be seen that over large areas where the terrain is level the holarctic and neotropical floras are divided by grassland. This grassland is being invaded from both sides which may be moving the vegetative cover toward a more natural condition (Wells 1970; Harris 1966). Usually the most aggressive invader is mesquite, while the exceedingly tolerant cactus and yucca are also widespread, not only in the grasslands but also well into holarctic formations, where sporadic disturbance will probably always provide them opportunities to grow. Possibly, given enough time without great stress, much of the mesquite woodland and savanna might be taken over by the neighboring juniper-oak-pinyon association. Almost no attention has been given here to the grass and other herbaceous species that particularly dominate the grassland areas. To be sure, each species has its habitat, but herbaceous plants are notorious for changing their distribution from one growing season to another following fluctuations in the climate and variations in disturbance, so they are not useful in defining floristic boundaries (Küchler 1972).

The last place in North America where the holarctic meets the neotropics is in southern Florida. Tropical forest occurs in "hammocks" or "bay heads" within the Everglades marshlands as well as along the Florida Keys and northward as far as Cape Canaveral on coastal limestone formations often next to the tidal mangrove. The hammocks are islands of edaphic rainforest around artesian springs, and the tropical forests elsewhere in Florida are probably all associated with high water table limestone structures. Hurricanes and cold winds usually keep these complex forests low in profile, and they are often overtopped by the more tolerant cabbage palms *(Sabal)* or live oak. Some sixty genera of trees occur within these associations and not elsewhere within the United States. More than a dozen families reach the United States only here. Most of the tree genera are confined to southernmost Florida, but about a dozen extend along the coast northward as far as Cape Canaveral, including one mangrove genus. It is notable that the only native cycad *(Zamia)* grows in this coastal strip. Prominent in Florida's tropical forests are several genera which are at home in both the tropics and the subtropics. These include magnolia, bay *(Persea,* Lauraceae), and holly *(Ilex,* Aquifoliaceae), as well as the cabbage palm. The only holarctic trees extending beyond the dominantly holarctic associations are the live oak, which also occurs in parts of Cuba, and certain pines. In Florida, *Pinus densa* stands grow in sandy disturbed areas in the tropical forest zone and are often seen being invaded by pioneering species of the tropical forest such as *Tetrazygia* (Melastomaceae), *Guettarda* (Rubiaceae), *Metopium* (Anacardiaceae), and *Chiococca* (a trailing vine, Rubiaceae). Other tropical pines present a similar situation in scattered areas from the Bahamas to the east coast of Central America. The forests of the southern fringes of Florida do not deviate from the floral character of widespread neotropical associations to the south.

The holarctic is well represented in Florida. On upland soils in the center of the peninsula many familiar trees are important, including oak, pine, sweet gum, maple, and hickory, along with the bridging genera, magnolia, bay, holly, and cabbage palm. Lesser plants are honey locust *(Gleditsia)* and elm as well as the smaller dogwood *(Cornus)* and hackberry *(Celtis)* and a long list of mostly holarctic shrubs and vines. Palmetto *(Serenoa)* is widespread particularly in disturbed areas. Flood plains and other wet areas add swamp cypress *(Taxodium),* willow *(Salix),* black gum *(Nyssa),* ash *(Fraxinus),* cottonwood *(Populus),* sycamore *(Platanus)* and *Planera* (Ulmaceae). Together these plants, along with further additions, extend northward into Alabama, Georgia, and the Carolinas. There is no transitional association separating the well-defined tropical forests from the equally well-defined holarctic forest, only that they share certain plants. The sharp boundary between these two floras in Florida could be regarded as edaphically controlled, but there can be no mistaking the segregation that exists between them. It is true that in large areas of southern Florida the two are separated by marshes and prairies filled with grasses, sedges, and other herbs. Practically all of these herbaceous plants are widely distributed beyond Florida. The more hardy holarctic trees invade the prairies or survive on coastal sandy areas, along with specialized shrubs and a few trees such as sand pine *(Pinus clausa)*.

## THE EURASIAN HOLARCTIC-PALAEOTROPICAL BOUNDARY

In the Old World the meeting of tropical and extra-tropical floras occurs within terrain even more accidented than in the New World, but otherwise the two segments of the boundary have much in common. Because I lack personal familiarity with the Eurasian situation it will be described in less precision than was presented for the boundary in America.

From the Atlantic to the Indian Ocean the primary areas of the holarctic and the palaeotropics are separated by the world's greatest desert, and the desert probably was there long before they came into being. Tenuous contact has been made along coastal and highland routes, particularly during pluvial times, but very few holarctic genera have become established south of the desert and only a handful of tropical genera are at home on the north side of the desert. In fact, most of the tropical genera which have species in the European holarctic probably penetrated from India, not Africa. An example of this is laurel as well as perhaps the edible fig *(Ficus carica)*. *Chamerops*, a scrub palm of the Mediterranean, apparently also has its closest relationships in Asia. Several important South African genera are found in the east African highlands and are a part of the European flora, such as heath *(Erica)* and perhaps olive *(Olea)*. Desert plants with holarctic relationships are a small minority but include one type of broom *(Genista*, Papilionaceae) and tamarix, among others. The actual boundary between the palaeotropics and the holarctic in Africa and Asia generally lies along mountain slopes.

In the Mahgreb the holarctic flora occupies the highlands and coastal regions (Map 22). A wide range of holarctic plants are

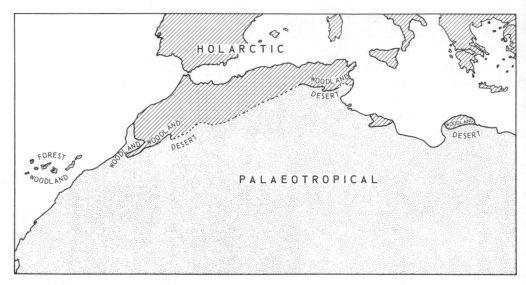

*Map 22.* Holarctic boundary in North Africa.

common, dominated by evergreen oak *(Quercus ilex* and cork oak,
*Q. suber)* (Walter 1968; Walter and Straka 1954; UNESCO 1968;
Mikesell 1960). Evergreen maple *(Acer monspessulanum)*, ash
*(Fraxinus parvifolia)*, poplar, cedar *(Juniperus oxycedrus)*, and
many lesser plants of holarctic affinities are regularly present
throughout the area. On poor soils *Pinus halepensis* prevails.
Around the drier margins of this association is usually found a
characteristic woodland with oleaster or wild olive *(Olea europaea)*,
carob *(Ceratonia siliqua*, Mimosaceae), pistachio *(Pistacia lentiscus)*,
palmetto *(Chamerops humilis)*, and juniper *(Juniperus phoenicia)*.
Endemic to the Mahgreb is the sandarac tree *(Tetraclinis articulata*,
Cupressaceae). Much of the woodland and forest has been altered
into a garigue (chaparral) in which heath *(Erica arborea)*, rosemary
*(Rosmarinus officinalis*, Labiatae), oleander *(Nerium oleander*,
Apocynaceae), rock rose *(Cistus* sp., Cistaceae), madrone *(Arbutus
uendo*, Ericaceae), sumac *(Rhus)*, occasional scrub oak *(Quercus
coccifera)*, and many other well-known Mediterranean shrubs and
herbs hold sway. Plains areas generally support grassland *(Stipa,
Lygeum)* which may be invaded from the margins by woodland
trees. On the high interior plains of Algeria scattered sage
*(Artemesia)* dots the grassland.

Tropical plants dominate dry valleys near the Mediterranean

and all of the Sahara. Next to the holarctic is found an association dominated by jujube *(Zizyphus lotus*, Rhamnaceae), thorn bush *(Acacia gummifera)*, *Launea spinosa* (Compositae), and succulent euphorbs. The date palm *(Phoenix dactylifera)*, now largely cultivated, favors springs in nature. Near the Atlantic coast the olive-like endemic *Argania sideroxylon* (Sapotaceae) is dominant. Other common plants are *Zygophyllum*, *Ephedra*, *Tamarix*, pistachio *(Pistacia atlantica)*, and the grasses *Stipa* and *Aristida*. Whether this association forms a woodland or constitutes desert is uncertain from available descriptions; what is clear is that it endures under distinctly more arid conditions and is characteristically less dense than the neighboring holarctic formation. The holarctic woodland is invaded for some distance by the *Acacia* and the succulent euphorbs, a situation analogous to that in the American southwest. Except for a few representatives along stream beds and the one *Pistacia* species, holarctic species can hardly be said to penetrate neighboring floras here at all.

The Canary Islands for all their isolation and endemism have a division of flora similar to that of the mainland. Forests, particularly of pine or laurel, alternate with brush made up of heath, rock rose, myrtle, broom *(Cytisus)*, and juniper. On lower slopes, particularly to the southeast, there is an arid flora of succulents (euphorbs and the composite *Kleinia)* along with the Canary Island palm *(Phoenix canariensis)* and a narrow strip of desert plants along the coast. There are some endemics in the laurel forest whose relatives are in distant homelands such as *Ocotea* and *Persea* (both Lauraceae), but the division between tropical and holarctic is quite clear.

Eastward, the holarctic maintains a toehold in both Tripolitania and Cyrenaica. It is fair to say that the natural vegetation here and in Tunisia has been so thoroughly disturbed over the years that not much is to be learned by observing present-day wild distributions (Le Honéron 1959; Murphey 1951). Yet the plants here generally continue the relationships further west.

The holarctic next appears in the Levant, again in the highlands and along the coast (Map 23). Woodlands are dominated by scrub oak, pistachio, carob, and juniper, with Aleppo pine also present. Widespread brush alternates involving oleaster, rock rose, oleander, madrone, and other characteristic Mediterranean shrubs. It is probably fair to say, however, that the floristic variety is reduced in comparison with northwest Africa. In the Jordan Valley

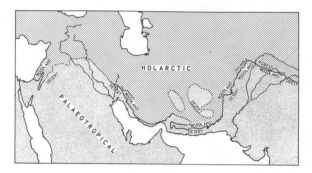

*Map 23.* Holarctic boundary in Southwestern Asia.

are to be found genera such as *Acacia,* "broom" *(Spartocytisus,*
Papilionaceae), and jujube growing possibly as woodland but giving
way rapidly to tropical desert in the drier valley bottom and in
areas to the south. The "broom" has holarctic affinities, the other
two are widespread tropical plants, while hardly a shrub genus
familiar in the holarctic is to be found in the desert. The slopes
where holarctic flora joins the tropical representatives are of
limited extent, for all along the eastern margin of the Levantine
highlands a grassland plain predominates, separating holarctic
woodland from tropical desert. In fact this grassland reaches eastward to the foot of the Kurdistan highlands and Zagros Mountains.
Sage frequently accompanies the grassland.

The mountains, then, that stretch from eastern Turkey to
Baluchistan, support a depauperate holarctic flora. The total lack
of pine in all of Iran is an amazing testimony of the depletion
which has occurred there (Critchfield and Little 1966; Bobek
1968). The wetter mountains of Iran have a typical holarctic
forest of oak, maple, walnut, hackberry, elm, pear *(Pyrus),*
almond, juniper, ash, sycamore, and various others. On dry hills
there is a woodland made up of pistachio, almond *(Prunus,*
Rosaceae), barberry *(Berberis),* honeysuckle bush *(Lonicera,*
Caprifoliaceae), *Lycium* (Solanaceae), and sage or worm-wood
*(Artemesia),* still strictly holarctic. The level ground of the high
interior plateau of Iran generally supports a grassland often dotted
with woodland shrubs, especially sage, or even just scattered
shrubs in the form of a desert. On the lower slopes of the mountains overlooking the Persian Gulf and to a limited extent in
valleys penetrating toward the interior there grows a large variety
of tropical shrubs. The date palm is cultivated here, and desert is

well developed along the coast. The division between highland holarctic plants and lowland tropical plants is not sharp, as might be expected with a much-disturbed vegetation growing on highly accidented terrain.

In eastern Afghanistan the pistachio-almond woodland grades into a different type, and new tree combinations appear in the more moist higher slopes (Schweinfurth 1957). On foothills in Pakistan a species of olive *(Olea cuspidata)* becomes the most important woodland tree in a transitional woodland. This is usually accompanied by the shrub varnish leaf *(Dodonaea viscosa,* Sapindaceae), which has a very broad distribution in the humid tropics. Also present are a palmetto *(Chamerops)* and the endemic *Reptonia buxifolia* (Myrsinaceae), adding to the east oleander *(Nerium),* the tropical *Adhatoda* (Acanthaceae), and a widespread tropical bean *(Dalbergia). Acacia* often penetrates this woodland which obviously has much in common with the Mediterranean woodland but is also largely tropical. Above this, west of Kashmir and into eastern Afghanistan, there is a live-oak savanna *(Quercus baloot)* which also recapitulates the Mediterranean paradigm. A common associate of the live-oak is a pinyon *(Pinus gerardiana)* and a variety of shrubs such as *Sophora griffithii* (Papilionaceae, this genus is largely tropical), *Daphne* (Thymelaeaceae), ash *(Fraxinus),* and sometimes elements from the almond-pistachio woodland which borders it to the southwest. At higher elevations various characteristically holarctic associations are found. The tropical association of southern Iran continues along the lower slopes of the mountains in southwestern Pakistan. A related woodland then extends onto the plains bordering the western Himalaya and from there south to Gujarat. Acacia continues to be the dominant plant in the woodland along with a variety of tropical shrubs such as *Calotropis* (Asclepiadaceae), capers *(Capparis),* mesquite *(Prosopis),* kunar *(Zizyphus), Salvadora* and others. Much of this woodland surrounding the Thar Desert has been converted into savanna or is cultivated where water is available.

In northern Pakistan the live-oak savanna gives way eastward to a pine forest *(Pinus roxburghii)* which follows the lower slopes of the Himalaya in a continuous belt as far as Nepal and then sporadically into eastern India on drier exposed sites. Upslope the pine forest grades into a rich holarctic forest of oak, conifers, and numerous less prominent but widespread plants. The neighboring woodland often extends under an open stand of pine near the lower margins of the pine forest. In the valley of the Sutlej River, however, the woodland is replaced by tropical sal forest. No more to the east does woodland form the northern boundary of the tropical flora; rather in east Asia holarctic mountains rise above a sea of tropical forest.

The westernmost sal forest is dominated by sal *(Shorea robusta,* Dipterocarpaceae) and includes a variety of tropical trees such as *Anogeissus latifolia* (Combretaceae), *Dalbergia sissoo,* and species of *Terminalia* (Combretaceae), *Ficus, Bauhinia, Cassia* (Caesalpinaceae), *Albizia* (Mimosaceae), *Adhatoda, Rhus* (Anacardiaceae, this genus is both tropical and holarctic), and many more. The sal forest is limited vertically, giving way almost abruptly to pure pine forest *(Pinus roxburghii).* The mountains here are deeply dissected so that tongues of sal forest penetrate northward, separated by pine-covered ridges. Upslope the pine gradually merges with and then gives way to a rich holarctic forest. First there appear various species of oak, then deodar *(Cedrus deodara,* Pinaceae), fir *(Abies pindrow),* white pine *(Pinus wallichiana),* and spruce *(Picea morinda).* Less common trees include walnut, maple, hornbeam *(Carpinus,* Betulaceae), horse chestnut, elm, and others. Undershrubs include *Rhododendron* (Ericaceae), yew *(Taxus),* and many others. Seemingly the pine is a buffer between a strong tropical flora on one side and an equally strong holarctic flora on the other.

Eastward in Nepal the forests change due to increased rainfall, and the pine belt becomes discontinuous. Wet sal forest, which reaches Assam, differs only in degree from the drier variety. Characteristically *Pandanus* (screw palm) joins the association. The *montane forest* also changes gradually. Chinquapin *(Castanopsis,* Fagaceae) is an important addition along with hemlock *(Tsuga,* Pinaceae), *Magnolia,* and arborescent *Rhododendron.* The two forest types are apparently well segregated, but the transition or boundary is widely obscured by cultivated land.

Starting at about Sikkim, the boundary between holarctic and tropical floras enters a zone of sufficiently heavy rainfall that on both sides there is a form of rainforest (Map 24). At this point any sharp differentiation breaks down. To be sure, at higher elevations the combination of plants is clearly holarctic, and at the base of the mountains the tropical flora reigns supreme. In between there is a zone of astonishing mixture. All sorts of things grow side by side that elsewhere are quite alien to one another. It would seem

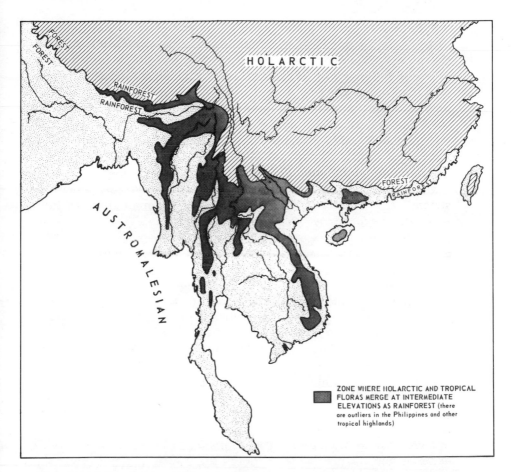

*Map 24.* Holarctic boundary in Southeastern Asia. The complex merging of floras in the highlands of Southeast Asia has no parallel in any other part of the world. A similar tendency in tropical rainforest highlands is, however, widespread.

that the gradually cooler temperatures here are not accompanied by any of the critical boundaries of moisture effectiveness that operate further west. The situation in Assam continues through northern and eastern Burma, northern Thailand, Viet Nam, and into southern China along very steep mountain slopes, for the most part (Davis 1964; Küchler and Sawyer 1968; Wang 1961). Widespread and characteristic tropical rainforest species extend to the lower slopes of these mountains, while upper forests contain well-known holarctic plants. It must be emphasized that the zone of transition is nowhere an extended area, being only a belt along the mountain slopes. At the same time we are dealing with a holarctic extension into fully tropical highlands, and the further into the tropics the less distinct is the boundary between holarctic highland plants and tropical lowland plants.

The temperate rainforest of highland southeast Asia is a complex of laurel-leafed evergreen trees with many genera represented but a few clearly dominant. The oaks *Castanopsis, Quercus,* and *Lithocarpus,* along with *Schima* (Theaceae), are most abundant. Several other characteristic families (and their most common genera) are Lauraceae *(Machilus, Phoebe, Cinnamomum, Beilschmedia, Cryptocarya),* Magnoliaceae *(Magnolia, Michelia, Manglietia),* and Hamamelidaceae *(Altingia, Bucklandia).* Other important trees include *Nyssa* (Nyssaceae), *Engelhardtia* (Juglandaceae), *Pieris* (Ericaceae), *Podocarpus* (Podocarpaceae), and *Eugenia* (Myrtaceae). Not a few of these are at home on both sides of the tropical-extra-tropical boundary in various parts of the world, and others are widespread tropical highland plants. Among the many less common plants found, many are typically tropical genera. Conversely, some holarctic genera extend even below the mixed zone in some places, particularly *Quercus* and *Castanopsis.* At higher elevations a majority of the important holarctic genera can be found. There are in eastern Asia, as in any other region, established species and genera whose relationships are otherwise outside the holarctic; examples have been given above. There are two pines in southeast Asia. One of these, *Pinus insularis,* is associated with exposed and disturbed sites often in the transition zone, while the other, *Pinus merkusii,* grows on poor soils and sometimes within regions of drier tropical forest.

Southeast Asia is the only place where the holarctic comes in contact with humid tropical floras on a broad front, but nowhere does this happen on level ground. The vast richness of both floras here, among other things, has suggested that this is where the modern angiosperm floras originated, with the holarctic flora being derived from the highland part and tropical floras from the lowland part (Takhtajan 1969). Conversely, this area may represent the most-favored region both for present-day growth and for opportunities for survival from the effects of climatic fluctuation. In any case, here the meeting of the floras is the most complex in the world.

## OTHER BOUNDARIES OF FLORISTIC REALMS

Other land boundaries of floristic realms than that of the holarctic are few and local. The next best candidate is the antarctic-neotropical meeting in South America. If the Australian flora can be taken at this rank, a boundary with the antarctic exists in Tasmania and with the malesian flora in Queensland, New Guinea, and a few nearby islands. Finally the Cape flora merits inclusion here although, in this case, no personal observations have been made, and published descriptions must be relied upon.

South of the neotropical flora in Chile the antarctic flora first appears in the coast range and on the slopes of the Andes as islands where conditions are more moist (Fuenzalida 1950; Oberdorfer 1960) (Map 25). These scattered bits of forest are found north of 31°S in the coast range and to about 34°S along the west slopes of the Andes, becoming more or less continuous by 35°S in both highland ranges. The main part of this forest is dominated by roble *(Nothofagus obliqua,* Fagaceae), especially in the central valley where it often appears in open park-like stands subject to periodic burning. Other *Nothofagus* species are sometimes present and become commoner further south. The most common associate is laurel *(Laurelia sempervirens,* Monimiaceae), while *Podocarpus salignus* (Podocarpaceae) is also characteristic. A group of species which not only occurs with roble but also dominates the isolated groves further north includes canelo *(Drimys winteri,* Winteraceae), olivillo *(Aextoxicon punctatum,* an endemic genus of Euphorbiaceae), avellano *(Guevina avellana,* Proteaceae), ulmo *(Eucryphia cordifolia,* Eucryphiaceae), and *Aristotelia chilensis* (Elaeocarpaceae). All of the above genera belong to the antarctic flora, but there are several associated vicariants of tropical genera, most of which tend to favor poorly drained places. These include lingue *(Persea lingue,* Lauraceae), luma *(Myrtus luma,* Myrtaceae), several species of *Myrceugenia* (also Myrtaceae), *Escallonia revoluta* (Saxifragaceae), *Fuchsia* (Onagraceae), and the bamboo *Chusquia quila.* The widespread *Berberis* (Berberidaceae) contributes representatives, and the Chilean genus *Azara* (Flacourtiaceae) is also present. The majority of the representatives of non-antarctic genera are bushes, and there are, of course, various other less common genera, both antarctic and tropical, to be found. This is a dominantly antarctic flora but with a generous secondary intrusive element. Along the margins of the forest is frequently found the

*Map 25.* Antarctic boundary in South America. Only an incomplete remnant of Antarctic elements is to be found in southern Brazil, where it is mixed with tropical elements.

Chilean cedar *(Libocedrus chilensis,* Cupressaceae) mixing in on both sides of the forest boundary or, on the cooler Argentine side of the forest, forming a woodland which faces the grasslands at the foot of the mountains.

North of the forest grow woodlands of predominantly tropical relationships. Oberdorfer identifies them as antarctic, but this can hardly be sustained by a study of the genera and their distribution.

The most common plants are probably peumo *(Cryptocarya rubra,* Lauraceae) and litre *(Lithraea caustica,* Anacardiaceae; this genus, though widespread in South America, is commonest in Chile), while the endemic boldo *(Peumus boldus,* Monimiaceae) is also characteristic of this zone. Other important species are quillay *(Quillaja saponaria,* Rosaceae, a small genus of Brazil and Chile), maiten *(Maytenus boaria,* Celastraceae), parqui *(Cestrum parqui,* Solanaceae), mitique *(Podanthus mitique,* Compositae, a small genus of Brazil and Chile), trevu *(Trevoa trinervata,* Rhamnaceae, a small genus of Bolivia and Chile), colliguay *(Colliguaya odorifera,* Euphorbaceae, a genus mostly in Chile but extending into Brazil), *Eupatorium salva* (Compositae), *Proustia pungens* (Compositae), *Colletia spinosa* (Rhamnaceae), *Schinus dependens* and *latifolius* (Anacardiaceae), and *Baccharis rosmarinifolia* (Compositae). Also present are the legumes *Adesmia, Sophora,* and *Psoralea,* as well as *Myrceugenia obtusa, Porlieria chilensis* (Zygophyllaceae), *Fabiana imbricata* (Solanaceae), *Escallonia* (Saxifragaceae), *Azara,* and *Kageneckia* (Rosaceae, a small genus of Peru and Chile). The nearest to antarctic affinities of any of these is the endemic woodland *Peumus* whose family is identified with the antarctic. The lauraceous *Cryptocarya rubra* and *Beilschmiedia miersii* (an antarctic genus) are associated with wet places near the forest. Several secondary genera have vicariant species in the forest and in the woodland including *Myrceugenia, Escallonia, Azara,* and *Chusquia,* all with tropical affinities except *Azara,* which is known only from Chile, but whose family is widespread in the tropics. Continuous woodland reaches to about 38°S in the central valley and as scattered islands as far as Osorno, although open grasslands often mark the major rain shadow areas in the central valley south of the continuous woodland zone. Much of the woodland is converted to a maqui by disturbance, as in the Mediterranean region.

There are several regional variations in the woodland of Chile. The open central valley at least as far south as Concepción, where not cultivated, is characterized by a thorn bush savanna with *Acacia caven.* Dry hills often support large cactus such as *Cereus, Echinocactus,* and *Opuntia.* Along the coast many inland woodland shrubs occur together with cactus and colorful yucca-like bromeliads such as *Puya coarctata* and *chilensis,* forming a narrow belt separating the forest from the sea to well south of Concepción. Wherever the two flora meet, central Chilean woodland and antarctic forest, they form contrasting formations, but, because of widespread disturbance, the forest may be fragmented and open to invasion in open areas by more demanding shrubs. Where flat land prevails, either formation near their frontier usually gives way to parkland, savanna, or even open grassland. Otherwise the boundary relates to elevation and soil moisture.

To the east, antarctic forest borders on grassland or woodland both above treeline and beyond the mountains, with grassland becoming more extensive toward the south. At the forest boundary lenga *(Nothofagus pumilio)* and ñire *(N. antarctica)* replace roble, while Chilean pine *(Araucaria araucana,* Araucariaceae) also comes to the forest edge roughly where roble gives way to lenga. The Patagonian scrub woodland is floristically strongly related to the woodlands of central Chile and areas further north, a majority of the genera being shared with central Chile and very few genera having an antarctic relationship. Some very widespread genera are prominent — *Berberis, Prosopis, Schinus, Buddleia* (Loganiaceae), *Ribes* (Saxifragaceae), and *Ephedra*. Genera shared with central Chile (and farther north) include *Colletia, Escallonia,* and *Adesmia.* Several Chilean woodland species extend, for the most part, only to the western fringes of Patagonia — *Maytenus boaria, Fabiana imbricata,* and *Azara microphylla.* Several common plants grow more or less in pillow-like aggregations — *Mulinum spinosum* (Umbelliferae, a genus restricted to Patagonia), *Chuquiragua aurea* (Compositae, the various species of this genus further north do not grow this way), *Cruckshanskia glacialis* (Rubiaceae, Patagonia and Chile), several *Azorella* (Umbelliferae, an antarctic genus), the Patagonian legume genus *Anarthrophyllum,* and the widespread neotropical *Verbena* (Verbenaceae, not usually in this form). Still other Patagonian shrubs are *Diostea* (Verbenaceae, to Chile and Paraguay), *Ovidia* (Thymelaeacea, to Chile), *Discaria* (Rhamnaceae, neotropical), and the endemic *Nardophyllum* (Compositae). The shrubs above the tree line in central Chile are mostly a continuation from Patagonia but are strong on "pillow" plants, of which there are a few additions including the endemic *Laretia* (Umbelliferae), the antarctic *Calandrina* (Portulacaceae), and *Pycnophyllum* (Caryophyllaceae, up the mountains to Peru).

A considerable area of the southern Parana Plateau in Brazil has a strong antarctic floristic element (Hueck 1966). The dominant tree is the Parana pine *(Araucaria angustifolia)* which overlaps with nearly pure stands of *Podocarpus lambertii.* Important associates are maté *(Ilex paraguayensis), Phoebe porosa* (Lauraceae), and *Cedrela fissilis* (Meliaceae). Smaller plants include *Schinus spinosus, Drimys winteri, Berberis laurina,* and species of *Weinmannia* (Cunoniaceae), *Eugenia* (Myrtaceae), and *Fuchsia.* A wide variety of neotropical plants mixes in parts of this forest. The eastern limits lie near the crest of the coastal escarpment, the southern limits are open grasslands, and the northern and western limits follow a rising contour to the north. Clearly this is a fragmentary outlier of the Chilean antarctic forest heavily mixed with neotropical plants. The northern and western boundary is not sharp, but grades into neighboring forests. Outlying islands occur in high areas even well north of Rio de Janeiro. Many of these genera are also found in high-elevation forests of the Andes from northern Argentina to Mexico, as has been mentioned earlier.

The only continuous area of antarctic flora in Australia occurs in western Tasmania (Schweinfurth 1962) (Map 26). Here there is

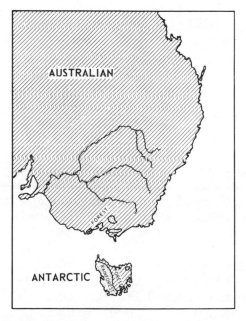

Map 26. Antarctic boundary in Australia.

found a temperate rainforest dominated by myrtle beech *(Nothofagus cunninghamii)* with which celery-topped pine *(Phyllocladus asplenifolius,* Podocarpaceae) and southern sassafrass *(Athero-*

*sperma moschatum*, Monimiaceae) are important associates. Understory plants include tree ferns *(Dicksonia)*, leatherwood *(Eucryphia billardieri)*, horizontal *(Anodopetalum biglandulosum*, Cunoniaceae, endemic), *Bauera rubioicles* (Cunonaceae, an Australian genus), *Acrademia franklinii* (Rutaceae, endemic), and at higher elevations the King William pine *(Athrotaxis selaginoides*, Taxodiaceae, endemic) becomes dominant. Many of these genera also occur in Chile and New Zealand, and only one strays beyond the antarctic floral region in Australia. On rocky ridges is found *Nothofagus gunnii* and along the tree line *Athrotaxis cupressoides*. There is also a fascinating antarctic tundra made up in part by large hard pillow plants, rather like fancy green boulders, among which grow a number of prostrate conifers with contrasting shades of bright green. The pillow plants are *Abrotanella fosterioides* (Compositae), *Donatia novaezelandiae* (Donatiaceae), *Phyllachne colensoi* (Stylideaceae), and *Pterygopappus lawrencii* (Compositae, endemic). Shrubs include *Orites aciculare* (Proteaceae), *Epacris serpyllifolia* (Epacridaceae, Australian), *Diselma archeri* (Cupressaceae, endemic), and the three podocarps *Microcachrys tetragona* (endemic), *Podocarpus alpina*, and *Microstobus niphophilus* (another species at waterfalls in New South Wales). Of these only *Epacris* extends significantly beyond the antarctic flora in Australia.

The drier parts of Tasmania support a typical Australian flora involving species of *Eucalyptus* (Myrtaceae), *Acacia* (the phylloidous group, Mimosaceae), *Callitris* (Cupressaceae), *Casuarina* (Casuarinaceae), *Banksia* (Proteaceae), and others. Shrubs or small trees which may invade disturbed rainforest areas include *Pomaderris apetala* (Rhamnaceae), *Phebalium squameum* (Rutaceae), *Anopterus glanulosus* (Escalloniaceae, to Victoria only), and species of *Olearia* (Compositae) and *Leptospermum* (Myrtaceae). Similar plants at higher elevation include *Melaleuca squamea* (Myrtaceae), *Gaultheria hispida* (Ericaceae), and *Pittosporum bicolor* (Pittosporaceae) together with the moor shrubs *Sprenglia incarnata* (Epacridaceae) and *Baeckia gunniana* (Myrtaceae). All of these genera except *Anopterus* are widely distributed in Australia and some well beyond but not in antarctic floras. The eucalyptus forest itself extends to higher elevations before giving way to mountain moors. Two snow gums — *Eucalyptus coccifera* and *E. pauciflora* — along with mountain gum, *E. dalrympleana*, form a twisted forest near the tree line.

The relationship between Australian and antarctic flora in Tasmania is tied up with fire. The eucalypt forests are quite inflammable and burn rather frequently. At least once in several centuries the rainforest itself gets burned, at which times moisture-loving but intolerant eucalypts such as mountain ash *(Eucalyptus regnans)*, alpine ash *(E. delegatensis*, the "alpine" applies north of Tasmania), and messmate stringybark *(E. obliqua)*, become established. These trees, especially the first two, become very tall (seventy-five meters and more) and stand well above the rainforest which returns underneath. Over time many of the eucalypts may disappear, but usually a few old giants keep watch even in the wettest parts of Tasmania. More frequent fire may encourage the blackwood *(Acacia melanoxylon)* to invade, making it also a common tree of this zone along with undershrubs mentioned above. Yet, rainforest, tundra, eucalypt forest, and moor are all distinct formations where each keeps its own flora, and, in spite of disturbance or perhaps because of it, the boundaries between them remain rather sharp. In Victoria and north into southern Queensland pockets of temperate rainforest cling to moist valleys where they are able to survive frequent fires that come from neighboring eucalypt forests. Large areas of potential rainforest on mountain ridges in Victoria belong to the magnificent mountain ash which challenges the redwood for the title of the world's tallest tree.

The Cape flora is largely confined to the Cape maquis in the southwestern corner of South Africa (Walter 1968; Good 1947) (Map 27). More than a third of the genera here are endemic, a remarkable concentration which merits further comment. To some degree this may be an artifact of classification, the lack of intermediates in this isolated flora leading to the erection of new genera. For comparison, two widely separated parts of, say, the holarctic, such as highland Mexico and highland southeast Asia, would duplicate, one compared to the other, much of the kind of distinctness found in the Cape flora, but, in this case they are tied together by the great mass of their flora of which they are two outliers. More important, probably, for the Cape has been its floristic history. Environmental fluctuations have apparently reduced South African floras to a few survivors followed by expansion of the available area again resulting in luxuriant speciation, as in Darwin's finches. One might ask why tropical plant species did not fill the available niches; of course, they did to some extent, but the presence of better adapted survivors has dominated the

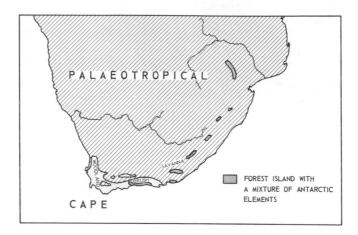

*Map 27.* Boundary of Cape Flora in South Africa. The forest islands with Antarctic elements resemble the situation in Brazil and are not to be considered extensions of the Cape Flora.

flora and its elaboration.

In spite of the endemism, an assessment of the relationships of the important plants of the Cape can be made. Probably the most characteristic family is Proteaceae, and, although a few species are spread across the tropics, the only other area of concentration is Australia, while the family is also present in New Zealand and Chile. A second very prominent family is Restionaceae, closely related to grass. This is also strongly developed in Australia and present in New Zealand, Chile, Madagascar, and the East Indies. The Cape flora is famous for the variety of Ericaceae which has developed, a family otherwise best known in the holarctic and in tropical highlands. Rutaceae is well represented in the Cape and, although quite a widespread family, has its other area of greatest variety in Australia. Four more very widespread families have one or more large endemic genus in the Cape flora, Compositae, Leguminosae, Rosaceae, and Rhamnaceae. The cupressaceous genus *Widdringtonia*, which is present, is most closely related to *Callitris* of Australia. About the only important woody genera of the Cape which intrude from the tropics are *Rhus* (Anacardiaceae), *Gymnosporia* (Celastraceae), and *Myrsine* (Myrsinaceae). There are several small endemic families and some endemic genera of Thymelaeaceae. It is no surprise that several genera primarily of the Cape flora extend into adjacent regions or, more particularly, into tropical highlands. There is no argument that the Cape flora is highly distinctive and is ultimately derived from a variety of sources, but the evidence suggests its strongest relationships lie with Australia.

East of the Cape there survives a forest remnant of which isolated elements exist even on Table Mountain behind Cape Town. This distinctive forest is locally called the Knysna Forest and is the southernmost stand of an association which occurs mainly as a mountain rainforest from southern Africa to Ethiopia. The most dominant trees are the podocarps *Podocarpus* and *Decussocarpus*, which are not found in Africa outside this association but are common in tropical highlands elsewhere, in the Melanesian rainforest in general, and the former also in Chile and New Zealand. Similar distributions characterize two other important genera, *Olea* and *Cunonia*. Associated genera shared with the Cape flora are *Widdringtonia* and the widespread *Gymnosporia*, *Myrsine*, and *Rhus*. Other widespread genera are *Myrica* (Myricaceae), *Plectronia* (Rubiaceae), *Ficus* (Moraceae), *Celtis* (Ulmaceae), and *Ocotea* (Lauraceae). The Knysna Forest itself contains a number of small endemic genera of various common families. Tropical African plants are well represented in this forest, which grows in South Africa as islands sharply distinguished from the surrounding flora. The character of this forest is reminiscent of the highland forest of southern Brazil, a tropical upland outlier of a more southern flora, except in Africa the more southern flora has long disappeared.

North of the Cape is found the Karroo flora, known for the development of desert succulents. The distinctive stone plants allied to *Mesembrianthemum* (Aizoaceae) are found only here, but their family is widespread. The large succulents, such as the cactus-like *Euphorbia* (Euphorbiaceae), *Aloe* (Liliaceae, resembling *Agave*), *Cotyledon* and *Crassula* (Crassulaceae), and *Portulacaria* (Portulacaceae), are familiar all over the drier parts of Africa as are most of the important shrubs, including *Euclea* (Ebenaceae), *Zygophyllum* (Zygophyllaceae), *Lycium* (Solanaceae), *Rhus*, *Acacia*, and *Salsola* (Chenopodiaceae). Several shrub genera of Cape composites enter the Karroo along with a few other Cape genera and many more tropical African plants. Clearly the Karroo flora belongs to the palaeotropics.

Besides the Karroo flora and the Knysna Forest, the Cape flora borders to a limited extent with "bush veld" savanna near Port Elizabeth. The scattered trees of this formation are strictly tropical and represent the southernmost limit of an extensive African landscape.

The widespread Australian flora borders sharply with rainforest to the east and the north. The nature of this very sharp boundary has been discussed earlier. Open eucalypt forest extends onto the southern fringes of New Guinea and onto Timor, while a related dry forest with *Melaleuca* (Myrtaceae), phyllodous *Acacia*, *Casuarina*, and *Callitris* occurs in New Caledonia. The continuous rainforest of New Guinea gives way to coastal strips in Queensland and to moist pockets with a few rainforest species further south. Although Australian flora contrasts strongly with the rainforest flora, they are ultimately related. Not only are there related genera, but the important Australian *Acacia* and *Casuarina*, for example, also have rainforest species.

The dry flora of Africa and of South America relate to the local rainforest much as does the Australian flora, but geographically they do not form a compact areal unit and have thus been given less attention as distinctive flora. A careful study would probably show consistently sharp boundaries like many already known to exist.

A tour of the land boundaries of floristic realms and subrealms shows conclusively that distinct boundaries do exist, which happily justifies the longstanding regionalization presented in the literature. But such confirmation is a step forward, for the lack of supporting description strongly suggests that previous delimitations were based on no more than an intuitive impression from sporadic observation. Different authorities disagreed as to where the boundary belonged, and bordering areas have been juggled about on maps rather cavalierly, which suggests a lack of attention to detail. Armed now with a more careful examination of the geography of flora it becomes possible to proceed to an analysis of the origin and character of major floristic regions.

# 10

# Origin and Character of Major
# Floristic Regions

IN ORDER to explain the origin of major floristic regions and thus illuminate their basic character, a sequence of factors will be considered. Almost every possible idea has been touched upon in some way in the literature, but no systematic evaluation has ever been offered.

At the outset it can be recognized that the land areas of the world offer diverse habitats and that an insignificant number of plant genera as well as few plant families even approach a cosmopolitan distribution. In part, at least, the limitations on the distribution of these taxonomic groups reflect the lack of adaptation among their members to some of the important natural environments. There is also the possibility that remote favorable environments have simply been beyond reach. As a result we find that the plants of the diverse regions of the earth differ markedly from one another. Because land areas are largely grouped into continental units, it follows that each continent should be floristically distinct merely because any arbitrarily selected world area of comparable size would be distinct, and the physical isolation of continents offers a convenient separation for dividing up the world flora. That the average geographic range of genera and families, in conjunction with continental isolation, is inadequate to explain most of the geography of plants can readily be seen when one considers that the flora of most of North America has far more in common with that of China and Europe than with the lowland flora of Mexico (Li 1952; Hultén 1958), which in turn resembles far more closely the flora of Argentina. These distinctions, furthermore, have persisted while floras have migrated first northward and then southward with pleistocene climatic fluctuations. Something more is at work.

Climatic differentiation offers a possible framework for floristic regionalization. Surely the plants of the desert differ taxonomically from those of the rainforest as do tropical plants from arctic regions. Most manuals of plant families go no farther than this in describing the distribution of plant groups, unless it be to refer to continents or major political units. Thus the plants of lowland Mexico are tropical and those to the north are not. Climate is important to plant distribution, and in some areas a major floristic change does correspond to the margins of the tropics, for example, assuming we know what that is. Some important exceptions, however, cast doubt on the proposition that climate is the major floristic determinant. While the neotropical flora seems to be confined to hot regions in North America, it extends into the coldest parts of South America (other than mountain tundra), with the genus *Prosopis*, for example, covering the entire range. The flora of Australia extends from unquestionably tropical environments in Queensland and New Guinea to genuine temperate conditions in Tasmania even to mountain moor. An impressive number of genera broadly transcend the boundaries of the tropics and are at home in the middle latitudes — or is it the other way around? There is no doubt that plant genera are not necessarily limited by temperature boundaries, while a majority of families have surely mastered this difficulty. Most genera in the drier parts of the west, furthermore, are also important in the humid east of North America. Although plant genera and families do not in most cases inhabit the complete range of possible climates, there is no particular climatic discriminant for flora. Even the compelling frost line is of limited meaning, for in most places tropical floras simply do not respect it, as can readily be seen by comparing the boundary of frost with the major floristic boundaries.

Even though there is no fixed set of floristic climates, environment, with a major emphasis on climate at the world scale, does play a significant role in the geography of flora. Within every major region such as a continent the flora can be seen to polarize with respect to one or more environmental gradients. The boreal flora of North America differs significantly from the subtropical flora, the arid flora of South America differs significantly from that of the rainforest. Wherever a plant group exploits one environmental pole it would tend to forsake the other as incompatible. A survey of plant genera and families shows this to be abundantly true. The midpoint in any polarization depends on the local gradient and its extremes, there is no invariable position. The two sides of a floristic gradient might then be thought of as phases of a larger flora, subrealms when realms are at hand. Polarization is certainly important, but it is of itself only a matter of degree, a gradient and not an adequate regional discriminant.

Isolation unquestionably brings about floristic discrimination, because lack of contact and interaction inevitably leads through time and mutation to differences. The distinctions between neotropical and palaeotropical flora can adequately be accounted for by the ocean of distance that separates them today. Once-connected floras have at various times been divided by diverse causes. The most absolute is the hiatus between eastern Asian and western American floras once connected across the Bering Strait and now displaced by changing climates to lower latitudes. The development of water bodies can also separate once continuous floras as can geologic change, such as the rise of the southern Andes, which produced a dry climate between southern Chile and southern Brazil. Isolation works its effects, which is no surprise. But the major floristic realms of the world are not primarily explained by isolation, even though they are in part. It is the land boundaries where distinct floras meet that validate the notion that there are meaningful floristic realms. These have still not been adequately explained.

The development of some sort of contact front between two floras which have come together where previously they have been separated has been suggested from time to time. Presumably a more aggressive flora would advance at the expense of a weaker flora until some sort of equilibrium was established along an environmental isoline. In order to cross the frontier a taxon would not only have to adjust to differing environment but would have simultaneously to contend with competition from the established populations, a double challenge not likely to be met readily. Certainly the southern holarctic boundary commends such an interpretation, the land masses to the south having been separate at a not so remote time geologically, and the boundary seems to follow some sort of temperature isoline. But this explanation can not apply to the very disjunct antarctic flora which occupies something of the same relationship on the other side of the tropical flora. Furthermore, for there to be a coherent "front" there must be some sort of systematic relationship between the elements of a flora. Otherwise different plants would find their limits in different places as some, at least, indeed do. And through time the front ought to break down as one after another taxon surmounts the barrier, unless somehow each is tied to the rest of the flora. In fact, floristic frontiers probably do dissolve with time; yet the holarctic boundary has been remarkably persistent.

After having observed many floristic boundaries in nature and having described more above, the conclusion emerges forcefully that such boundaries are at once usually formation boundaries. Here is the necessary link that holds a floral assemblage together at its boundary. It is not just a matter of environmental degree; at a formation boundary an advancing taxon must invade a wholly new environment whose niches are largely already filled. No wonder that floras maintain their distinction over extended time spans. This relationship has not been utterly overlooked in the past; there are many casual references to formation differences along a particular floristic boundary. In fact some attempt was made to combine the two concepts, but this had to be abandoned because it was obvious that many, perhaps most, formation boundaries are not major floristic boundaries, nor had either boundary concept been carefully examined and understood. It turns out that the particular two formations which confront one another differ from one part of a boundary to another. In North America, for example, tropical desert borders on holarctic woodland in the west, while in eastern Texas tropical woodland penetrates to the limits of holarctic seasonal forest, and in Florida it is tropical rainforest in edaphic outposts that confronts the holarctic which here is seasonal forest. Only occasionally do similar formations from different floras come to face one another. Apparently in the case of two opposing floras involving the same formation one is almost certain to be more aggressive and simply advances until a different formation is encountered. That is to say, the lack of a formation difference usually produces an untenable boundary.

It is also manifest that major floristic boundaries tend to run along mountain slopes. Granted, there is no great dearth of available mountains, yet there are almost no examples of a floristic boundary crossing an open plain. Few plains are so large but that they might easily be captured wholly by a particular local flora. There are a number of quasi-exceptions to this assertion.

Except in the wettest and driest places, plains are usually found to be grass covered, separating contrasting floras (and floristic) on either side. Who is to say where the formation boundary belongs in a grassland? A mountain slope provides a strong environmental gradient that surely helps to maintain floristic distinctions even in those few cases where there is no formation boundary. As a matter of fact, the most indistinct floristic boundary discovered was in Southeast Asia where mountain rainforest grows above lowland rainforest and temperature can be the only variable. Between mountain slopes and formation distinctions nearly all major floristic boundaries are adequately accounted for, as well as, in at least some cases, the considerable differences that attach to major phases of a floral realm.

Floristic realms are real and therefore have meaning. In part they represent a legacy of the past. Obviously the various parts of a realm have had unity even where they are disjunct today. The contact between dissimilar realms is also suggestive, even though the explanation may not so readily be produced. In the case of the holarctic there is reason to believe it has occupied similar environments to the present condition for some considerable time separate from the tropical floras. As the Gondwanna land masses impinged upon the Laurasia of the holarctic the separately developed floras came into intimate contact. Their boundary today probably reflects more the general position of their initial contact in terms of prevailing environments than it does any sort of specific climatic divide. However, the antarctic flora in Chile and in Tasmania seems to be as sharply differentiated from more northerly floras, and its origin can in no way be explained by continental drift. In fact, it is the present disjunction of the antarctic flora which is explained by continental drift, at least in part. An important clue here is that both in Patagonia and in Tasmania the neighboring floras extend into the coldest zones where conditions are drier; by comparison it is as though the neotropical flora predominated into Alberta. The situation here is more probably a function of formation discrimination, the same as that which separates the Australian flora from the adjacent rainforest flora. In spite of disjunction today the antarctic flora can be traced northward from New Zealand through New Caledonia and into highland New Guinea where no sharp division between the highland flora and lower floras can be made.

The fact that the world flora can be divided into several largely independent kingdoms means that there exists a refreshing diversity. Not only are there different vegetation formation responses to environmental differences, but each kind of formation has developed independently at least once in each of several regional kingdoms. Of course, each kingdom does not necessarily contain every possible formation, but there are, nevertheless, several examples of each kind. The holarctic woodlands of North America are made up of entirely different plants than are neotropical woodlands, and these have next to nothing in common with Australian woodlands. If one should visit the various dry summer subtropical regions of the world one cannot help being impressed by the physiognomic similarity of the vegetation cover in spite of their remote locations one from another. The forms of desert plants in Africa, including cactus-like euphorbias, strongly resemble the plant forms in arid tropical America. It becomes possible to appreciate and understand the general nature of each kind of vegetation formation because there exist several independent examples of each of these systems.

Finally, by way of conclusion, a new look can be taken at the classification of world flora. Clearly, the most profound divisions are those between the holarctic and the various tropical floras together with the distinctions seen in southern South America and South Africa. The separation of Africa from South America is enough to make the neotropics distinct from the palaeotropics. Less agreement attaches to the separation of tropical Asian floras from Africa because there are some small relationships. The areas are essentially disjunct and certainly quite dissimilar, and I feel that not separating them is misleading and unnecessary. Considering the polarized phases of the neotropics and of the African palaeotropics, it seems logical to assign Australia as the arid phase of the Asian tropics, inasmuch as its floristic relationships are just as strong (or weak as the case may be). In fact, the antarctic flora is even more strongly related to the Asian tropics and also qualifies as a floristic phase or subrealm, cool in this case. Thus I would propose four plant kingdoms — holarctic, neotropical, palaeotropical, and austromalesian (Map 28).

The holarctic flora occupies almost the entire extra-tropical land area of the northern hemisphere. Its subrealms, in fact, are not strongly developed. The boreal phase has often been distinguished and can be accepted as one subrealm. The arid phase in North America hardly merits distinction, but the arid phase of

BOREAL
HOLARCTIC
HUMID
ARID
NEOTROPICAL
ARID
ARID
HUMID
ARID
ANTARCTIC
HUMID
HOLARCTIC
BOREAL
ARID
HUMID
PALAEOTROPICAL
HUMID
ARID
HUMID
CAPE
HUMID
HUMID
AUSTRALIAN
AUSTROMALESIAN
ANTARCTIC
BOUNDARIES OF REALMS
BOUNDARIES OF SUBREALMS
TROPICAL HIGHLANDS WITH
MIXED OR PURE EXTRATROPICAL
FLORAL ELEMENTS

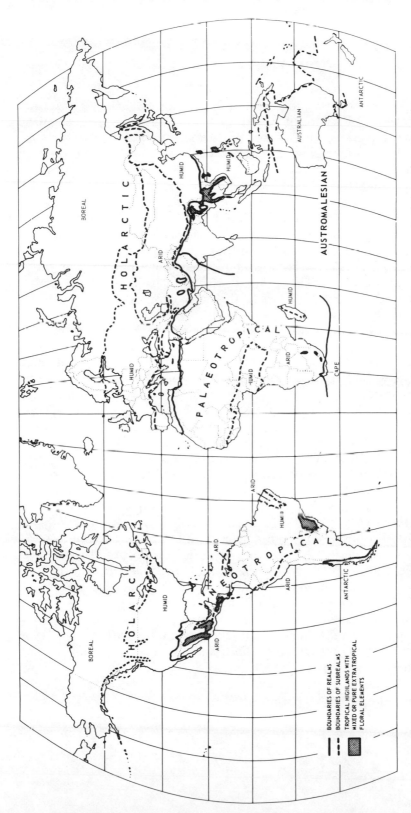

*Map 28.* Floral realms and subrealms. A few changes appear here compared to traditional maps both in major categories and in the location of boundaries. For the most part the map corresponds to previous maps.

the Mediterranean and Turkestan perhaps qualifies as a second subrealm. There are, of course, several separate easily recognized holarctic regions, such as eastern North America and eastern Asia, that differ primarily at the species level and represent a lower rank in floristic regionalization.

The neotropical and palaeotropical floras divide readily each into an arid and a humid phase, each making a well-differentiated subrealm not, however, geographically compact. Wet vegetation extends along orographic coasts well removed from the main body of the rainforest. Dry areas are found both north and south of the equatorial rainforest regions and extend into rain-shadow areas. The dry flora of Pakistan (Meher-Homji 1970) and even of central Burma (Davis 1964) belongs to the palaeotropics.

The austromalesian realm has several subrealms. The humid tropical subrealm extends from India to the Pacific islands with several regional variations. The arid subrealm of Australia is compact, but the Cape flora must be considered as a separate subrealm thanks to its long history of isolation from the rest of the realm. The antarctic subrealm is the most disjunct in the world, being found in Chile, Tasmania, New Zealand, and several isolated antarctic islands.

This treatment has produced few new boundaries, but there are some shifts in emphasis. At the kingdom level, there is a reduction, with the antarctic, the Cape, and the Australian realms all being combined together with the Asian tropics to form one single realm. The Asian and African tropics have been separated before, as they are here. A major contribution is calling attention to the distinction between arid and humid floras in America and Africa. Attempts have been made to do this before at some level in the classification, but workers were bedeviled by the lack of compactness of the resulting divisions. A compact region may be satisfying and easy to delimit, but the insistence on this sort of geographic "convenience" is a bit amateur and not defensible in this case. These differences merit recognition at the same level accorded to compact Australian flora. It is hoped that a more balanced treatment has now been produced.

# Bibliography

Ackerman, E. A. "The Köppen Classification of Climates in North America." *The Geographical Review* 31 (1941):105-11.

American Geographical Society. *Map of the Americas*. New York, 1933.

Andree, Richard. *Allgemeiner Handatlas*. Leipzig, 1906.

Axelrod, D. I. "Origin of Deciduous and Evergreen Habits in Temperate Forests." *Evolution* 20 (1966):1-15.

Bartholomew, J. G. *The Advanced Atlas of Physical and Political Geography*. Oxford, 1917.

Beadle, N. C. W. "The Misuse of Climate as an Indicator of Vegetation and Soils." *Ecology* 32 (1951):343-45.

Beard, J. S. "Climax Vegetation in Tropical America." *Ecology* 25 (1944): 127-58.

Bentham, George. *Labiatarum genera et species*. London, 1832-36.

Billings, W. D. "The Shadscale Vegetation Zone of Nevada and Eastern California in Relation to Climate and Soils." *American Midland Naturalist* 41 (1949):87-109.

Blumenstock, David I., and C. W. Thornthwaite. "Climate and World Pattern." *Climate and Man*. Yearbook of Agriculture, 1941. Washington, D.C.: United States Department of Agriculture, 1941, pp. 98-127.

Blydenstein, John. "The Tropical Savanna Vegetation of the Campos of Colombia." *Ecology* 48 (1967):1-15.

Bobek, H. "Vegetation." *The Cambridge History of Iran I, The Land of Iran*, W. B. Fisher, ed. Cambridge: At the University Press, 1968, Chapter 8, pp. 280-93.

Bonpland, A., and A. de Humboldt. *Nova genera et species plantarum*. Paris, 1815.

Boyko, H. "On the Role of Plants as Quantitative Climate Indicators and the Geo-Ecological Law of Distribution." *Journal of Ecology* 35 (1947): 138-57.

Braun, E. Lucy. *Deciduous Forests of Eastern North America*. Philadelphia: Blakiston, 1950.

Brown, Robert. "General Remarks, Geographical and Systematical on the Botany of Terra Australis." *A Voyage to Terra Australis*, Matthew Flinders. London, 1814, Vol. 2, pp. 533-613.

Buffington, Luc, and Carlton H. Herbel. "Vegetation Changes on a Semi-Desert Grassland Range." *Ecological Monographs* 35 (1965): 135-64.

Butland, G. J. *The Human Geography of Southern Chile*. London: George Philip and Son, 1957.

Cain, Stanley A. *Foundations of Plant Geography*. New York: Harper, 1959.

——, and G. M. Oliveira Castro. *Manual of Vegetation Analysis*. New York: Harper, 1959).

Chatterjee, D. "Tropical Vegetation of Eastern India." *Study of Tropical Vegetation, Proceedings of the Kandy Symposium*. Paris: UNESCO, 1958, pp. 61-67.

Chisholm, George G., and C. H. Leete, eds. *Longman's New School Atlas*, new ed. New York, 1908.

Clements, Frederick E. *Plant Succession and Indicators*. New York: Hafner, 1963; first published 1916.

——, and V. E. Shelford. *Bioecology*. New York: Wiley, 1936.

Cockayne, L., and E. P. Turner. *The Trees of New Zealand*, 4th ed. Wellington: New Zealand Government Printer, 1958.

Cole, Monica. "Distribution and Origin of Savanna Vegetation in Brazil." *Geographical Journal* 126 (1960):168-79.

——. "Vegetation and Geomorphology in Northern Rhodesia: An Aspect of the Distribution of Savanna of Central Africa." *Geographical Journal* 129 (1963):290-310.

Corporación de Fomento de las Producción. *Geografía Económica de Chile*. Vol. 1. Santiago, 1950.

Cowlin, R. W., P. A. Briegleb, and F. L. Moravets. *Forest Resources of the Ponderosa Pine Region*. Misc. Publication 490. Washington, D.C.: United States Department of Agriculture, 1942.

Critchfield, W. B., and E. L. Little. *Geographic Distribution of Pines of the World*. Misc. Publication 991. Washington, D.C.: United States Department of Agriculture, 1966.

Cumberland, Kenneth B. "A Century's Change: Natural to Cultural Vegetation in New Zealand." *The Geographical Review* 31 (1941):525-54.

Dansereau, Pierre. *Biogeography*. New York: Ronald, 1957.

Daubenmire, R. "Vegetation: Identification of Typal Communities." *Science* 151 (1966):291-98.

Davies, J. L. "A Vegetational Map of Tasmania." *The Geographical Review* 54 (1964):249-53.

Davis, John H. "The Forests of Burma." *Sarracenia* 8 (1964).

de Candolle, Alphonse. *Introduction à l'étude de la géographie botanique.* Bruxelles, 1837.

_____. *Geographie botanique raisonné.* Paris, 1855.

_____. "Constitution dans le règne végétal de groups physiologiques appliqués à la géographie ancienne et moderne." *Archives des sciences physiques et naturelles* 50 (1874).

de Candolle, Augustin. "Essai Elementaire de Geographie botanique." *Dictionaire des sciences naturelles.* Vol. 18. Paris, 1820.

de Laubenfels, David J. "The External Morphology of Conifer Leaves." *Phytomorphology* 3 (1953):1-20.

_____. "The Status of 'Conifers' in Vegetation Classifications." *Annals of the Association of American Geographers* 47 (1957):145-49.

_____. "World Vegetation." Appendix C, pp. 442-43, and map, pp. 16-17, in Preston E. James, *One World Divided.* New York: Blaisdell, 1964.

_____. "A Revision of the Malesian and Pacific Rainforest Conifers, I." *Journal of the Arnold Arboretum* 50 (1969):274-369.

De Martonne, E. *Traité de Géographie Physique.* Vol. 3, 4th ed. Paris: Armand Colin, 1927.

Denevan, William. "The Upland Pine Forests of Nicaragua." *University of California Publications in Geography* 12 (1961):251-320.

Diels, Ludwig, *Pflanzengeographie.* Leipzig, 1908; 5th ed. rev. by F. Mattick, Berlin: De Gruyter, 1958.

Dogra, P. D. "Gymnosperms of India II, Chilgoza Pine *(Pinus gerardiana Wall.).*" *Bulletin of the National Botanic Gardens* 109 (Lucknow, India, 1964).

Drude, Oscar. "Die Florenreiche der Erde." *Ergänzungshefte zu Petermann's Mittheilungen* 74 (1884).

_____. *Atlas der Pflanzenverbreitung.* Abteilung V., *Berghaus' Physikalisher Atlas.* Gotha, 1887.

_____. *Handbuch der Pflanzengeographie.* Stuttgart, 1890.

DuReitz, G. Einar. *Zur methodologischen Grundlage der modernen Pflanzen-soziologie.* Upsala: Akad. Abhandlungen, 1921.

Eckert, Max. *Die Kartenwirtenschaft.* Vol. 2. Berlin and Leipzig: De Gruyter, 1925. "Die pflanzengeographische Karte," pp. 385-411.

Egler, Frank E. "The Nature of the Relationship between Climate, Soil, and Vegetation." *Proceedings of the Ninth Pacific Science Congress* 20 (Bangkok, 1958):50-56.

Eiten, George. "Habit Flora of Fazenda Campininha, São Paulo, Brazil." *Simpósio sôbre o cerrado.* São Paulo: The University Press, 1963, pp. 179-231.

_____. "The Cerrado Vegetation of Brazil." *Botanical Review* 38 (1972): 201-341.

Engler, A. *Versuch einer Entwicklungsgeschichte der Pflanzenwelt.* Leipzig, part I, 1879; part II, 1882.

_____. *Syllabus der Pflanzenfamilien.* 7th ed. Berlin, 1912; 2nd ed., 1898.

_____. *Die Entwicklung der Pflanzengeographie in den letzten hundert Jahren.* Berlin, 1899.

_____, and Ludwig Diels. *Syllabus der Pflanzenfamilien,* 11th ed. Berlin: Borntraeger, 1936.

_____, and Oscar Drude. *Die Vegetation der Erde.* Leipzig, 1896 ff.

Eyre, S. R. *Vegetation and Soils, A World Picture.* London: Arnold, 1963.

Ferri, Mario Guimarães. *Contribuição ao Conhecimento da Ecologia do Cerrado e da Caatinga.* Vol. 195. University of São Paulo, 1955.

Finch, V. C., and G. T. Trewartha. *Elements of Geography.* New York: McGraw-Hill, 1936.

_____, G. T. Trewartha, A. H. Robinson, and E. H. Hammond. *Physical Elements of Geography.* 4th ed. New York: McGraw-Hill, 1957; other eds., 1936-67.

Forestry and Timber Bureau, Department of the Interior, Commonwealth of Australia. *Forest Trees of Australia.* Canberra: Forestry and Timber Bureau, 1957.

Fosberg, F. R. "What Should We Map?" *Méthodes de la Cartographie de la Végétation,* Colloques Internationaux du Centre National de la Recherche Scientifique. (Paris, 1961):23-32.

_____, B. J. Garnier, and A. W. Küchler. "Delimitation of the Humid Tropics." *The Geographical Review* 51 (1961):333-47.

Franklin, J. F., and C. T. Dyrness. *Vegetation of Oregon and Washington.* Portland: Pacific Northwest Forest and Range Experiment Station, 1969.

Fuenzalida Villegas, Humberto. "Biogeografia." *Geografia Economica de Chile,* I. Santiago: Corporación de Fomento de la Producción, 1950, Chapter 7, pp. 371-428.

Fullard, Harold, and H. C. Darby. *Aldine University Atlas.* London: Aldine, 1969.

Fuson, Robert H. *The Origin and Nature of American Savannas.* Geographic Education Series, 2. Norman, Oklahoma: National Council for Geographic Education, 1963.

Good, Ronald. *The Geography of Flowering Plants.* London: Longmans, 1947; 2nd ed., 1953.

Goodall, David W. "The Continuum and the Individualistic Association." *Vegetatio* 11 (1963):297-316.

Graebner, P. *Lehrbuch der Allgemeinen Pflanzengeographie.* 2nd ed. Leipzig: Von Quelle und Meyer, 1929.

Grigg, David. "The Logic of Regional Systems." *Annals of the Association of American Geographers* 55 (1965):465-91.

Griggs, R. G. "Timberlines as Indicators of Climatic Trends." *Science* 85 (1937):251-55.

_____. "The Timberlines of Northern America and Their Interpretation." *Ecology* 27 (1946):275-89.

Grisebach, A. R. H. "Über den Einflusz des Klimas auf die Begrenzung der natürlichen Floren." *Linnaea* 12 (1838):159-200.

———. "Die Vegetations-Gebiete der Erde, übersichlich zusammengestellt." *Petermann's Mitteilungen* 12 (1866):45-53.

———. *Die Vegetation der Erde nach ihrer klimatischen Anordnung.* Leipzig, 1872.

———. "Die Wirksamkeit Humboldts im Gebiete der Pflanzengeographie und Botanik." *Gesammelte Abhandlungen und Kleinere Schriften zur Pflanzengeographie.* Leipzig, 1880, pp. 557-84.

Grubb, P. J., and T. C. Whitmore. "A Comparison of Montane and Lowland Rainforest in Ecuador, III. The Climate and Its Effects on the Distribution and Physiognomy of the Forests." *Journal of Ecology* 54 (1966): 303-33.

Haddon-Guest, Stephen, John K. Wright, and Eileen M. Teclaff. *A World Geography of Forest Resources.* New York. Ronald, 1956

Hanes, T. A. "Succession after Fire in the Chaparral of Southern California." *Ecological Monographs* 31 (1971):27-52.

Hardy, M. E. *The Geography of Plants.* Oxford: Clarendon, 1920.

Hare, F. Kenneth. "Climate and Zonal Divisions of the Boreal Forest Formation in Eastern Canada." *The Geographical Review* 40 (1950):615-35.

———. "Climatic Classification." *London Essays in Geography,* L. D. Stamp and S. W. Wooldridge, eds. London: Longmans, Green, 1951, Chapter 7, pp. 111-34.

———. *A Photo-Reconnaissance Survey of Labrador-Ungava.* Memoir 6. Ottawa: Geographical Branch, Department of Mines and Technical Surveys, 1959.

Harris, David R. "Recent Plant Invasions in the Arid and Semiarid Southwest of the United States." *Annals of the Association of American Geographers* 56 (1966):408-22.

Harshberger, John W. *Phytogeographic Survey of North America.* Leipzig, 1911.

Heinselman, Miron L. "Forest Sites, Bog Processes, and Peatland Types in the Glacial Lake Agassiz Region, Minnesota." *Ecological Monographs* 33 (1963):327-74.

Herbertson, A. J. "The Major Natural Regions: An Essay in Systematic Geography." *Geographical Journal* 25 (1905):310-12.

Herzog, Theodore. "Pflanzengeographie." *Handbuch der Geographischen Wissenschaft,* 11, Part 2. Potsdam: Akademische Verlagsgesellschaft Athenaion, 1933, pp. 1-80.

Hills, Theo L. *Savannas: A Review of a Major Research Problem in Tropical Geography.* Savanna Research Project, Savanna Research Series 3. Montreal: McGill University Press, 1965.

———, and R. E. Randall. *The Ecology of the Forest/Savanna Boundary.* Savanna Research Project, Savanna Research Series 13. Montreal: McGill University Press, 1968.

Hinman, Russell. *Eclectic Physical Geography.* New York, 1888.

Holloway, John T. "Forests and Climate in the South Island of New Zealand." *Transactions Royal Society New Zealand* 82 (1954):392-410.

Holmes, C. H. "The Broad Pattern of Climate and Vegetational Distribution in Ceylon." *Study of Tropical Vegetation, Proceedings of the Kandy Symposium.* Paris: UNESCO, 1958, pp. 99-114.

Hopkins, Brian. *Forest and Savanna.* London: Heinemann, 1965.

Hueck, Kurt. *Mapa de la Vegetación de la República de Venezuela.* Mérida: Instituto Forestal Latinamericano de Investigación y Capacitación, 1960.

_____. *Die Walder Sudamerikas.* Stuttgart: Gustav Fischer, 1966.

Hultén, Eric. *The Amphi-Atlantic Plants and their Phytogeographical Connection.* Stockholm: Almquist & Wiksell, 1958.

Humboldt, A. von. *Essai sur la geographie des plantes.* Paris, 1805.

_____. *De distributione geographica plantarum secondum coeli temperiem et altitudnem montium prolegomena.* Paris, 1817; reprinted from Bonpland and Humboldt 1815.

International Congress of Geography. *Le Probleme des Savannes et Campos dans les Regiones Tropicales — Colloquium.* Comptes Rendus du 18 Congrès International de Géographie, Vol. 1. Rio de Janiero, 1956.

James, Preston E. *Regional Geography.* Ann Arbor: Edwards Brothers, 1929.

_____. *An Outline of Geography.* Boston: Ginn, 1935.

_____. *Latin America.* New York: Odyssey, 1942.

_____. "Trends in Brazilian Agricultural Development." *The Geographical Review* 43 (1953):301-28.

Johannessen, Carl J. "Savannas of Interior Honduras." *Ibero-Americana* 46 (1963).

Jones, C. F. "Types of Vegetation." *Goode's School Atlas.* Chicago: Rand McNally, 1923, pp. 6-7.

Keay, R. W. J. *Vegetation Map of Africa, Explanatory Notes.* Oxford: The Clarendon Press, 1959.

Kendall, H. M., R. M. Glendenning, and C. H. MacFadden. *Introduction to Geography,* 3rd ed. New York: Harcourt, Brace & World, 1962; other eds., 1951-67.

Kimble, G. H. T., and Dorothy Good. *Geography of the Northlands.* New York: American Geographical Society and Wiley, 1955.

Köppen, W. "Versuch einer Klassifikation der Klimate, vorzugsweise nach ihren Beziehungen zur Pflanzenwelt." *Geographischen Zeitshift* 6 (1900): 593-611.

_____. "Klassifikation der Klimate nach Temperature Niederschlag, und Jahreslauf." *Petermann's Mitteilungen* 64 (1918):193-203.

Küchler, A. W. "A Geographical System of Vegetation." *The Geographical Review* 37 (1947a):233-40.

_____. "Localizing Vegetation Terms." *Annals of the Association of American Geographers* 37 (1947b):197-208.

_____. "A Physiognomic Classification of Vegetation." *Annals of the Association of American Geographers* 39 (1949a):201-10.

_____. "Natural Vegetation." *Goode's School Atlas*, 8th ed. Chicago: Rand McNally, 1949b.

_____. "Classification and Purpose in Vegetation Maps." *The Geographical Review* 46 (1956):155-67.

_____. "Vegetation Maps in Geographical Research." *Professional Geographer* 11 (1959):6-9.

_____. *Potential Natural Vegetation of the Coterminous United States.* American Geographical Society serial publication 36. New York, 1964.

_____. "Analyzing the Physiognomy and Structure of Vegetation." *Annals of the Association of American Geographers* 56 (1966):112-27.

_____. *Vegetation Mapping.* New York: Ronald, 1967.

_____. "The Oscillation of the Mixed Prairie in Kansas." *Erdkunde* 26 (1972): 120-29.

_____. "Problems in Classifying and Mapping Vegetation for Ecological Regionalization." *Ecology* 54 (1973):512-23.

_____, and J. O. Sawyer. "A Study of Vegetation near Chiangmai, Thailand." *Transactions of the Kansas Academy of Science* 70 (1968):281-348.

Larson, James. "The Vegetation of the Ennadai Lake Area, N.W.T., Studies in Subarctic and Arctic Bioclimatology." *Ecological Monographs* 35 (1965): 37-59.

Le Honèron, H. N. *Recherches ecologiques et florestiques sur la vegetation de la Tunisie méridionale.* Mémoire No. 6. Université d'Alger, Institute de Recherche Sahariane, 1959.

Leighly, J. "Climatology since the Year 1800." *Transactions of the American Geophysical Union* 30 (1949):658-72.

Lemée, G. *Precis de Biogeographie.* Paris: Masson, 1967.

Li, Hui-Lin. "Floristic Relationships between Eastern Asia and Eastern North America." *Transactions of the American Philosophical Society* 42, part 2 (1952):371-429.

_____. "Present Distribution and Habitats of the Conifers and Taxads." *Evolution* 7 (1953):245-61.

Linton, D. L. "Vegetation." *The American Oxford Atlas.* New York: Oxford University Press, 1951, pp. viii-ix.

Major, Jack. "Review of Flora and Vegetation of the Aleutian Islands." *Ecology* 43 (1962):351-52.

Martius, K. F. P. von. *Historia naturalis Palmarum.* Vol. 1. Lipsiae, 1831-50.

Mather, John R., and Gary A. Yoshioka. "The Role of Climate in the Distribution of Vegetation." *Annals of the Association of American Geographers* 58 (1968):29-41.

McIntosh, Robert P. "Ecosystems, Evolution and Relational Patterns of Living Organisms." *American Scientist* 51 (1963):246-67.

———. "The Continuum Concept of Vegetation." *Botanical Review* 33 (1967): 130-87.

McLintock, A. H., ed. *A Descriptive Atlas of New Zealand.* Wellington: Government Printer, 1960.

Meher-Homji, V. M. "Some Phytogeographic Aspects of Rajasthan, India." *Vegetatio* 21 (1970):299-320.

Melchior, Hans A. *A. Engler's Syllabus der Pflanzenfamilien.* 12th ed. Vol. 2. Berlin: Borntraeger, 1964.

Merriam, C. H. *Life Zones and Crop Zones.* Biological Survey Bulletin 10 Washington, D.C.: United States Department of Agriculture, 1898.

Meyen, F. *Grundriss der Pflanzengeographie.* Berlin, 1836.

Mikesell, Marvin. "Deforestation in Northern Morocco." *Science* 132 (1960): 441-48.

Monk, Carl D. "An Ecological Significance of Evergreenness." *Ecology* 47 (1966):504-505.

Montoya Maquin, J. M. "El acuerdo de Yangambi (1956) como base para una nomenclatura de tipos de vegetación en el trópico americano." *Turrialba* 16 (1966):169-80.

Morgan, W. B., and R. P. Moss. "Geography and Ecology: The Concept of the Community and its Relationship to Environment." *Annals of the Association of American Geographers* 55 (1965):339-50.

Murphey, Rhodes. "The Decline of North Africa Since the Roman Occupation: Climatic or Human." *Annals of the Association of American Geographers* 41 (1951):116-32.

Newbigin, Marion I. *Plant and Animal Geography.* London: Methuen, 1936.

Nichol, A. A. *The Natural Vegetation of Arizona.* Technical Bulletin 127 Tucson: University of Arizona Agricultural Experiment Station, 1952.

Norin, B. N. "The Problem of the Wooded Tundra and the Long-Term Study of its Various Aspects Under Field Conditions." *Problems of the North* 8 (1965):57-66.

Oberdorfer, Erich. *Pflanzensoziogische Studien in Chile.* Weinheim: Cramer, 1960.

Pacific Southwest Forest and Range Experiment Station. *Soil-Vegetation Surveys in California.* Sacramento, 1958; rev. 1969.

Parsons, James J. "The Miskito Pine Savanna of Nicaragua and Honduras." *Annals of the Association of American Geographers* 45 (1955):36-63.

Penck, A. "Versuch einer Klimaklassification auf physiographische Grundlagen." *Sitzungs Berichte der Akademie der Wissenschaften* 1 (1910): 236-46.

Pennington, T. D., and Jose Sarakhan. *Árboles Tropicales de México.* Mexico City: Instituto Nacional de Investigaciones Forestales, 1968.

Philbrick, A. K. *This Human World.* New York: Wiley, 1963.

Phillips, W. S. *Vegetational Changes in the Northern Great Plains.* Tucson: University of Arizona Press, 1963.

Pickering, C. "The Geographical Distribution of Animals and Plants, part 2, Plants in their Wild State." *United States Exploring Expedition* 15. Salem, 1876, with map.

Polunin, Nicholas. *Introduction to Plant Geography.* New York: McGraw-Hill, 1960.

Poore, M. E. D. "The Method of Successive Approximation in Descriptive Ecology." *Advances in Ecological Research* (1962):35-68.

——. "Problems in the Classification of Tropical Rainforest." *Journal of Tropical Geography* 17 (1963):12-19.

Puri, G. S. "Vegetation and Soil in Tropical and Subtropical India." *Tropical Soils and Vegetation, Proceedings of the Abidjan Symposium.* Paris: UNESCO, 1961, pp. 93-102.

Rattray, J. M. *The Grass Cover of Africa.* Rome: FAO, 1960.

Raunkiaer, O. "Types biologiques pour la géographie botanique." *Bulletin of the Royal Academy of Science of Denmark* 5 (1905):347-438.

——. *The Life Forms of Plants and Statistical Plant Geography.* Oxford: The Clarendon Press, 1934.

Raup, Hugh M. "Trends in the Development of Geographic Botany." *Annals of the Association of American Geographers* 32 (1942):319-54.

Richards, P. W. *The Tropical Rainforest.* Cambridge: At the University Press, 1952.

Robbins, R. G. "The Anthropogenic Grasslands of Papua and New Guinea." *Symposium on the Impact of Man on Humid Tropics Vegetation.* Canberra: UNESCO, 1962, pp. 313-29.

Rübel, Eduard. *Pflanzengesellschaften der Erde.* Bern: Huber, 1930.

Rubner, K. "Die Forstlich-klimatische Einteilung Europas." *Zeitschrift für Weltforstwirtschaft* 5 (1938):422-34.

Sarlin, P. *Bois et Forêts de la Nouvelle-Caledonie.* Nogent-Sur-Marne (Seine), France: Centre Technique Forestier Tropical, 1954.

Sauer, Carl O. "Grassland Climate, Fire, and Man." *Journal of Range Management* 3 (1950):16-21.

Schimper, A. F. W. *Pflanzengeographie auf physiologischer Grundlage.* Jena, 1898; English ed., *Plant Geography upon a Physiological Basis,* trans. by W. R. Fisher, published at Oxford in 1903.

——, and F. C. von Faber. *Pflanzengeographie auf physiologischen Grundlage.* 3rd ed. Jena: Fischer, 1935.

Schmithüsen, Josef. *Allgemeine Vegetationsgeographie.* Berlin: Walter de Gruyter, 1959.

Schouw, J. F. *Grundträg til en almindelig Plantegeografie.* Kopenhagen, 1822; Atlas, 1824. *Grundzüge einer allgemeinen Pflanzengeographie.* Berlin, 1823, including atlas.

——. "Pflanzengeographie." *Berghaus Physikalischem Atlas.* Part 5. Gotha: J. Perthes, 1838.

———. "Momente zu einer Vorlessung über die pflanzengeographischen Reiche." *Linnaea* 8 (1833):625-52.

Schroeter, C. "Ueber Pflanzengeographischen Karten." *Actes du Troisieme Congrès International de Botanique, Bruxelles 1910*, Vol. 2, *Conférences et mémoires*. Brussels, 1912, pp. 97-154.

Schweinfurth, Ulrich. "Die Horizontale und Vertikale Verbreitung der Vegetation im Himalaya." *Bonner Geographische Abhandlungen* 20 (1957).

———. "Studien zur Pflanzengeographie von Tasmanien." *Bonner Geographische Abhandlungen* 31 (1962).

Shantz, H. L., and C. F. Marbut. *The Vegetation and Soils of Africa*. New York: American Geographical Society, 1923.

Shantz, H. L., and R. Zon. "The Natural Vegetation of the United States." *Atlas of American Agriculture*. Washington, D.C.: Department of Agriculture, 1924.

Sigafoos, Robert S. "Vegetation of Northwestern North America as an Aid in Interpretation of Geologic Data." *Geologic Survey Bulletin* 1061 (Washington, 1958).

Soares, Lucio de Castro. "Limites Meridionais e Orientais da Área Ocorrência de Floresta Amazônica em Território Brazilero." *Revista Brasilera de Geografía* 15 (1953):3-122.

Takhtajan, Armen. *Flowering Plants — Origin and Dispersal*. Edinburgh: Oliver and Boyd, 1969.

Thiselton-Dyer, W. T. "Lecture on Plant Distribution as a Field for Geographical Research." *Proceedings of the Royal Geographical Society* 22 (1898).

Thornthwaite, C. W. "Grassland Climate." *Publications in Climatology* 5 (1952):1-14.

Tikhomirov, B. A. "Principal Stages of Vegetation Development in Northern U.S.S.R. as Related to Climatic Fluctuations and the Activity of Man." *Canadian Geographer* 7 (1963):55-71.

Tosi, Joseph A. "Climatic Control of Terrestrial Ecosystems: A Report on the Holdridge Model." *Economic Geography* 40 (1964):173-81.

Trewartha, G. T. *An Introduction to Climate*. 3rd ed. New York: McGraw-Hill, 1954.

Troll, Carl. *Studien zur vergleichenden Geographie der Hochgebirge*. Bonn: The University, 1941.

UNESCO. *Vegetation Map of the Mediterranean Region*. Paris, 1968.

Unstead, J. F., and E. G. R. Taylor. *Philip's Series of Comparative Wall Atlases*. London, n.d.

Van Steenis, C. G. G. J. "The Delimitation of Malaysia and its Main Plant Geographical Divisions." *Flora Malesiana*. Ser. I, vol. I, chapter III (1950): lxx-lxxv.

———. "Results of the Archibold Expeditions, Papuan Nothofagus." *Journal of the Arnold Arboretum* 34 (1953):301-74.

_____. *Vegetation Map of Malaysia.* Haarlem: UNESCO, 1958*a*.

_____. "Tropical Lowland Vegetation: The Characteristics of its Types and Their Relation to Climate." *Proceedings of the Ninth Pacific Science Congress* 20. Bangkok: Secretariat, Ninth Pacific Science Congress, 1958*b*, pp. 25-37.

Vasek, Frank C. "The Distribution and Taxonomy of Three Western Junipers." *Brittonia* 18 (1966):350-72.

Vidal, P. de la Blanche, and L. Gallois. *Geographie Universelle.* Paris: Armand Colin, 1927-46.

Wace, N. M. "The Units and Uses of Biogeography." *Australian Geographical Studies* 5 (1967):15-29.

Wagner, Hermann, and Emil von Sydow. *Sydow-Wagners Methodischer Schul Atlas.* Gotha, 1888; 7th ed., 1897.

Wagner, Philip L. "A Contribution to Structural Vegetation Mapping." *Annals of the Association of American Geographers* 47 (1957):363-69.

Walter, Heinrich. *Die Vegetation der Erde.* Jena: Gustav Fischer, Vol. I, 1962, Vol. II, 1968.

_____, and H. Straka. *Arealkunde.* Stuttgart: Eugen Ulmer, 1954; 2nd ed., 1970.

Wang, Chi-Wu. *The Forests of China.* Maria Moors Cabot Foundation, Publication 5. Cambridge, Mass.: Harvard University Press, 1961.

Weaver, John E., and Frederick E. Clements. *Plant Ecology.* 2nd ed. New York: McGraw-Hill, 1938; 1st ed., 1929.

Webb, L. J. "A Physiognomic Classification of Australian Rainforests." *Journal of Ecology* 47 (1959):551-70.

Weberbauer, A *Phytogeography of the Peruvian Andes.* Field Museum of Natural History, Publication No. 351, Botanical Series 13 (1936):13-81.

Wells, Philip V. "Physiognomic Intergradation of Vegetation on the Pine Valley Mountains in Southwestern Utah." *Ecology* 41 (1960):553-56.

_____. "Scarp Woodlands, Transported Grassland Soils, and the Concept of Grassland Climate in the Great Plains Region." *Science* 148 (1965): 246-49.

_____. "Postglacial Vegetational History of the Great Plains." *Science* 167 (1970):1574-82.

White, C. T. "Ligneous Plants Collected in New Caledonia, Introductory Note." *Journal of the Arnold Arboretum* 7 (1926):74-76.

White, Keith L. "Structure and Composition of Foothill Woodland in Central Coastal California." *Ecology* 47 (1966):229-37.

Whittaker, Robert H. "Recent Evolution of Ecological Concepts in Relation to the Eastern Forests of North America." *American Journal of Botany* 44 (1957):197-206.

_____. "Classification of Natural Communities." *Botanical Review* 28 (1962): 1-239.

_____. *Communities and Ecosystems.* New York: Macmillan, 1970.

Whittaker, Robert H., and W. A. Neiring. "Vegetation of the Santa Catalina Mountains, Arizona: A Gradient Analysis of the South Slope." *Ecology* 46 (1965):429-52.

Willdenow, Carl L. *Grundrisz der Kräuterkunde*. Berlin, 1792; 5th ed., 1810.

Williams, J. E. *Prentice-Hall World Atlas*, 2nd ed. Englewood Cliffs, N.J., 1963.

Williams, R. J. "Vegetation Regions." *Atlas of Australian Resources*. Canberra: Australian Department of National Development, 1955.

Womersley, J. S., and J. B. McAdam. *The Forests and Forest Conditions in the Territories of Papua and New Guinea*. Port Moresby: Government Printer, 1957.

Wood, Walter. "Flat Grasslands and Hilly Forests, Why?" *Annals of the Association of American Geographers* 48 (1958):298.

Wulff, E. V. *An Introduction to Historical Plant Geography*. Waltham, Mass.: Chronica Botanica, 1950.

Zon, R., and W. N. Spearhawk. *Forest Resources of the World*. New York: McGraw-Hill, 1923.

# Index

MAPPING THE WORLD'S VEGETATION

*Regionalization of Formations and Flora*

Was composed in 10-point IBM Selectric Century Medium, leaded two points,
by Metricomp Studios, Grundy Center, Iowa; with display type
in Century Expanded by Dix Typesetting Co., Inc., Syracuse, New York;
printed offset on Perkins & Squier 55-pound Litho
by Vicks Lithograph and Printing Corporation, Yorkville, New York;
Smyth-sewn and bound over boards in Columbia Bayside Vellum by
Vail-Ballou Press, Inc., Binghamton, New York;
and published by

SYRACUSE UNIVERSITY PRESS
Syracuse, New York 13210